THE LANDY ERA

THE LANDY ERA

FROM NOWHERE TO THE TOP OF THE WORLD

LEN JOHNSON

M

MELBOURNE BOOKS

Published by Melbourne Books
Level 9, 100 Collins Street,
Melbourne, VIC, 3000
Australia

www.melbournebooks.com.au
info@melbournebooks.com.au

Title: The Landy Era: From Nowhere
to the Top of the World
Author: Len Johnson
ISBN: 9781877096938

A catalogue record for this
book is available from the
National Library of Australia

NATIONAL
LIBRARY
OF AUSTRALIA

Front cover photo: John Landy races at Olympic Park,
Melbourne, in 1956. The crowds flocked to see him run.

Back cover photo: John Landy is at the rear of the field
early in the 1956 Victorian mile title at Olympic Park. He won
in 3:58.6, the first sub-four minute mile ever run in Australia.

To Brian Lenton, for the inspiration,
and to my family, Anne, Tim and Michael,
for the indulgence.

Acknowledgements

This book grew out of a conversation with Ron Clarke, Trevor Vincent and Neil Robbins the day after a memorial service for Les Perry in 2005. Subsequently, Ron's suggested book plan became the basis for the project.

John Landy was happy to collaborate on a book on his era and was generous in giving his time for interviews and allowing unfettered access to his athletics memorabilia, chiefly the comprehensive scrapbooks kept on his career by his mother, and others, and his collection of photographs. Most of the latter came originally from contemporary newspapers and wire services.

Tom Roberts, Geoff Warren, John Plummer, Albie Thomas and Dave Power were all interviewed by me, as were Jim Bailey and Brian Hewson when they came to Melbourne for the 50th anniversary of the 1956 Melbourne Olympic Games.

Special thanks to Al Lawrence who, though he lives in Houston, sent me a copy of his unpublished autobiography (*Chew with my mouth shut …*), copies of his photographs and countless recollections of *The Landy era*.

Pat Clohessy provided copies of his correspondence with John during the formative stages of Pat's running career and wrote of John Landy's influence on those who followed him (in this regard, nothing could be more revealing than Merv Lincoln's quote after the Santry Mile: "Wouldn't John Landy have liked to be here. He can take a lot of credit for what we did here. He was the pioneer … if he hadn't inspired Herb and myself, we wouldn't even be here.")

Tom Roberts, who ran in the first sub-four minute mile race in Australia, provided much early information and guidance of the way to proceed. Barrie Almond who, like Al Lawrence and Jim Bailey, now lives in the USA, was happy to chat about his experiences with John and the influence John Landy had on his career.

Melissa Campbell and Con Lannan, archivists at Geelong Grammar and Geelong College, respectively, assisted with access to material contained in their records, as did Virginia Boyd (president of Dookie United Football and Netball Club) and Sarah Parker (Dookie College) about John Landy's time at Dookie College.

Professor Per-Olof Åstrand sent an account of John Landy's visit to his Stockholm laboratory way back in 1954 (complete with his report at the time) and Gus Macmillan, a handy miler himself in his heyday, filled in aspects of his father, Don's, career.

Thanks too to Phil Dwyer, without whose help and guidance this book would not have got to the draft stage, and to Julian Dwyer for helping me find Melbourne Books.

Lastly, thanks to David Tenenbaum, Marleena Forward and Ning Xue at Melbourne Books.

Len Johnson
13 January, 2009

Foreword

by Ron Clarke

There is no doubt the catalyst for the turnaround in Australian distance running was John Landy and his feats at Olympic Park in the summer of 1952–53. At that time I, for one, was a keen footballer and cricketer who only ran in the school cross-country one Wednesday afternoon in July each year, and the school sports every October.

I must have had some distance talent from the start as I was never beaten in my age group in cross-country and managed to win all age groups, including the open, from the time I was twelve years old in year two of secondary school (1949). Yet, typical of the time, I never thought of joining an athletic club or doing anything else but playing football all winter and cricket all summer.

The London (1948) and Helsinki (1952) Olympic Games came and went with not much of a passing thought except to marvel at the feats of Emil Zatopek and Marjorie Jackson in the athletics, Russell Mockridge and Lionel Cox in the cycling, and feel sorry for John Marshall, who failed to win the swimming Gold medals we all expected. Judy Joy Davies and Marjorie Quade (together with Quade's boyfriend, water polo competitor Peter Bennett, also a St Kilda footballer) were others from that era whose feats made us all proud of being Australian and taking on the world. The names of athletes John Landy, Don Macmillan, Les Perry and coach Percy Cerutty were known but no one in our circles really knew what they looked like … they were just names in the newspaper.

However, John Landy's 4:02.1 recorded at Olympic Park on an

ordinary interclub race one hot day in December 1952 — a time within one second of the world record — changed all that. Suddenly, the sports fans in Melbourne became interested in athletics. Landy's continued assault of Gunder Hägg's supposedly invincible world record, combined with the debate as to whether the human body could ever run so fast for so long as to break four minutes for the one mile distance, aroused the interest of us all.

By then, I was 15 and had just finished my Leaving Certificate at Essendon High School. As Essendon had dropped their matriculation classes three years earlier due to lack of numbers, those of us who wanted to continue with our education had the choice of Melbourne or University High. Up until then, every Australian Olympic distance runner (from 800 metres upwards) from Ted Flack in 1896 to Don McMillan and John Landy in 1952 had emerged out of the private school system, with the exception of Les Perry, who discovered his talent for running while participating in army competitions at the end of World War II.

In 1953 at Melbourne High I, too, was taking much more of an interest in "track and field", as I had learned to refer to athletics. For the first time in my life, all my races on the track were timed. I easily won the school and interschool cross-country, then I won the 220, 440, 880 and the mile on the same afternoon at the school athletic sports, the last two in school record times. I became a bit of a king, receiving the type of attention usually only devoted to the captain of the senior football team at Essendon.

I'm certain others around the same age, all over the country, also started to acknowledge that competing in track and field had some distinct challenges and attractions. I began to break some state, and then Australian, junior records, culminating in world best times for the one, two and three mile events (there was no such thing as world records for juniors back then). I transferred my devotion from cricket to track although nothing I, or Landy, ever did could get me away from playing football during the winter months rather than competing in cross-country.

I met some of the top runners, including John Landy. I'll always remember first meeting John in a dressing room at Olympic Park when he introduced himself with the words going something like: "Well done Ron. I'm John Landy and, although he will probably not remember me, I raced your brother Jack in the Australian Junior Championships in January 1948 at the St Kilda football ground when we were both kids and he beat me." Actually, John was Associated Public Schools (APS) champion in 1947, at 18 years of age, whereas Jack was just 14 and more interested in the triple jump and the sprints. John went on to be a world champion whereas Jack never ran another 880 again until after he retired from football and competed at the Stawell Gift meeting as a 36-year-old.

Neil Robbins, a Les Perry protégé at Williamstown athletic club and one of Landy's fellow competitors in the 1954 Commonwealth Games in Vancouver, took me under his wing and introduced me to Austrian coach Franz Stampfl, whose group Neil also joined in preparation for the 1956 Olympics 3000 metres steeplechase. Landy was out there doing his heroics, and Dave Stephens broke the Australian six miles record on the grass track at the Junction Oval in St Kilda (better known to me then as the St Kilda football ground) running in bare feet — an event I actually witnessed.

Stephens's performances, and the selection of Melbourne as the Olympic venue for the 1956 Olympics, convinced the legendary Hungarian distance stars Tabori, Rozsavolgyi and Iharos, together with their esteemed coach, Mihaly Igloi, to tour Melbourne in 1955 and take on Dave Stephens, who was equal to the task. The Victorian Amateur Athletic Association (VAAA) was flush with funds at the time and so was able to finance their visit. It was great athletics and to see it in the flesh was exhilarating for a teenager now completely involved in the challenge of seeing just how fast he could run.

I have to admit I never thought I would ever be competing internationally on a level equal to the Hungarians. Frankly, I just didn't think about it; my sporting ambitions were solely focused on joining my brother Jack in playing football with Essendon. But it was fun pushing the barriers. In fact, up until I joined Stampfl's squad, I never trained for track but for the odd session with Neil Robbins and his friends. The first thing Franz did when he saw me was put me on a diet: no sweets, ice cream, potatoes or bread — all foods I loved to eat. Whether it was the regular daily training or the diet, or a bit of both, I quickly dropped more than a stone (just over six kilograms) and started to challenge the world junior records.

I remember interclub during those days as being most exciting. Everybody competed at the same venue so we could all compete with, if not against, Australia's top athletes; we could see how fit they were, how much they enjoyed their sport and how approachable they were. When Olympic Park was closed in preparation for the Olympics we moved to Collingwood with the funniest shaped track I ever did see. The 440 hurdles stretched in a straight line parallel to the road, with the hurdles seemingly going on forever. The circular events started on the same track but then went around a tiny circle, about 220 yards around, so the computations for the various distances were quite complex. Of course, the field was all grass. It wasn't until after the Olympics that some suburban tracks started to emerge.

There was much excitement and urgency about the place. Franz gathered quite a collection of high jumpers, throwers, sprinters and distance runners about him, all of whom trained at the new track Professor Rawlinson (an ex-javelin thrower) had persuaded the university authorities to build. Merv Lincoln, another ex-Melbourne High student, was developed by the mercurial Austrian from an ordinary runner into a world champion. Yet another who improved greatly under Stampfl's tutelage was Ron Blackney, who flourished into an Australian steeplechase champion after languishing for many years as an average interclub athlete. Then there was Hec Hogan, already an Australian champion sprinter but taken to new heights under Stampfl (he placed third in the Olympic 100 metres in 1956 and remains our only ever male Olympic 100 medalist). I remember that everyone, after they finished their own training, had to race Hec over 30–40 yards a few times before they showered. In all Hec would have 50 to 60 starts each night, giving his opponents anything up to 20 yards start, with lots of banter and bets being won and lost.

The influence of Landy breaking the world record and the four minute mile was momentous (even if he lost the race to do it first to Roger Bannister, helped by none other then Franz Stampfl, in an artificial time trial rather than a race). Of course, the interest created by Landy was heightened by the coming Olympics. Soon, a young West Australian, inspired by the Olympics and egged on by Percy Cerutty, broke all my junior world times and quickly went on to become our greatest ever Olympic miler. His name was Herb Elliott.

It was the spirit that prevailed at the time that was so inspiring. Les Perry, one of our greatest Olympians, organised track meetings at his club's track in Williamstown where he was the chief attraction, the promoter, and sold most of the tickets at the gate. His enthusiasm was infectious, as was that of his clubmates, Neil Robbins, Geoff Warren, Dave Stephens and many more.

Percy Cerutty also contributed. Even his bitter rivalry with the "Austrian import" Franz Stampfl was good press, with the distance athletes dividing into opposing groups. Herb Elliott's phenomenal success boosted Cerutty's stocks enormously but the renegade coach's own erratic behaviour discouraged many potential athletes from visiting Portsea where he had established his training headquarters.

I remember persuading my father and brother to take me across the city to a Cerutty lecture at Caulfield Racecourse one Sunday morning in January 1954. At one point, Cerutty took me to one side, knowing I had broken a few school distance records the previous year, to give me a personal demonstration. He took me some 400 metres away up the track because, he said, he was always "being spied upon by professional coaches", pointing to my father and brother. When I told him who his "spies" were he was pretty unimpressed; in fact I don't think he believed me. I determined I would wait until I met a coach I could believe before committing to any sort of a training program.

Another principle I had at an early age was to look to compete against older athletes in open races rather than be satisfied with winning in restricted competition. My father had always preached that competition was always more important than results. "Always keep stretched if you really want to improve" he used to tell both Jack and me. So I have never been that impressed with junior champions; it's what they do with their talent that matters. In 1957, Herb Elliott showed just how true that philosophy was when he took on the world as a teenager and won. Later, Gerry Lindgren, Bruce Kidd and Jim Ryun all went on to prove it, too.

Interestingly, 16-year-old Herb Elliott (I was almost exactly eleven months older) thrashed me in the 1955 Australian Junior Championships in Adelaide. Then he dropped a piano on his foot at the beginning of the next season (1955–56) and so was out of the scene until his father, worried his talented son was lapsing into a surfing lifestyle, paid for Herb to come to Melbourne, stay with Cerutty, and watch the Olympics. According to his biography, Herb looked at the heroics being displayed before him by the likes of Ronnie Delany and Vladimir Kuts and said "I can do that," and set out to do so. I watched the same great runners and said "I could never do that," and focused on football yet again.

But I believe I was the exception. Hundreds of youngsters were inspired by the challenge of track and field. Schools became better organised, cinder and all-weather tracks were built, interclub became better organised, and the competitions in all events improved in standards. By the time I returned to the sport seriously, again led into it by Les Perry, its popularity was at its peak.

I found it much more enjoyable the second time around. I joined Glenhuntly, where the club dressing rooms were located at the same Caulfield Racecourse where Percy Cerutty so disillusioned me. Now running became a pleasure more than a challenge. It was an exciting era and I have wondered ever since why I ever did prefer football when I was so much more talented as a runner. What would have happened had I tried cross-country running when I was 18 instead of waiting until I was 25? Who can tell?

I do know that when I did get more involved in 1961, even though I was losing most of my events in the beginning, the satisfaction of establishing new personal bests, the joys of competition and in simply running through the countryside or along the beach — joys that others must have been encountering for all those years — had me regretting my earlier short-sightedness.

It was a wonderful era for track and field in Australia, especially in Victoria. And it all really started that December day in 1952 when the great John Landy discovered his destiny.

1

From Nowhere: Setting the Scene

What role do tradition and culture play in creating sporting success? It is the sort of question that can be discussed endlessly over a cold beer or glass of red wine without ever arriving at a definitive conclusion. The ancient Greeks' military messengers, for example, were the inspiration for the modern Olympic marathon.

Fat lot of good it has done them. Aside from the first modern Olympics — when Spiridon Louis's victory in the race from Marathon to Athens was celebrated by the Crown Prince running the final metres by the athlete's side — Greece does not have a marathon medal. Nor, alas, has Hellas ever produced a swag of world-class middle or long-distance runners.

Another example can be found further north. There was no running culture to speak of in Finland at the turn of the 20th century. Yet in the next 20 years, the tiny Baltic nation had thrown up the first of a string of Olympic champions who swept all events from 1500 metres to the marathon. Hannes Kolehmainen and Paavo Nurmi were the forerunners of several generations of "Flying Finns". From Stockholm in 1912 to Berlin in 1936, Finland won so many Olympic medals — overwhelmingly in distance running — that it challenged the USA for Olympic supremacy. As much as anything, the Finns were motivated by nationalism and a fierce desire to make a statement on behalf of a country that won its independence after long struggles against its dominant neighbours Sweden and Russia.

Similarly, the waves of African runners who now dominate world distance running had no previous tradition or culture to draw on. The first Kenyan runners competed internationally in the 1950s. Within a decade, the likes of Kip Keino, Neftali Temu and Ben Jipcho were winning gold medals and breaking world records. Kenya's great east African rival Ethiopia progressed with equal rapidity. Mamo Wolde, a future Olympic marathon gold medallist, went to the 1956 Melbourne Olympic Games as a 4×400 metres relay runner. Four years later, Abebe Bikila, running barefoot over the cobblestones, won the marathon at the Rome Olympic Games.

Again, no tradition, but nationalism played a role. Kenyans were encouraged into long-distance running by British colonial masters. Like Australians at cricket, beating the colonising power was motivation in itself, and Britain was always a power in running events. And geography helped, too. The Kenyan and Ethiopian runners were largely drawn from the Rift Valley: living a nomadic existence at high altitude developed an ideal endurance base for distance running.

Once established, tradition and culture help sustain activities through the cyclical ups and downs. Kenya, for instance, has had several hiccups in its athletics development, notably when it did not participate in the 1976 and 1980 Olympic Games in support of boycotts, the first by African states against New Zealand's sporting links with South Africa, the second an American-led boycott over the Soviet intervention in Afghanistan. But once Keino and others had scaled the first peak, others saw what was possible and sought to emulate the pioneers (the rewards that sporting success brought in an undeveloped economy were not insignificant, either).

The Flying Finns were the distance-running phenomenon of the first third of the 20th century. The rise and rise of the Africans dominated the last third of the century and has continued apace into the 21st. In between, the focus of world attention was on the race for the four-minute mile.

Many sporting barriers are surmounted almost before people

start to think of them as significant. Bikila, for instance, broke the two hours and fifteen minutes, 2:14.00 and 2:13.00 "barriers" in one hit when he won his second Olympic title in Tokyo in 1964. Australia's Derek Clayton broke 2:12.00, 2:11.00 and 2:10.00 in one go when he ran 2:09:36 in 1967. The four-minute mile, or sub-four minute mile to be more exact, was not like that. The concept was simple to grasp — four laps of a quarter-mile track at an average of one minute per lap. Expectation built up because the achievement of this simple feat went from seeming inevitable to perhaps even being physiologically impossible.

The delay imposed by World War II had a lot to do with this. As milers got faster and faster through the 1920s and 1930s, a "sub-four" seemed a matter of natural progression. Even through the war years, the performances of Arne Andersson and Gunder Hägg from neutral Sweden suggested it was only a matter of time. The two compatriots had batted the record back and forth while the rest of the world fought, and Hägg held it at four minutes 1.4 seconds at the end of 1945. But then the two Swedes were disqualified for accepting illegal payments and stagnation set in until three relative failures from the 1952 Helsinki Olympic Games got into the act.

England's Roger Bannister had been Britain's great hope in Helsinki. Britain had indulged the talented young medical student as he stubbornly plotted his own path to the 1952 Games. He loomed as one of the favourites for a gold medal in the 1500 metres, but the relatively late and (to Bannister, anyway) unexpected addition of a semi-final round to the Olympic program relegated him to a disappointed fourth place. The critics, who had largely held off as Bannister prepared in his own way for Helsinki, now unleashed. Stung by the criticism and motivated by his own failure, Bannister resolved to continue for two more years, with the goal of becoming the first man to break four minutes as his primary incentive.

Wes Santee of America was even more bitterly disappointed by his Olympics. The University of Kansas runner qualified for the team in the 5000 metres but was pulled off the starting line in the 1500 trial, officials saying he was not good enough to first run against Emil Zatopek in the 5000 and then come back to run the 1500. Nor would the unbending US Olympic officials allow Santee to switch events. It was the first of many clashes he would have with them, ultimately at the cost of his amateur career.

Santee was eliminated in the heats of the 5000 metres. He resolved to prove the officials who had prevented him from running his best event wrong. What better way than being the first man to break four minutes?

Australia's John Landy got to Helsinki only after public monies were raised for his fare through the efforts of his father, his club, and his coach, the eccentric and controversial Percy Cerutty. He made major breakthroughs on his Olympic trip, and made observations of his own that would see him develop dramatically soon afterwards. In the Games, however, Landy was, like Santee, a heat runner only.

Failure had a galvanising effect on each of these three young men. Within months, they became the protagonists in the renewed chase for the sub-four minute mile.

If culture and tradition do play a part in sporting performance, Landy represented a stark contrast to the other two. Bannister and Santee each had tradition to draw on; Landy, and his generation of Australian runners, had to establish their own.

Bannister had been a diffident young boy who found confidence through running. He went to Oxford in 1946 to study medicine, but the summer before that the then 16-year-old teenager had a formative athletic experience. Bannister went with his father to the White City Stadium, in the west London suburb of Shepherd's Bush, the stadium that had staged the 1908 Olympic Games athletics competition. The purpose of the trip was to see British miler Sydney Wooderson race against Andersson. Wooderson was an unprepossessing athlete, both in personality and stature. Small and bespectacled, he looked more like an articled clerk than one of the world's best milers. Before Andersson and Hägg had got together, Wooderson had held the mile world record.

The 1945 meeting was the first international in Britain since the end of the war. As Bannister and his father neared White City the approach roads were packed; 50,000 were already inside the ground and the gates had been closed. "The crowd in front was determined to surge its way in," Bannister wrote some years later (*The Four-Minute Mile*, Roger Bannister, 1994 edition, The Lyons Press). "Someone pushed over a barrier, a police cordon broke, and before I recovered my breath I was inside the coveted ground, happy to stand for four hours."

Once inside, father and son witnessed a classic battle between the tall, blond Andersson and the diminutive Wooderson. Deemed unfit for active service, Wooderson had served in the Army Pay Corps during the war years. Illness — severe rheumatism that caused doctors to advise him he would never run again — and service meant he had barely trained. In 1945, less than a year after that gloomy prognosis, Wooderson had reduced his British record to 4:04.2 in losing to Andersson in Gothenburg. This night at White City, he again fell to the barrel-chested Swede, 4:08.8 to 4:09.2.

The result scarcely mattered. The teenage Bannister had found a hero. "As boys we all have our sports heroes," he wrote in *The Four-Minute Mile*, "and Wooderson from that day became mine."

When Bannister went up to Oxford the following year (1946), he immediately went to the Iffley Road track. "This was the track on which three Olympic middle-distance runners had trained — [Arnold] Strode-Jackson [the 1912 Olympic 1500 metres champion], [Tom] Hampson [the 1932 Olympic 800 metres champion], [Jack] Lovelock [New Zealand's 1936 1500 Olympic champion] ..." wrote Bannister. "It lay peaceful yet defiant, as if unwilling to yield its secret to any who were not prepared to toil up its steep gradient and break their spikes on the rough brick that protruded in places." He did not run that day, but did on a return visit.

Bannister also encountered a groundsman. "I remember Lovelock well," said the groundsman to Bannister. At this stage, Bannister did not know who the legendary Kiwi was. "He had such a powerful stride," the groundsman-sage continued. "I think you might become a runner. But I'm afraid that you [Bannister] will never be any good. You just haven't got the strength or the build for it."

Whether he was motivated or devastated by the groundsman's disparagement is hardly the point. Bannister was inspired by Wooderson. As a boy, he had one of the world's best in his own country; as a student, he ran on the track graced by three gold medallists and countless other Olympians. If he sought his inspiration, he needed only to look around.

Santee could not quite draw from such a deep well of tradition, but for the son of a Kansas farmer, he did not fare too badly by comparison to the Englishman. The mid-west state of Kansas may seem unpromising territory for runners, but the University of Kansas has seen several success stories, both before and since Wes Santee arrived in 1950.

The most notable before Santee's time was Glenn Cunningham. Nick-named variously "The Elkhart Express", for his home town, and "The Iron Horse of Kansas", or "The Kansas Flyer", for his state, Cunningham had held the world record in the mile and was the Olympic silver medallist behind Lovelock in Berlin in 1936.

Foremost among the Kansas greats to follow Santee are Billy Mills, the part-Sioux Indian who upset Australia's Ron Clarke to win the 1964 Olympic 10,000 metres and Jim Ryun, the youngest-ever sub-four minute miler, a world record holder in the mile, the 1500 metres and the 880 yards and arguably the greatest of the Kansas middle-distance trinity of Glenn Cunningham, Santee and Ryun.

The athletic ghosts may well have been many at Oxford and Kansas when Bannister and Santee began their careers as senior athletes, but there was precious little to inspire young John Landy from Australian history.

When Edwin Flack, an Australian accountant working in London, won the 800 and 1500 metres at the first modern Olympic Games, he was garnered with laurel wreaths and showered with praise. Reportedly, he was dubbed "the lion of Athens". Regardless of the aptness of this soubriquet, it was one that could in no way describe Australian distance running. Even if Flack were a lion, Australian distance running turned out to be a mouse that roared rather than a jungle king.

In subsequent Olympics, Australian representation at middle and long-distance running was sporadic and results mediocre. Athletes ran the distance events at the various Games, but it was more in the hope they would do well rather than the expectation. Ignoring the Intercalated Games of 1906 held in Athens on the 10th anniversary of the revival to bolster the near terminally-ill modern Olympic movement, it took five attempts before an Australian finished an Olympic marathon and, even then, Victorian Thomas Sinton Hewitt could do no better than 30th in Antwerp in 1920.

Greg Wheatley finished fourth in the 1500 at the 1906 "Games", but it was 32 years after Flack before another Australian reached an Olympic middle-distance final, William "Tickle" Whyte of Victoria finishing eighth in the 1500 in Amsterdam in 1928.

No Australian added a medal to Flack's two in the ten editions of the Games from Athens 1896 to Helsinki 1952. Stanley Rowley of New South Wales won one for Britain in Paris in 1900, running in the cross-country team. Rules governing nationality were obviously far more lax then, but all sprinter Rowley had to do was present himself at the start, jog a hundred metres and then pull out, his presence required only to give Britain sufficient numbers to form a team.

Flack's importance to the Australian Olympic movement was that his decision to go to Athens from London (where he worked and also ran with the Thames Hares and Hounds Harriers) for Baron Pierre de Coubertin's revival of the ancient Greek Olympic Games established Australia's unbroken line of Olympic representation. This tradition — carelessly jeopardised by Prime Minister Malcolm Fraser's (ultimately unsuccessful) campaign in favour of the US boycott of the 1980 Moscow Olympics — was heavily emphasised in the successful Games bids of both Melbourne in 1956 and Sydney in 2000.

If Edwin Flack initiated an Australian Olympic tradition, he palpably did not start one in his preferred events. For 50 years, virtually nothing happened at Olympic level. Whyte, as noted, made the 1500 final in 1928.

Pre-war, there were limited signs of improvement. Whyte's feat of making an Olympic final was matched by two more Victorians — Alex Hillhouse in the 5000 metres in Los Angeles in 1932 and Gerald Backhouse in the 800 metres in Berlin, 1936. The first British Empire Games got going in Hamilton, Canada in 1930, but even within that less competitive environment, success was modest. Home ground advantage at Sydney in 1938 produced nothing more than a silver to Backhouse in the one mile.

Despite the mediocre level of performance at championship level, however, there was some basis for the success that would come in the post-World War II era. Competition was well established, even if its best practitioners were not world-class. There was a healthy club system in both Victoria and New South Wales. Australian private schools embraced the concepts of muscular Christianity, and the consequence was an emphasis on healthy sport, as espoused in the English schools which they so closely emulated.

In Victoria, Edwin Flack had the benefit of both. He attended Melbourne Grammar School and also joined the Melbourne Hare and Hounds club (established by former Melbourne Grammar pupils) and competed in early cross-country races.

The oldest Victorian race, the ten miles cross-country championships, was established in 1892. Held at Caulfield Racecourse, home of the Melbourne Racing Club and the Caulfield Cup, it was quite an occasion. "The race was regarded as a socially accepted event," Victorian athletics historian Bert Gardiner wrote some years ago, "like the important horse races. Many men in top hats and evening suits were seen following the race on horseback. Ladies stayed on course to watch 100 and 440 yards handicaps, and listen to orchestras on lawns playing high-class music. Often 25,000 attended. With few cars and no motorbikes, cyclists were considered daring speedsters and runners appeared very fast." Caulfield is totally surrounded by suburbs now, and has been for more than 50 years. Then, it was a vastly different place, with open paddocks dotted between the houses on the course's perimeter.

A few strips of grass and parkland aside, such a cross-country run has long since been swallowed up by suburban sprawl. Major roads such as North Road and Jasper Road are not negotiable by runners other than with extreme caution. Nonetheless, turn of the century Harriers could race around the area with abandon. Flack himself was twice placed third in the ten miles, in 1892 and 1893. Melbourne Hare and Hounds won the teams' race.

Track races were also common, first on the goldfields and then in the major cities. Mostly these were handicap races, with more emphasis on hiding one's form until an opportune (read lucrative by way of winning both a cash prize and wagers on the side) moment than revealing it. Nor were the tracks anything flash. Walter George, the English record breaker billed as "athletics' first superstar" visited Australia for a series of races in 1887. The American, Lon Myers, and world-leading sprinters Harry Hutchens and Tom Malone were also in Australia at the time, leading British sporting papers to run stories of how four or the world's greatest runners were now assembled in "the Antipodes".

"What lucky dogs the cornstalks are," carped *Sport & Play*, referring to sports fans in Sydney and Melbourne. Clearly, the English sports paper thought, gold money aside, Australia had little to offer such athletes and lacked the sophistication to appreciate them.

Rob Hadgraft, in his book *Beer and Brine, the Making of Walter George, Athletics' First Superstar* (Desert Island Books, 2006), writes that in Australia cricket was accorded a much higher priority than athletics, even with such runners on hand. "There was some difficulty in securing venues as the local cricket season was in full swing and most Aussie running tracks surrounded cricket pitches. Myers understood only too well that cricket and running didn't mix, for while taking a training spin on the grass track at the Melbourne Cricket Ground, he had to swerve to avoid a flying cricket ball and pulled a leg muscle in the process."

The situation had not much changed when Dr Otto Pelzer, the German who held the world records in the 1500 metres and 880 yards, visited Melbourne for the national championship held on the Melbourne Cricket Ground. At the conclusion of his visit, Pelzer, a school teacher in Germany, wrote an article for the Melbourne *Herald*. "I have criticised your grass tracks, which should be of cinders to get the best result," he wrote. "I have been astonished at the great number of fine athletes you have in this country, but it is not fair to them that they should be trained to run on the wrong tracks." A quarter of a century later, when Franz Stampfl took up his appointment as coach at Melbourne University, things had changed — though not much. The first thing the man who had masterminded Bannister's sub-four minute mile asked — no, pleaded — for was first-class tracks.

JOHN LANDY

RUNS AT

FOOTSCRAY OVAL

IN THE TWILIGHT ATHLETIC MEETING

WEDNESDAY EVENING, 1st DECEMBER

6.30 p.m. to 8 p.m.

IN A 3,000 METRES	In Same Race Aust. and Vic. Champions
RECORD ATTEMPT.	GEOFF. WARREN NEIL ROBBINS
7.30 P.M. SHARP	LES PERRY DAVE STEPHENS

16 ALL-STAR EVENTS

FEATURING ALSO

KEVIN GOSPER

N.S.W.

Empire Games 440 yds. Champion and Record Holder

★ LEN McRAE	880 yds.
★ JOHN VERNON	HIGH JUMP
★ BARRY DONATH	SHOT PUTT
★ CEC WRIGHT	POLE VAULT
★ TED ALLSOPP	WALK

AND VICTORIA'S CHAMPION WOMEN SPRINTERS

HAVE AN EARLY OR LATE TEA OR REFRESHMENTS AT THE GROUND
BUT . . .

DON'T MISS THIS GREAT CARNIVAL

ADMISSION 3/- - - CHILDREN 1/-

ENSIGN PRESS, PRINT, 1-5 VICTORIA STREET FOOTSCRAY

From the visit of Walter George in 1887 to Franz Stampfl's arrival in 1955, the standard of Australian tracks was an issue. This poster promotes a meeting featuring Landy and other prominent athletes at Melbourne's suburban Footscray Oval, an Australian Rules football ground.

If cricket restricted access to track and field athletes, however, the positive side was that it also provided big venues in which to stage events. From the 1890s to World War II, and a little beyond, major Australian meetings were regularly conducted on the MCG and Sydney Cricket Ground or the adjoining Sydney Sports Ground.

Sometimes the crowds matched the venues. In 1949, 23,000 spectators went to the MCG to see a women's meeting with Fanny Blankers-Koen, the Dutch woman who had won four gold medals at the previous year's London Olympic Games, the star attraction. Blankers-Koen suffered a shock loss to a young Lithgow sprinter named Marjorie Jackson on that trip. Similarly, a local middle-distance athlete would occasionally upset a visitor.

International stars made infrequent appearances in Australia. When they did come — usually for major events such as Melbourne's 1935 Centenary Games — they were competing out of season and sometimes compounded this by being out of shape as well. Thus, "Tickle" Whyte and Alex Hillhouse defeated Pelzer over a mile at the Melbourne Cricket Ground in 1930. Pelzer, who held the world records for the 880 yards and 1500 metres at the time, was stung badly enough to make sure he gained revenge on Whyte in the 880 yards the following day.

From the late 1920s on, performances were gradually improving. Whyte (1500 metres in 1928), Hillhouse (5000 metres in 1932) and Backhouse (800 metres in 1936) made the final of their events at three consecutive Olympics. This hardly represented a groundswell, however.

In 1928, Whyte became Australia's first Olympic middle-distance finalist since Flack. After being run out in the heats of the 800 metres, he made the final of the 1500, finishing eighth. He finished second in the mile at the first British Empire Games in Hamilton in Ontario, Canada in 1930, and two years later he had turned professional. He was second in the Grampians Stakes, a handicap race of two miles, at the 1932 Stawell Gift meeting. (Two years further on, Whyte left the professional running ranks, this time to take up track cycling. He had been handicapped out of professional running, he told a journalist.)

Hillhouse made a more lasting contribution to amateur athletics. At the 1930 Empire Games he was second in both the three miles and the two miles steeplechase (an event which was promptly abandoned at Empire level and did not reappear on the program until the 1962 Empire and Commonwealth Games in Perth). In Los Angeles in 1932, towards the tail end of the era of the Flying Finns, Hillhouse finished sixth in his heat of the 5000 metres. In the final, he was 10th in a race controversially won by Lauri Lehtinen of Finland (in a close finish, Lehtinen veered out in the final straight, seeming to block the American silver medallist Ralph Hill). "Alex Hillhouse, the Victorian, put up a plucky fight in the 5000 metres, finishing in [tenth] place," reported the Melbourne *Sun*.

Hillhouse ran for the Melbourne University club at that stage and, subsequently, for Geelong Guild. He also taught physical education at Melbourne Grammar School through the 1940s and remained active in Victorian interclub athletics for many years. Hillhouse was a product of the Geelong private schools, attending Geelong College. In 1929, when Hillhouse won the Australian cross-country championship, Backhouse, who was five years his junior, won the mile at the Associated Public Schools (APS) Sports in Melbourne.

Backhouse was something of a singular character, religious but not sanctimonious, following his own ideas on training and racing, but generous in giving his time to train schoolboy athletes. He was a man described as "the life of the party", invariably the last to leave, by a clubmate.

In a 1975 article, part of a "Salute the Brave" series, veteran *Sporting Globe* journalist Jim Blake profiled Backhouse under the heading, "The Pathfinder for John Landy and Herb Elliott". "He Died

Too Soon", ran the sub-heading. (Backhouse was killed in a wartime aircraft crash in England in December 1941 at the age of 29.)

Jack Biggins, a life member of St Stephen's Harriers, the club for which Backhouse ran, felt that Backhouse "trained according to his mood". In 1997, Biggins wrote in a letter to one of Backhouse's descendants seeking information on his career: "His training routine was of his own making, not always regular or hard working."

Hillhouse described some of Backhouse's unorthodox training sessions to Blake, including some surprising post-party runs. "I remember going home by all-night bus along St Kilda Road. He was going to East Malvern and I was going to Brighton. We were in full evening dress … white tie and tails. At St Kilda Junction Gerald said good-night, jumped off the bus, tucked his tails in his trousers, pulled his socks over his trousers and ran the rest of the way home up Wellington Street and Dandenong Road to East Malvern. He was wearing dancing pumps!

"Another night after a party at Frankston he ran home to East Malvern in his tails and pumps — over virtually the marathon distance of 26 miles 385 yards."

Blake observed that Backhouse was an extraordinarily acute judge of the ability of his opponents. He sensed when they would have race-eve jitters. "When the worrying type gets up in the morning they are mentally and physically tired," Backhouse said.

Backhouse often went to a party the night before a race, arrived home late, went straight to bed and slept, Blake wrote. He would then arrive on the starting line relaxed. He adopted similar tactics when the gun went off, dropping to the back of the field and then moving up gradually as the race progressed. Almost invariably, he would win with a well-judged finishing sprint.

Backhouse told his own story in an "interview" (it reads more like a personal profile) with *The Sporting Globe* published a week after the 1935 Centenary Games. The precede to the story told how, the previous winter, he had left a party at 1am and run eleven miles home, arriving at 3am, before finishing sixth in the Victorian Ten Miles Cross-Country Championship. "The desire to do something that savoured of the spectacular or displayed physical activity found its outlet for me through two channels," said Backhouse, who was delicate and frail as a child. "One was in competition of speed ... and the other in the fascinating adventure of going a long way on foot. That eleven miles run home before the 1934 cross-country race seemed to be a turning point for me."

Another long run set him up for his Centenary Games performances (he won the 880 yards and the mile). "I became stranded at Mt Eliza, and ran the distance of 30 miles to my home in under three-and-a-half-hours. This convinced me that my stamina, at all events, was right. To the many people who have inquired how I became prominent so suddenly I can only say that I still run the same race as I did five years ago — hang near the leaders, if possible, and tear away at the finish — also, if possible.

"I have never suffered from nerves before or during a race. This is probably because, although confident of my physical fitness, I am always prepared for defeat. Naturally my ambition is to represent Australia at the next Olympic Games ... If I am to compete at the Games it is for the selectors to name the distance."

Eccentric Backhouse may have been, and his tactics unorthodox, but he won many races, starting with that APS mile. He had been selected to run the mile late when his school's original selection fell sick. He ran like a substitute, too, until he swept to the lead in the last half-lap. At Victorian championship level, Backhouse won the 880 yards in five out of six years from 1935 to 1940 and the mile five times out of the six. Twice he was Australian 880 yards and mile champion and, as well as reaching the final of the 800 metres in Berlin, he was second in the mile at the 1938 Empire Games in Sydney.

After the Berlin Games, Backhouse ran, and won, an 800 in Cologne. He defeated several of the Olympic finalists in doing so, making him the first Australian winner of an international middle-distance race since Flack in Athens 40 years earlier. On the same trip, Backhouse was a member of an Empire 4×880 yards relay team that finished behind a USA team at an Empire versus USA match at the White City in London. The Americans set a world record, with the Empire team also well under the previous mark.

If it was not exactly the sort of glorious tradition that Bannister experienced at Oxford, or the winning tradition Santee entered at the University of Kansas, at least Backhouse and his contemporaries had some modest successes to point the way for the post-war generation.

There was also a flourishing club system. Backhouse ran for St Stephen's Harriers, the strongest club in Victoria and, arguably, Australia as well. As Jack Biggins recounts in a summary of the club's first 90 years, St Stephen's was formed in 1908 "from a group of young lads who were members of St Stephen's Church of England, Richmond". It must have been a period of sporting upheaval in Richmond, then a working-class suburb whose social history was published under the title *Struggletown* (Janet McCalman, Hyland House Publishing, 1998). In the same year, Richmond Football Club joined the Victorian Football League; the "Tigers" remain one of the Australian Football League's most passionately supported teams. The St Stephen's Bible class, Biggins continues, "were looking for a recreational sport to occupy their spare time. Parents vetoed football [as] too rough, cycling equipment too expensive, tennis [for] lack of courts, so athletics was adopted."

After a slow start, St Stephen's — SSH as it is still widely known — flourished, particularly in middle-distance events and cross-country. From 1919 to 1949, the club was cross-country champion of Victoria in all but two winter seasons. In those days, the winter season started with a pack run at one of Melbourne's major racecourses. One year, St Stephen's had 116 participants, a record, and more than the combined membership of many rival clubs.

SSH often looked for opportunities to promote itself, chiefly by attempting long-distance relays. In September 1929, 23 runners, each doing five miles daily, ran from Melbourne to Sydney in a little under 55 hours. Two years later, 78 runners covered 262 miles 125 yards in a 24-hour relay around Richmond. In 1934, the club sent a team to Adelaide for the South Australian ten-mile cross-country championships and afterwards a team of 23 ran home in a relay that took a touch over 54 hours. Backhouse was a member of this group.

Prominent members of the club included Edgar Tanner and Charles Moses, who went on to become an MP and Australian Olympic Federation president, and chairman of the Australian Broadcasting Commission, respectively. Many club members competed in the Olympic Games and Empire Games. Five SSH men were in the 1924 Paris Olympic team. On the club's 51st birthday in 1959, Jim Blake hailed St Stephen's in *The Sporting Globe* as "one of the strongest athletics clubs in Australia".

SSH was still a major power in Australian distance running well into the 1960s when club member Derek Clayton set two world records for the marathon distance. However, SSH was not the only strong club. Malvern Harriers was the winter champion club in the only two years that the men from St Stephen's did not win the title. Melbourne Harriers, for whom "Tickle" Whyte competed, was another power. Glenhuntly eventually supplanted SSH as the distance-running power in Victoria and Williamstown, Preston and the Geelong Guild club were also in the mix.

Coaching was another matter. There were some successful coaches in sprints, but for the most part distance running coaches held to the prevailing orthodoxy that too much training made athletes stale. Backhouse partied hard and raced hard but, like the rest of his contemporaries, did not train hard — not, at least, by the standards of a Craig Mottram.

Clubs, regular competition and healthy participation rates all formed a basis for further success. But until John Landy and his contemporaries came along, it was a case of all launching pad, no rocket.

2

Percy Cerutty and the War Years

" I've come down to have a run with you. I used to be a member here."
Diffidence was not a hallmark of Percy Cerutty. He did few things
with understatement. Regardless, his simple line of introduction to
a group of Malvern Harriers after he walked into their clubrooms
one spring evening in the year of 1942 presaged one of the most
significant moments in Australia's rise from obscurity to leadership
in world middle-distance running.

Cerutty may well have gone on to enlighten the bemused
Harriers that his name was pronounced "Like sincerity, only without
the sin." He often used to tell people that, though throughout a
controversial career many would come to question the implication
behind the statement.

Brash, outspoken and known as much in his post-Rome years
for his fiery appearances as a wind-him-up-and-stand-back panellist
or interview subject on early Australian television shows as for his
coaching, Cerutty polarised views. Normally, that could be taken to
mean half the world loved him, the other half loathed him; but with
Cerutty, it sometimes seemed that half the world disliked him, the
other half disliked him intensely.

Few were neutral. John Landy, among the group of disillusioned
Helsinki Olympians who subsequently split with Cerutty, never
had anything to do with him again, throwing all his many
communications into a bin, unopened. Yet Landy acknowledges
Cerutty as a "beacon on the hill sort of personality" and as the
catalyst for Australia's success in the era.

Cerutty guided Herb Elliott to a win, in world record time, in the 1960 Rome Olympic 1500 metres. He is one of only two men to have coached an Australian to an Olympic middle or long-distance track gold medal — the other, ironically, was his bitter rival Franz Stampfl with Ralph Doubell in the 1968 Olympic 800 metres.

"Unlike other coaches of the day, Cerutty could actually do himself what he asked his athlete to do," Landy says. "So here was this grey-haired 51-year-old who could run a marathon in three hours, and 4:50.0 for a mile."

He looked the part, too. Noted Melbourne journalist and writer Keith Dunstan relates his meeting with Percy on a visit to Portsea. "At 64 he had curly white hair, a fine moustache and a tiny tuft of beard just under his bottom lip," Dunstan wrote in his chapter on Cerutty in *Ratbags*. "If you tried to pinch a piece of flesh anywhere on his body it wouldn't have worked. He looked like an ageing romantic lead of the nineteen thirties who had been progressively starved."

John Landy, too, was impressed on first meetings. "At first, Percy to me was a breath of fresh air. You had to be very impressed with his verbosity and enthusiasm. He was less impressive on the third or fourth hearing because you felt you had heard it all before." Yet Landy certainly acknowledges his initial debt to Cerutty. When he made his first mile breakthrough to 4:14.6 in 1951, he gave the coach a picture of the finish inscribed: "To Perce, the bloke who made it possible."

Landy continues: "[Cerutty] set his sights on the international scene. He just assumed that people in Australia weren't going to do these great things, so you had to look at what was being done overseas." Other coaches looked to Europe, too, but through the prism of the cultural cringe. Their training ideas were derivative, automatically deferring to Europe; their attitude to physical training that too much of it risked burn-out.

Cerutty, on the other hand, looked to Europe like the young athletes who quickly fell into his thrall. Like them, he took inspiration from the old world — none more than the charismatic Czech runner, Emil Zatopek, who trained harder than his rivals and was re-writing the record books — but his response was not to copy. It was to say that anything others could do, Australians could do better. According to John Landy: "Cerutty's basic message at that time was right. You could train consistently and in fact just get stronger. In this he anticipated the theories of people like Hans Selye, which showed that the body can adapt to repeated stresses."

(Hans Selye was a Hungarian-born Canadian endocrinologist. In 1936, he proposed that there was a universal three-stage response to stressors, such as illness or infections. Stage one is *alarm*, stage two is *resistance* or *adaptation*, stage three, *exhaustion*. Practically, the body reacts to an external stimulus, tries to cope with or adapt to it, but is ultimately exhausted by the effort. He described the response as the General Adaptation Syndrome. What this means for training is that the body will react to physical stimulus, and will initially try to adapt to it. If the stimulus is managed, the body need not reach the state of exhaustion/depletion. In other words, repeated training need not lead to breakdown; adaptation will occur if the body is not overloaded.)

"You have to see Cerutty in the context of the time when coaches were greatly concerned about overtraining," Landy continues, "about becoming stale, muscle-bound or even being burnt out by doing too much. Two or three days a week of about an hour or so for each session was about the limit."

Cerutty also had access to the latest news from Europe — what Zatopek was doing, or the Hungarians under Mihaly Igloi, or Bannister and the British. One of the sources for this information was *Sporting Globe* journalist, Joe Galli.

"Joe Galli [was] thick-set and a heavy smoker," says Geoff

Warren, another early member of Cerruty's gang. "He didn't fit [in with] any of Perce's tenets. But he was Percy's ear on the international scene, especially Europe. He was the one who brought us first news about what Zatopek did, made us aware of how good Zatopek was, how he was coming to the top and putting himself beyond anyone else at the time.

"Joe Galli had this connection with two Czech journalists. He used to bring us all the Zatopek news and also used to have a column in World Sports [a British athletics publication]. The international section had a little Australian bit and if we saw our name in that we got a bit puffed up. Joe Galli was the one who brought to Perce's attention what was happening in Europe. Perce seized on this, and particularly Zatopek, and we tried to emulate his training."

Galli, and other journalists, were repaid with plenty of stories. Percy Cerutty was a sure-fire bet for a yarn, whether it be on one of his athletes' prospects, or his own exploits. Early in 1951, for example, Cerutty told Galli: "Before the Olympic Games next year, the best of my boys will be running world-class times, and by 1953 they will be showing us times that are today world records."

Cerutty's return to the Harriers in 1942 followed his recovery from a near complete physical and mental breakdown. Three years earlier, Cerutty had been a "shambling shell", as Graeme Kelly wrote in his sympathetic work (*Mr Controversial*, Stanley Paul, 1964). "He was pitiably weak, for years of sickness had culminated in a severe nervous breakdown," wrote Kelly. "He had failed to respond to medical treatment and after this most recent collapse, his third, there seemed little hope for him." The initial medical prognosis was that Cerutty would never work again, and may have no more than two years to live. A more sympathetic physician told Cerutty that, in effect, he had to save himself, to find the answers from within.

Cerutty did just that. He took six months' leave from his job at the old Post Master General's department. He gave up the smoking which, if it ever did do anything to ameliorate his migraine headaches, did so at an even higher cost to his fragile health. He changed his diet — radically. Physical exercise, once he was able to get back to it, banished the migraines. Now Cerutty turned to study, exploring philosophy, physiology and nutrition with equal zeal. This would eventually lead to a holistic approach to training. More importantly, it led to a cure for his own varied ailments.

He joined the Melbourne Walking Club, tackling long and arduous treks, among them an ascent of Mt Howitt (1742 metres) in the Victorian High Country in an hour and a half. During 1945, Cerutty ran 100 miles in 24 hours, becoming only the third Australian to achieve the feat. In December of the same year, a fortnight before his 51st birthday, he ran his first marathon, completing the distance in just over three hours. The following year, he finished behind four New South Wales runners in the Victorian championship marathon, winning the title as the first Victorian across the line. His time of 2:58:11.0 was a mere second outside the state record.

Not long after that, Cerutty formalised his first training group. He was willing to take on anyone who sought his advice. He put a brass name-plate on his Domain Road apartment: "Percy Wells Cerutty — Conditioner of Men."

Never a coach in the strictest sense of the word, Cerutty was more about implanting a philosophy than the nitty-gritty of telling his charges how many miles or fast repetitions of the track they should run or how many weights they should lift. "Don't forget, the schedule is the product of the top-man," Cerutty told Les Perry. "Rarely is the top-man the product of his schedule." (In *Ratbags*, Dunstan cites a favourite Cerutty line: "What's the use of a body that can run a four-minute mile if the brain can't appreciate the beauty of a sunset across the sea?")

The first fruits of success came when some of Cerutty's charges — Les Perry, John Pottage, Bob Prentice and Don Macmillan among them — made the 1950 Auckland Empire Games team. However, it was the Olympic Games in Helsinki just over two years later where Cerutty's influence really began to be noticed. Perry, Macmillan and Prentice all made the team, as did Landy, who had joined the Cerutty "gang" on the recommendation of Gordon Hall. A Geelong Guild teammate of Landy's, Hall was one of the coach's talent spotters.

The trip was a learning experience for coach and athletes. When we look for the Australians who embraced the notion that athletes from this part of the world could be competitive at the highest international levels, we start with Cerutty. The coach's whole message to his athletes was that they should believe in their own potential. He held his first Portsea summer training camp in December 1951. Geoff Warren was one of those who attended. "Each one came away … believing more in their ability," he told author Graem Sims (*Why Die? The Extraordinary Percy Cerutty 'Maker of Champions'*, Lothian Books, 2003).

Cerutty had a more specific message for Macmillan, who was at that stage already a qualifier for Helsinki. "The four-minute mile, Olympic gold, it was there for Macmillan if only he *believed* he could grasp it. Like most Australians, he was only lacking in confidence — the only thing holding him back was the belief that he couldn't hold his own against the world. Now he had the chance to show for all time that he was as good as anyone else, *anywhere*." (*Why Die?*)

Yet the Helsinki trip saw the beginning of disillusionment for the athletes. They all recognised the need to learn, yet they were uneasy at the way Cerutty went about things. The desire to boost his own reputation, even at the expense of these men preparing for the biggest competition of their young lives, was too transparent.

Some believe this eagerness to place himself at the centre of things may have spoken to Cerutty's underlying insecurity. He never lost it. One way or another, the entire group fell out with Cerutty at, or soon after, Helsinki. He still had influence, but his impact on »

A few Facts about Portsea, and the
INTERNATIONAL TRAINING CENTRE

PORTSEA is the Premier Seaside Resort in the State: Ideal as to climate and terrain it offers conditions not excelled anywhere in the world. Known for its delightful scenery, as for its athletes, Portsea is now world famous.

The only World Records in Middle-distance and Distance running ever in the history of athletics in Australia — all made by Portsea trained athletes. The only Gold Medals won by Australia — in events above the 440 yards, in the history of the British Empire Games — won by athletes trained on Portsea techniques. The only medals for running by male athletes won in Olympic Games won by Portsea athletes.

The Centre is 60 miles from Melbourne, beautifully and ideally situated for its purpose. It is conducted by Athletic Coach Percy Cerutty, Australia's only OFFICIAL Olympic Games Coach.

Coach Cerutty at 51 years of age became Victorian Native Marathon Champion and record holder. He holds Australian Long Distance records and ran from Portsea to Melbourne in a little over eight hours at over fifty years of age.

Recognised as the World's Leading Coach of runners, all sport and field games, sprints, jumps and hurdles are catered for. Portsea-trained athletes hold or have held all the world records for the One Mile, Two Mile, Three Mile, Four Mile and Six Mile track distances; as well as the World Record for the 1,500 metres (three times).

It can be said that practically all the State and Australian Champions in Australia for many years now have been trained by or according to the methods taught at Portsea and now widely used throughout Australia.

Amongst the athletes to have visited Portsea for training are numbered athletes from England, Canada, the United States of America, Malaya, New Zealand, as well as all States of the Commonwealth. World class athletes in other countries visited have been taught and are too numerous to mention here.

SUCCESS CAN BE YOURS !

Percy Cerutty had to generate an income from coaching. Here he outlines the terms and conditions for "athletes and sportsmen, or those interested in becoming fit". Alcohol and nicotine were banned, dates not allowed, and visitors were expected to perform up to two hours of "chores" a day in addition to the three training sessions and one to two hours of sleep!

Don Macmillan

Don Macmillan was an imposing physical specimen. One hundred and ninety centimetres tall, weighing over 80 kilograms, he literally towered over most of his competitors.

When Macmillan broke the Australian national and all-comers record in November 1951, *The Sporting Globe*'s Jim Blake wrote (on 1 December 1951) about Macmillan almost with reverence. Blake had great knowledge of school sport and knew Macmillan was the third generation of middle-distance talent in his family. "Australia's brilliant mile runner and new record holder Donald Macmillan is the fourth member of his family to excel at the mile," wrote Blake. "His grandfather in Scotland set the fashion and this has been carried on by his father and an uncle at Geelong College where Donald made his first records.

"Donald Macmillan has the unique honour of holding both the Australian schoolboy record for the mile (4:27.0) and the Australian senior all-comers' record (4:09.0). Don's grandfather, Mr T. Macmillan, was prominent in the mile and cross-country races when at Aberdeen University (Scotland). His father, Dr Wilfred Macmillan, broke the Associated Public Schools record for the mile in 1916. An uncle, Mr J. R. T. Macmillan, was third in the APS mile in 1922.

"Both Donald and his father set new standards for Victorian schoolboys in the mile," Blake continued. "The father was the first to break 4:40.0. Thirty years later Don was the first to break 4:30.0." Blake alluded to Don Macmillan's "tons of stamina" developed by football and rowing.

In a 2002 interview at his home in Red Hill with Geelong College historian Harley Dickinson, Macmillan recalled a music teacher who "pushed me into something which I felt I could not do but found I was able to [do], that led me on to other things. My football suddenly came good, I certainly tried other things, and we started the cross-country." Macmillan almost beat one of the school's best all-round sportsmen in the cross-country, further enhancing his self-confidence.

At the 1945 Geelong College sports, he broke the school record for the 880 yards and then, expecting to run around five minutes, won the mile in 4:36.0. At the Combined Sports, Macmillan made the amateurish mistake of trying to take on the best runner in the field, Bill Ramsay, in the first lap of the 880. Macmillan led at 440 in 54.5 — "I could never run that fast in my life" — before hitting a "brick wall". Ramsay, who would go on to represent Australia in the Olympic 800 metres in London in 1948, won in 1:59.1. Macmillan struggled in third, but was also under two minutes. His father, who had come down to watch, told him to bide his time in the mile. He did, winning in 4:34.0.

In 1946, Macmillan was in no-one's shadow. He won the half mile then took aim squarely at the mile. His main rival was a boy named Ian Johnson, from Scotch College, whose coach, perhaps mindful of the previous year's half mile, called loudly "Let Macmillan go," when Macmillan went to the lead from the start.

"I thought I would show him, and I took off," said Macmillan. Macmillan's father, waiting at the 220 yard mark of the lap, had always advocated even-paced running. When he called out, "That's alright, keep going," Macmillan knew the pace was OK. He said the same on the second and third laps and then called "Go like hell!" on the last. Macmillan did go like hell; he ran 4:27.0, a British Empire record for a schoolboy. "I suddenly felt very tired," he told Dickinson. "I hadn't even noticed it."

In his first year at university, Macmillan confided to a running friend that things were going hopelessly with his course work. The friend, Les Perry, said: "I've got a bloke I'm talking to. He's terrific. Why don't you come along and meet Percy." (*Why Die?* Graem Sims, p.89.)

And so, Don Macmillan, the best schoolboy miler in the British Empire, joined up with Percy Cerutty.

» his home Olympic Games four years later was limited. In a very real sense, Herb Elliott rescued Cerutty's coaching reputation, the coach needing the champion athlete every bit as much as the athlete needed him.

There is no doubt coaches got a raw deal in Australian Olympic and Empire Games teams at the time, not only in athletics, but also in swimming. Yet accounts of trips to Helsinki, Cardiff, Rome, Perth and Tokyo all suggest Cerutty went out of his way to provoke officials, then cashed in on the resulting controversy. Even Cerutty's most celebrated success — Elliott's gold medal in a world record in the Rome Olympic 1500 metres — may have had a touch of this.

Cerutty's promise to Elliott that he would wave a towel at 200 metres to go if he was on world record pace and his subsequent action in leaping a moat, hotly pursued by the local *carbanieri* to do just that, have overwhelmingly been interpreted in a favourable light. Cerutty had done this for Elliott before, yet how much help could it realistically have been in Rome? How could Elliott be sure of even seeing Cerutty? Besides, at that stage of the race, he was already eyeballs out and had been since making his surge for home more than 400 metres earlier. In the light of his earlier group's Helsinki experience, perhaps this should be interpreted as the coach again trying to put himself at the centre of events.

Two years later, at the Empire and Commonwealth Games in Perth, an on-air observation by former Trinidad sprinter Mike Agostini as he and Cerutty sat on the same panel that Landy had been a "self-made champion" triggered a flurry of demeaning mutual insults. Then, in Tokyo at the 1964 Olympic Games, Cerutty intruded on Ron Clarke's final minutes before the 5000 metres final, choosing an oft-used tactic to try to goad him into a big performance. "You've got no hope Clarke, you always were a weak bastard," was Cerutty's barb. Even ignoring the fact that Cerutty had no place even talking to Clarke, it was a ploy as transparent as it was ill-timed. Cerutty was putting himself in a no-lose situation. If Clarke won, he could claim some of the credit; if he lost — well, at least he could say he was right.

Cerutty was always capable of being his own worst enemy. He could contradict himself, too. Landy recalls him telling one runner not to train too hard in winter — "What does a snake do [in winter]?" he asked. "It hibernates," — then, minutes later, firing another up to work harder with stories about Zatopek training knee-deep in the snow in the depth of a Prague winter.

Nevertheless, he got things moving and then iced the cake with Elliott's gold medal. With those achievements for bookends, a lot else can be forgiven or overlooked. "The whole question of Cerutty and how important he was really has to be looked at in terms of when he was saying and doing these things," says Landy. "It was a time when very little was understood about fitness and there were many false ideas about fitness. He was the apostle of hard work, and non-stop hard work. Today, what he said wouldn't mean a thing because people have gone past it, [training methods are] far more sophisticated, but it worked then."

As there often is, there was a resonance between Australia and New Zealand at this time. Around the same time that Cerutty was developing his training system in Australia, a former rugby player named Arthur Lydiard was coming to the fore as an athletics coach on the other side of the Tasman. Lydiard, like Cerutty, evolved his system from a little acquired knowledge, a lot of self-experimentation and a mountain of intuition. Where the Australian's break-throughs were as much on the mental side as the physical, Lydiard's system was firmly based on endurance.

Lydiard, like Cerutty, had the advantage of being able to hold himself up as proof of what he was saying. Taking up running near the age of 30, he made the 1950 Empire Games team in the marathon and then won the New Zealand title three years later, just short of his 36th birthday. Through his marathon training, Lydiard made the intuitive leap to realise that the fitter he got the faster he ran. After several disappointing races when his training indicated he should have run well, he concluded that he needed to taper his training before he raced.

And, like Cerutty, he intuitively understood psychology and motivation. When he sensed his young charges were in awe of a track session performed by one of their rivals just before the Rome Olympics, Lydiard snorted derisively: "The silly bugger's left it all on the track."

Finally, because Lydiard's system was more formulaic — an endurance base, followed by a period of hill bounding for strength, a period of speed-work and all topped by the racing phase — it was easier to grasp than Cerutty's regime. Lydiard's was a complex system delivering pretty well everything a distance runner needed.

Through Elliott, Cerutty brought home one gold medal from Rome. Lydiard-trained athletes took two — Peter Snell in the 1500 metres and Murray Halberg in the 5000 — and Snell went on to break Elliott's mile world record and to an 800 metres–1500 metres double in Tokyo four years later.

Sport continued throughout the war years — it was regarded as vital to national morale — but many formal competitions were suspended. Athletics followed the prevailing trend, conducting no national championships between the women's titles in Perth in 1940 and 1946. When national competition resumed with the cross-country championships in Queensland, Hugh Weir, the president of the Amateur Athletic Union of Australia, stressed the union's support for the war effort while reassuring all athletes that competition would be resumed with all possible speed. The cross-country championships would, Weir felt sure, "usher in a new era of amateur athletics more brilliant that than of the pre-war period".

Weir was right, in the long run, with the next 20 years to bring

Australia's greatest success in Olympic history to that point. But if some of the conditions for greater success in middle- and long-distance running were in place, it would take a while for anyone to take advantage of them.

The first Olympic Games after the war, held in London in 1948, saw just one Australian representative in events from 800 metres to the marathon. Bill Ramsay, who came from the family that founded the "Kiwi" boot polish company, ran in the 800 metres. He made it through the heats, but was eliminated in the semi-finals. Ramsay was another product of the Geelong schools — captain of athletics and open champion at the school sports of both 1944 and 1945 at Geelong Grammar.

The war was a watershed for Australia. For the first time in our history, Australian troops were involved in battles which, as they and the nation saw it, were critical to our national survival. Singapore, regarded as an impregnable fortress, fell to Japanese forces that had advanced along the Malayan peninsula with terrifying rapidity. An entire Australian division was among the garrison forced to surrender and march off to captivity in the notorious Changi Prison. In 1942, Australians halted the Japanese land forces along the mountainous Kokoda Track and critical naval battles were fought at Midway and in the Coral Sea. Darwin was bombed, as was Broome, and Japanese midget submarines penetrated Sydney Harbour's defences in a raid that set Australian nerves jangling.

"After the fall of the bastion of Singapore it was impossible to doubt that Australia had vital interests in the world — including our national survival — that did not always coincide with Great Britain's," former Prime Minister, the Hon. Paul Keating, said in a 2002 speech on the 57th anniversary of the death of wartime PM John Curtin.

As a result, Australia emerged from the conflict with a new spirit of independence and confidence. This translated onto the sporting scene. Allied to this confidence was the fact that the war had less direct impact on Australia than on Europe and the rest of the world and, consequently, the country recovered much more quickly.

"We Australians weren't riven by war," remembers John Landy. "Not that we'd come out unscathed — we'd lost many men in overseas combat, but continental Australia was untouched except for Darwin, food was abundant and we had this all-year round climate. Much of the rest of the world was affected, and we had a chance." (In fact, Darwin was not the only town that was bombed, but it was the largest population centre to experience air raids. Other towns bombed included Katherine, Wyndham, Derby, Port Headland, Broome and Townsville. John Landy was simply making the point that the direct physical impact of war on Australia was limited.)

Whatever the explanation, there was a flowering of Australian talent in the post-war era, both in the sports in which the nation had been traditionally strong, and in new ones. The first signs were seen clearly at the London Games. Only two golds were won, but the 13 medals overall reflected a depth not seen in any of ten earlier editions of the Games. The highest previous tally had been seven.

In the best athletics performance since Flack's double, John Winter won the high jump and there were silver medals to Theo "Bill" Bruce and George Avery in the long and triple jump, respectively. Sprinter–hurdler Shirley Strickland came away with three medals — bronze in the 80 metres hurdles and 100 metres, silver in the 4×100 relay — a prelude to the Australian domination of women's sprinting over the next two Olympiads. It should have been four medals, as judges placed Strickland fourth in the 200 metres. The photo-finish machine, in use, but which did not at that time have to be consulted by the judges, showed the Australian was third.

Over the next decade and more, Australians also excelled on the tennis courts, the golf links, the cycling velodromes, the pools and the motor racing tracks of the world. At the end of it all, journalist

Harry Gordon wrote a book, *Young Men in a Hurry*, which profiled the athletes and coaches who had been most prominent in this unprecedented success.

Ramsay aside, not much was yet happening in middle-distances. That, too, was about to change. The men who would take Australia to international pre-eminence over the next ten years were starting to make their mark, even if none yet stood out as potential world-beaters.

John Landy, for one, was still at school at Geelong Grammar. He would come both to embody and to lead Australia's race to the top of the world. For the minute, however, he was a handy schoolboy sprinter who also did well at Australian Rules football.

In 1948, his final year at school, Landy won the open mile at the Associated Public Schools Combined Sports. Early the following year, he ran the junior mile at the Victorian championships held on the St Kilda Cricket Ground in Melbourne, finishing fourth. At his own school, Landy also won the 440 yards, the 880 and was cross-country champion. But his winning mile time at the combined sports was well outside the Australian schoolboy record. (That record had been set two years earlier by Geelong College student Don Macmillan. A giant of a lad, Macmillan had run the mile in 4:27.0.)

Les Perry, who would become one of the major influences on Australian distance running, had done a little running at school but then rediscovered his ability while on active service. Sport continued during the war, both at home and as inter-services competitions wherever significant numbers of Australians were stationed. At one of these meetings in Morotai, Papua New Guinea, Perry was narrowly beaten in two races by Neville McDonald. He had no idea who McDonald was, but a mate enlightened him. He was the best distance runner in New South Wales, his mate said.

Indeed, McDonald won the three miles at the 1948 national titles. But it was Perry who stole the show, dashing to the front in the final lap and appearing to have the race won until he stumbled and fell, a victim of the heat and the custom of running distance races in the middle of the day. Perry's courage and commitment impressed onlookers, including Landy and Geoff Warren, another youngster from Melbourne's western suburbs who would show his talent in years to come.

Momentum was also building north of the Murray. Victoria, through Whyte, Hillhouse and Backhouse and been pre-eminent in the 1930s, but the pendulum swung back New South Wales' way in the immediate post-war years. Like Victoria, New South Wales had a strong interclub system. The leading runners raced against each other week in and week out, to the benefit of all. Among those making their mark were John Plummer, Jim Bailey, Dave Power and Al Lawrence. Albie Thomas would soon follow. There were influential coaches; Plummer, Power and, especially, Thomas were influenced to some extent either by Cerutty directly, or by Jack Pross, a Sydney coach who embraced his philosophy.

Al Lawrence, who eventually went on to a bronze medal at the Melbourne Olympics in the 10,000 metres, ran for the Botany club. As Lawrence tells it: "Australia had never been in the vanguard of world track and field; most 'experts' on the 'wide brown land' claimed that the Australian climate was simply unsuitable to produce champions in this discipline." Some, however, "refused to accept the standard reasons for the country not [being] able to produce track and field champions". Cerutty was one, and among the members of the Botany club was another such: Cecil "Chicks" Hensley.

"He [Hensley] ridiculed the notion that the Australian 'climate' was the culprit that prevented the country from producing world-class athletes, constantly preaching that it was a lack of 'method', not 'climate', that accounted for the conspicuous lack of Australian names in record books and Olympic results." (Al Lawrence, … *Chew with My Mouth Shut*, 1992.)

Hensley was club captain and Mayor of Botany when Lawrence

first met him. Botany (later Randwick-Botany), St George and Western Suburbs were the dominant clubs in Sydney interclub competition. They were fiercely competitive, too, though sometimes athletes would cross boundaries to train together.

Albie Thomas was a Cerutty protégé. Though he made visits to Percy's camp at Portsea, they mostly discussed his progress via correspondence. He describes Cerutty's contribution as "mental". "He never set you a training program," Thomas says. "He'd give you ideas. It was like [what] Elliott was doing, fartlek and free running and track work. One of the things I did different from Lawrence and Power was they'd do quantity and I'd do quality. I'd get up to 65 miles a week, 100 kilometres, and they were doing 100 miles or so. I tried it once and didn't like it."

Thomas lived in Kogarah then, and still does. He did a lot of his training in a local parkland area, and still utlisises it for the squad of juniors he coaches. "You'd get to know every bump in the park. So I'd write every week or two and say, 'I've done this, done that', and he'd write back and give comments. 'Yeah, this is good, keep that going, do that.' Never a program would come back; it was actually inspiration [sic]."

Separation might have been an essential element of the Thomas–Cerutty union. Like everyone else, Thomas occasionally cringed at Cerutty's behaviour. He describes catching up with the coach when competition took him to Melbourne: "You'd go to the athletics and Percy would say something. You'd wish you could crawl under the seat and not be with him, not know him." But, Thomas continues, Cerutty had a generous side. "He was staying with us when [Thomas's wife] Nola had Trish [their first child]. We had this old Feltex on the floor with holes in it. We came home from hospital and Percy had put a carpet square down. He'd paid for it himself; he'd give you his last quid.

"People say he was eccentric. Yes. He might have been, but I'd say he was ahead of his time. If he'd been much later with the ideas he was promoting, he'd have been a millionaire."

If there was an on-track leader in New South Wales, it was probably John Plummer. "He had a hell of an influence," says Thomas. Al Lawrence writes of the competitive experience he picked up running against Plummer and his Western Suburbs teammates: "Western Suburbs runners ran as a team in distance events, and I learned more about race tactics in one season of racing against them than in the combined years of my entire competitive career ... Although generally legal in their race tactics, their combined presence in a race was a difficult obstacle to overcome."

Plummer won the Combined High Schools mile in 1945 and progressed from there to interclub. "I entered the school championships for the first time at age 16 and by 17 I was winning the CHS. So it was purely luck that I ever got into running." He looked to make his mark at the 880 yards and mile at first and gradually got his times down. He was good enough to make the Empire Games team for Auckland in 1950 and, after a short-lived "retirement", came back to just miss the 1956 Olympic team at 5000 metres.

Plummer credits the strong interclub competition for the rise in standards in NSW during the late 1940s and early 1950s. He was influenced by Cerutty — "I was always amazed at his fitness and his philosophy," — but did not go to Portsea as Thomas and another Wests runner, Alex Henderson, did. He put his study and work as a chartered accountant first. "I corresponded with Cerutty," says Plummer. "We printed his letters in the club magazine. I got reports back from people like Alex Henderson and Albie. But I could never find the time, and the inclination, to do it [go to Portsea]. Because you were strictly amateur in those days, you could never see a living in it. People finished at age 30. You had no real inducement other than the joy of your hobby and wanting to be the best you could be. There was no professionalism, just those who were ambitious and wanted to do it. That was their aim in life and they got stuck into it and they did better than those who sat back and said 'Right, I'm enjoying it, but I'm not going to take it too seriously.'"

Whatever else you might say about Percy Cerutty, few would deny his gift for inspiring people to "get stuck into it" and take it seriously.

3

Schoolboy Champion

In 1945, John Landy was attending Geelong Grammar School. Situated on the shores of Corio Bay just outside the city of Geelong, the school had a proud tradition of rearing successful distance-runners. Gerald Backhouse had been a pupil there before the war and the athletics captain in 1945 was Bill Ramsay. Don Macmillan was at Geelong College, a few miles away in Geelong.

The rural setting made sport one of the preferred (one of the few, in reality) activities for Geelong Grammar students. More sensitive souls may even have called the environment harsh. Indeed, the school's most famous former pupil, Prince Charles, was held to have been sent there by his father, Prince Phillip, Duke of Edinburgh, precisely because its setting mirrored the unforgiving surrounds of Gordonstoun, the Scottish boarding school he had attended at the same age. The story is probably apocryphal: Charles actually spent his Geelong Grammar year at the school's Timbertop campus.

Keith Dunstan, for many years one of the most-loved chroniclers of Melbourne life through his "A Place in the Sun" column (in the *Sun News Pictorial*, the morning tabloid that was Melbourne's biggest selling newspaper) and other journalistic endeavours, was definitely one of those sensitive souls who found the environment harsh. The chapter of his autobiography detailing his four years at GGS is titled, simply and bleakly, *Siberia*. (*Keith Dunstan: No Brains at All*, Keith Dunstan, Penguin, 1990.) "Banishment to Geelong Grammar I saw as a disaster of major proportions," he writes.

The school was rigidly structured into houses. There were five houses in the senior school — the "Geelong" house for local students, the other four for the boarders. "Those in a house lived as separate entities, like inmates of a severe guest-house."

"Day-release" for boarders came on the weekends, when they were relatively free. "We could bicycle anywhere within 30 kilometres of the school … In 1939–40 there were 12 kilometres of open space between Corio and Geelong."

Dunstan continues: "The dictum of Dr Arnold, headmaster of Rugby, was never let a boy be idle. Geelong Grammar boys were always running, and at the Combined Sports the pale blues never won the athletics title but always did well in the long distance events. If normal sports … were not possible in stormy Corio weather, there were always cross-country runs in their place."

There were compensations. Geelong Grammar's headmaster was Dr J. R. Darling, who forged a reputation as one of Australia's foremost educators. He ensured the school offered as wide a variety of experiences as possible.

The schoolboy Landy had been a respectable sprinter. "I usually won or came second or third in my age from seven onwards, so I suppose I was reasonably quick," he told Brian Lenton (*Off the Record*, Brian Lenton, 1981). Landy's winning time in the Associated Public Schools' mile was 4:43.8. It was well outside the record 4:27.0 run by Don Macmillan two years earlier. (Within the next eight years, both Ron Clarke and Herb Elliott would run considerably faster as juniors.) Yet it was by no means the run of a slouch. Indeed, *The Age* accorded the mile run top billing in its report on the Monday following the race, though this was prompted — some things never change — by associated controversy.

"The mile was the most exciting event of the day," the paper reported. "There were many checks in a roughly-run race, and P. B. Quin (Xavier), who was second past the post, was disqualified after an inquiry, for alleged interference. The winner, John Landy

(G.G.S.), ran an excellent mile. He led for half the distance with a long effortless stride, and finished courageously to overtake Quin just before the line. Landy's time of 4.43.8 was good. He was also second in the 880."

All five Melbourne papers of the time routinely reported on the school sports competitions. School sport was frequently played at major venues and major events — football matches were often curtain-raisers to Victorian Football League games — and it was widely reported in the newspapers.

John Bartram, Australian Olympic sprinter in 1948, was one of many schoolboy athletes to compete at the APS Combined Sports on the MCG. He ran for Wesley in the 1939 sports, one of several held on the arena during that decade. Bartram lost that day to Ian Gillon of Melbourne Grammar, but he remembers the "tremendous thrill" of running on the same ground where Don Bradman batted for Australia and the top teams fought out the VFL football finals each year.

The year Landy won, the sports were held at Melbourne's Scotch College, as they had been when Macmillan won two years earlier. The College oval sits in a natural bowl, the chapel towering above it on one side, and is reasonably sheltered. It has its own athletics tradition. One year, Tony Sneazwell, the first man to clear seven feet in the high jump in Australia, competed there; another time Ron Clarke ran a two-mile trial on the grass track in 8:42.0 against a school 4×880 yards relay team that ran 8:36.0.

The crowd in 1948 was variously estimated at between 9000 and 11,000 in the newspaper reports. More reliably, the "gate" was £611, which was donated to the Public Schools' Charities Fund. In any case, the publicity and acclaim for a successful schoolboy athlete was far more extensive then than it is now. The spotlight may be more intense these days, but its range is far more restricted, says John Landy. "There was far more interest then, relatively. That may seem strange with all the media coverage of sports today but there are far more sports now and athletics is much lower on the totem pole. [Newspapers] would write stories about prominent young athletes and you'd get a whole page given over to whom was likely to win the high jump or the 100 yards at the private school Combined Sports or High School Sports."

In contrast, school sport is barely reported these days, according to Landy. If publicity is part of the oxygen swirling around talented young sportsmen and women, then potential athletes are breathing much thinner air than potential AFL draftees, Landy says.

Professionalism is another issue. When John Landy was contemplating running versus football back in the early 1950s, money was not really part of the issue. Neither football nor running was an alternative to a professional career. Footballers were paid, but not much. "They were moving out of the 'three quid a match' stage, but not a lot more," Landy says. (Three quid was the equivalent of six dollars when Australia converted to decimal currency in 1966.) Indeed, it was not uncommon for football players to retain their amateur status so as not to carry any stigma into their subsequent careers in the professions. Many who did just that played in an Australian Rules exhibition match at the 1956 Melbourne Olympics.

The professionalisation of major sports has changed all that. Under the current collective bargaining agreement, for example, the minimum annual salary for a player drafted into an AFL club is around AUD$40,000, with bonus payments of up to $6300 if the player participates in more than ten games in his first year. Increasingly, the average AFL draftee has attended a private school (often on a sports scholarship) and makes a choice in favour of football ahead of alternative careers. In 1950, if a medical student broke his hand badly playing football he compromised his future earnings potential. Now, the money he might earn from sport in the meantime represents substantial compensation.

Some athletes wind up making a living out of athletics, but not many. Without even publicity to compensate, it is an unequal choice, according to John Landy. "You can't expect young kids to aspire to athletics, which is most unlikely to provide a professional career, if you don't cover junior athletics in any way. That's a very important thing to me. If a kid is at school and he starts doing well at athletics, and he goes to the Combined Sports and runs 48 seconds for 400 metres it's not even reported. But if he happens to be a reasonably nifty footballer he'll attract attention. What's the point of staying in athletics?"

Among recent AFL players, there are plenty who showed promise at athletics. Anthony Koutoufides was an under-age national champion in both the 110 metres hurdles and the decathlon before opting for a career at Carlton Football Club. The Clarke brothers — David (Geelong and Carlton) and Tim (Hawthorn) — were outstanding athletes, too. David won the U16 400 and 800 metres titles at the 1996 Australian championships before following the AFL development pathway. Tim won national under-age steeplechase titles before joining Craig Mottram in the junior (U20) team at the 1999 world cross-country championships in Belfast.

Nic Fosdike, a member of Sydney's 2005 AFL premiership team, was another who stuck with his athletics as long as he could. In 1997, he finished a close third in the U18 1500 at the national championships behind Alastair Stevenson, who has represented Australia at world junior championships and world cross-country, and Adrian Blincoe, who ran for New Zealand at the 2008 Beijing Olympic Games. David Spriggs, who played for both Geelong and Sydney, won the U15 800 and 1500 metres double at the Australian All-Schools championships, and both West Coast Eagles captain Chris Judd and St Kilda co-captain Luke Ball were prominent athletes with their schools in age group competition.

Fortunately, when John Landy made his choice, the financial

inducements to pursue football over athletics were not as overwhelmingly tilted in football's favour as they are today. The possibility of making the 1952 Olympic team against the possibility of "three quid a match" — with neither offering a career — was not a financial "no-brainer".

That would be Landy's *final* choice. When he started his agricultural science course at Melbourne University in 1949, Landy was more interested in pursuing football than athletics. He trained with Melbourne Football Club's Thirds (for players under 19 years of age) with a view to getting an invitation to train with the seniors. It was an understandable ambition for a young man keen on football. Melbourne was a powerful club and only a few years away from building a team that would win five of the six premierships from 1955 to 1960.

As a result, Landy did little athletically in 1949. "I won the freshers' mile at Melbourne University but I didn't take athletics very seriously. I joined (athletics club) Geelong Guild, but I don't think I ran at all in 1949; I was tied up in study."

The pattern continued into 1950, when Landy did a year at Dookie Agricultural College. Dookie is a town near Shepparton, about 160 kilometres north of Melbourne. The college has always fielded a football team; back then, it played in the Central Goulburn Valley Football League. "I went to Dookie, as the second practical year of an Agricultural Science course," John Landy recalls. As with most second-year "ag" science students in those days, the emphasis was not so much on study as on enjoying everything a year in "the bush" had to offer.

Landy competed in running events at Dookie, but he rarely won. The gun runner in his time at the college was Len McRae, a quarter-miler/half-miler type. "Len McRae won almost everything," Landy remembers. The one exception — almost — was the cross-country. "I led all the way but had no idea where the course was. I led them all off the course and came 26th." Winning races at Dookie may not have attracted too much publicity. McRae went on to win several Victorian half-mile championships. One of his subsequent victories over Landy would attract far more publicity, as it would be the mile champion's first domestic loss for two years.

Overall, Landy's impact on athletics while at Dookie was minimal. The book on the college's first 100 years reports: "Landy did not distinguish himself as a miler while at Dookie ... Diploma student James Johnstone won the mile in 1950 in 4:40.6 sec with Landy second, although Landy won the mile event for College in a C grade provincial championship in Melbourne in a race which was not even timed!" (*Dookie College, The First 100 Years* by Roger Aldridge, 1986.)

Landy's fledgling football career and elements of his future athletics career came together coincidentally on the first weekend in September 1950. The back page of *The Shepparton News* reports Landy's win in the Central Goulburn Valley League's best and fairest (he polled 32 votes to win by eight) and Dookie's triumph over Boys' Club in a semi-final. The front page of the same edition, however, features a prominent report on the visit to Shepparton by Les Perry to run the Victorian five-mile cross-country championship. Perry, who had been to the Empire Games in Auckland earlier that year with Cerutty's first group of successful athletes, heaped praise on the locals. In all his experience in the Commonwealth, Perry is reported as saying, the local course layout, its markings, and the club organisation was the best outside Sydney. The hospitality to the runners was unsurpassed in his experience, Perry was further reported as saying.

Like many a young Victorian before or since who has at some stage nurtured football ambitions, or even dreams, John Landy would love to have made the big time in the sport. "I would like to think I could have done better at football, but I was certainly not going to have a career in League football." Among other things, he believes he was too light.

Over the coming years, Les Perry would have a far greater influence on the second-year agricultural science student than Australian Rules football ever did. Even before Landy left Dookie to resume his studies in 1951 at Melbourne University, a couple of results were pointing the way forward. "I ran a two-mile relay in Shepparton and ran inside ten minutes. In November 1950 I came back to Melbourne a couple of times for runs at Olympic Park. That showed I had some potential. I ran for Geelong Guild in a couple of mile events but was far behind."

One of Landy's club-mates was Gordon Hall. "I met Gordon Hall, who was a Geelong hairdresser, at Olympic Park. He said, 'You've really got to get on to a program of hard training.'"

Hall was also a member of Cerutty's group. Indeed, he is credited with establishing one of the staple Portsea runs — the "Hall Circuit" of just under a mile and a quarter. According to Graem Sims (*Why Die?*): "Hall had stayed in the shack one weekend with his wife and new baby and, not wanting to stray too far from the camp, had run repetitions on this particular circuit." The Hall Circuit became one of the Portsea benchmark runs.

"[Gordon Hall] gave me some ideas," Landy says. "The ideas were very crude but worked like a charm. One day, go out and run six miles; next day, go out and run some sprints with short intervals between them. I didn't have a clue what he meant by 'with a short interval between them', so I ended up running 50 metres at a jog then sprinting 50 metres for as far as I could, and I'd go for half a mile, three-quarters of a mile and be absolutely stuffed, and the next day I'd run cross-country, or attempt to."

It was pretty much Landy's first organised training and the dividends would not be long coming.

4

From the Central Goulburn Valley Football League to an Olympic blazer

There was little sign of the birth of an Australian distance running era at the fourth British Empire Games in Auckland in 1950. In events from 880 yards to the marathon, no Australian won a medal. Traditional middle- and long-distance powers England and New Zealand shared the bulk of the medals.

The more discerning observer might have noted the depth of Australian representation. Five managed a fourth place finish — David White in the 880 yards, John Marks in the mile, Alan Merrett in the three miles, John Davey in the six miles and Gordon Stanley in the marathon. The previous edition of the Games, in Sydney in 1938, had even bigger representation, but this was to be expected at home.

Further investigation would have revealed that a solid nucleus of the middle and long-distance contingent belonged to the Cerutty group. There was Don Macmillan in the mile, Les Perry in the three miles, Stanley in the marathon and John Pottage in the six miles and marathon. Another finisher in the Auckland marathon would go on to have more influence than any of them. Arthur Lydiard came twelfth for New Zealand. He would go on to coach Olympic champions Peter Snell (800 metres in 1960, 800 and 1500 in 1964) and Murray Halberg (5000 metres in 1960), revolutionising middle- and long-distance training in the process.

Among the non-finishers was Tasmanian Bill Emmerton. He would eventually make his mark, too, as an ultra-distance runner, chiefly for his runs across California's infamous Death Valley. None of the athletes showed sensational results in Auckland. Athletes and coach together were on an upward curve, however.

It was a promising environment for John Landy to enter on his return from Dookie. Acting on Hall's advice, he had already started to modify his training and it did not take long for his results to show improvement. As with most athletes who are not champions from their very first race, this improvement first showed itself in small ways.

The first positive sign was beating runners who had previously beaten him. "There were two brothers by the name of Stanes, running for St Stephen's Harriers, who were good runners. They were miles in front of me previous to that, and I came past them in the straight and won in about 4:28.0." One of the brothers, Roley Stanes, was indeed a promising runner. Early in the 1950–51 Australian season he defeated Bill Ramsay and David White over 880 yards. A couple of weeks later, Stanes pushed Les Perry close in a mile race. Perry ran 4:18.8 with 19-year-old Stanes estimated to have run 4:20.0. *The Age* reported that Stanes "seems to have the makings of a star miler". The report went on: "Although he had been running fast 880s, Stanes' performance on Saturday surpassed all expectations, and his time … is believed to be the fastest by any boy of his age in Australia."

A second positive sign for Landy was beating someone with a reputation. "I ran against Dave White, a former national 880 yards champion, who'd come fourth in the 880 at the Empire Games in Auckland, and I beat him. People were saying, 'who's this guy?'" White, as noted, was an 880 specialist. Just before Christmas 1950 he had run the fastest half mile of the Australian season to that point. Early in the New Year, however, Landy beat him over a mile in 4:31.6.

The final positive sign came in winning a race with some extra meaning attached. "I ran a scratch mile in bare feet in 4:19.0 on grass about a week later. I missed the national championships but they put me in a Victorian team to race against New South Wales and I beat Dave Power in 4:21.0."

Inter-state matches were big events in the 1950s, the rivalry between Victoria and New South Wales the most intense of all the states. The matches were normally held on holiday weekends, as was this one, on 10 March, the first day of the Labour Day long weekend. Landy not only beat Power, one of the emerging young runners from New South Wales, but also Perry's young protégé Geoff Warren.

Landy appeared on the scene just as Warren was poised to be the next big thing, although Warren had become aware of Landy some time earlier. At a glance, they did not appear to have much in common, Landy having had a private school education and coming from a solid middle-class background, and Warren a self-described "bumptious adolescent" from Melbourne's working-class western suburbs.

As Warren tells it, however, Landy's innate decency and genuine interest in others overwhelmed any social distinctions. "John appeared when I was a youngster — 17 or 18. I had started to think I was something, as kids do, get a bit full of themselves. I was a bit jealous of John, this boy from Geelong coming onto the scene. Then I met him, had a few races with him and it completely overcame any sense of jealousy. From then on I could only revel in any success that he had. [There was] just something about John, you could not think of having anything other than friendly rivalry with him. Even as a youngster it came out then; [he was] just a wonderful guy."

Also running for New South Wales in the match was John Plummer. A member of the 1950 Empire Games team, Plummer was something of a leader for his state colleagues. He was captain of the strong Western Suburbs club and, although he never went there for training camps, had corresponded with Cerutty and helped introduce some of his ideas.

For John Landy and other emerging runners, however, Olympic »

Dave Power

Dave Power came into Plummer's orbit when Power moved down to Sydney to work for the Commonwealth Bank. Power was born and grew up near Maitland in the Hunter Valley and went to the Marist Brothers College there.

"Wednesday was sports day," he said in November 2006. "My grandparents owned and ran the local movie theatre and, rather than play sport, I used to 'wag it' and go to the pictures most sports days."

The arrival of a new sports master, a Marist brother who ran an athletics club at Hamilton, Newcastle, changed that. Dave joined the school rugby league team. Through football, "I found I had a bit of toe," says Power. "I started winning school sprints." The sports teacher started a running club in Newcastle. In those more sectarian times, a Catholic club was frowned upon, so Dave joined the Achilles club. He first "got fired up" reading about Zatopek's exploits.

Power left school at the end of 1947. He worked at the local dairy company, but when it closed down moved to Sydney to work at the Commonwealth Bank, joining the branch at the corner of Pitt and Hunter Streets. He gradually moved up from sprints, but only to 880 and mile. He started to win state titles and national medals, finishing third behind Macmillan and Perry in the 1950–51 championships.

Training was not sophisticated. "We had a club night at Concord Oval," Power remembers. "Other times I'd go from the bank to Rushcutters Oval if I knew someone was training there. We had club races at Concord on a Wednesday night. One of those was a turning point for me. I went in a 220 [yards race] and on the bend [I] was spiked in the Achilles tendon. I folded like a deck of cards. I couldn't walk on the injured leg for a while and was off running for probably three months. At that stage I used to run in the summer and played A-grade rugby [union] for Western Suburbs in the winter."

The injury meant a forced break from football that in turn led to Power moving further up in distances. "During that time I came into contact with [Sydney coach] Jack Pross. He talked me into running cross-country and got me to go up to a gymnasium in King's Cross for weight training. I ran my first cross-country race up at Lane Cove, got halfway and I pulled out. Jack said, at the least, I was supposed to finish. So that was the start of my cross-country and going over to longer distances. At the end of that season I got selected in the NSW team and went over to Perth and won the national title on a sandy course."

That, in turn, would eventually lead to Empire Games gold medals in the six miles and marathon in 1958 and an Olympic bronze medal in the 10,000 metres in Rome two years later. "If I'd stayed in sprinting I never would have run for Australia," says Power.

Then again, you never know. "I suppose I've always been a determined bugger — never give up."

» dreams were pipe dreams back in the summer of 1950–51. At that point it was more about getting established.

Don Macmillan was the gun runner, though he had had a disappointing time of it at the Empire Games. Like most Australian athletes, Macmillan started his season with the first round of interclub competition. On 6 November 1950 *The Age* reported on his first run of the season. His target, the report stated, was to break the Australian record of 4:11.6 for the mile. In those days, the national record was the fastest time run by any athlete in Australia. The record holder was Jim Alford, the Welshman who had beaten Backhouse in the 1938 British Empire Games in Sydney.

Macmillan held the Australian native record at 4:15.8. "He has been doing distance work for the last month under veteran coach Percy Cerutty," the report continued, "and his style, stamina and judgement of pace have improved. He has concentrated on building up his strength so that a competition mile weekly during the season will constitute most of his training."

Macmillan ran an "easy" 4:29.8 to open his 1950–51 season and continued to win races. John Marks, who had finished fourth (with Macmillan seventh) in the Empire final, was also in form.

Macmillan, hurdler Ray Weinberg and sprinter Murray Morris had been invited to New Zealand for the Christchurch Centennial Games in late December, 1950. By this stage, *The Age's* athletics correspondent was wondering where Macmillan's form had left him. The report on the round of interclub competition conducted the day before the trio left indicated that Weinberg and Morris "both showed themselves to be in excellent physical condition and they should improve greatly on the faster New Zealand tracks". Macmillan, on the other hand, "failed badly" and was "disappointing". Harking back to the Games in February that year, the paper reported: "He [Macmillan] ran as he did when he failed miserably at the Empire Games and appeared a stale runner."

Macmillan won his race in 4:30.2, marginally slower than the opening run reported on so optimistically just six weeks earlier. The report said he was "obviously worried about his form halfway through the race … He appeared mentally tired and upset by his form."

At first glance, it appears to be the work of a highly perceptive reporter. Or perhaps our *Age* reporter was regurgitating the words of one Percy Cerutty, Macmillan's coach and a man not unknown for firing a psychological barb at one of his athletes before a big competition. Whatever the case may have been, Macmillan duly went to New Zealand where his opponents included one R. G. Bannister of Oxford and England. Bannister had not run in the Empire Games, but he enjoyed his visit to New Zealand ten months later, despite the arduous long-haul flights he and a small group of athletes had to endure.

The party stopped off in Sydney before the final leg. "Sydney Bridge [sic], ranked as one of the wonders of the modern world, raised barely a murmur of excitement in us," Bannister wrote in an account of the trip in his book, *Four-Minute Mile*. "And the little we saw of the city itself spelt brashness and Coca-Cola to our insensitive minds."

In Christchurch, Bannister's opponents in the mile were headed by Wim Slijkhuis, the Dutchman who had won that year's European championships 1500 metres. Bannister won in 4:09.9. It was his fastest time; the fastest mile ever run in the Southern Hemisphere and he had run it on a grass track. He was pleased.

So, too, was Macmillan, who belied his "poor" form by taking second place. After the race, Macmillan teased the Englishman with the remark, "You only become really friendly with your opponents after you've beaten them." (*Four-Minute Mile*, Roger Bannister, 1955.) It all sounds a little too friendly, especially for an Australian sportsman. Graem Sims has the same quote in his book *Why Die* but in his version Macmillan adds, "See you in Helsinki."

While the visiting athletes were in Australia en route to Christchurch, efforts were made to get them to run at a meeting in Melbourne in January 1951. On the same day *The Age* reported on Macmillan's "disappointing" run, the newspaper also reported that the efforts had failed. Had the plan come off, Bannister and Landy could have met under vastly different circumstances than those that would prevail when they finally did race in the 1954 British Empire Games.

Others were running well in the 1950–51 Australian season. Les Perry opened up with a personal best over a mile, running 4:23.2 late in November. Perry defeated Macmillan in the race, his effort reported as "surprising, as he [Perry] has been regarded more as a three-mile runner". A week later, Perry underlined his improvement at the shorter distance by running 4:18.8, a Victorian interclub record. On 16 December, he turned to his specialty, defeating Empire Games representative Ken Macdonald over three miles in 14:27.8, a new Victorian record.

On the resumption of competition after Christmas, Macdonald

turned the tables, defeating Perry in 14:28.0 in what were described as "unpleasantly hot conditions". That hiccup aside, Perry continued on his way. He beat Empire Games fourth place-getter John Marks over a mile, set a new Victorian record for two miles in the Victoria–New South Wales match and then split Macmillan and Landy in an invitation mile two days later.

Jim Bailey, another of the NSW athletes breaking through, came down to Melbourne for an invitation run at the end of January, 1951. It was a rewarding visit: Bailey won the 880 yards in 1:56.2, fastest in Australia for the season, ahead of White and Marks. Bailey had already been competitive at national level for a number of years, taking a number of national title placings at 880 yards. He had also shown a penchant for creating controversy.

John Landy was by no means the best of this group on revealed performances. They were all improving, but he had improved quicker than any of them. And he wasn't done yet.

Once the championships were contested and the interclub season completed, the next phase of the Australian season was university and inter-varsity competition. This, too, was a far bigger thing in the 1950s than it is now — indeed, current Federal Government changes to compulsory union fees have put university sport in mortal danger. Back then, university sport generated widespread media coverage. With Landy and Macmillan both attending Melbourne University, they clashed in both the intra- and inter-varsity championships in May 1951.

Like interclub, the aim of university sport was to win points for your faculty, your college or your university. *The Argus* of 5 May 1951 reported Landy finishing a yard behind Macmillan in the 880 yards at the Melbourne University championships, running 1:59.2. On the same day, Landy beat Pottage in the three miles. Earlier in the championships, Landy was second to Macmillan in the mile. Don ran 4:23.0 and won by a mere three yards. "[Macmillan] was fully extended by John Landy, who is the most promising young miler in Australia," reported *The Age*.

Fewer than three weeks later, the inter-varsity championships were held in Hobart. Australia's southernmost state capital is hardly the place most conducive to middle-distance running, but Macmillan, Landy and John Plummer turned on a memorable race in the mile. Macmillan won in 4:15.2, with Landy slashing his previous best by seven seconds with 4:16.0 to finish in second place and Plummer another eight yards back in third. *The Mercury*, Hobart's daily paper, reported that "Macmillan defeated Landy by five yards after a desperate 100 yards struggle with Plummer along the back-stretch in the final lap."

Two days later, Macmillan won the 880 from Landy and Plummer and Landy won the three miles. People were now getting to have a fair idea of who "this guy" (Landy) was. Landy's ambitions were adjusted accordingly. He had come into the season with his schoolboy best of 4:43.0, run 4:31.0 in his first race and then improved all the way to 4:16.0. "All this happened in a very short space of time," says John Landy. "I scrapped the idea of playing footy, and with the [Olympic] Games on the next year I decided to have a go. Because of the speed with which I'd come up, people said I'd have a chance [of getting in the team]."

Landy trained solidly, if not particularly scientifically, all through the Melbourne winter. Most of his training was done in Central Park, across the road from his parents' East Malvern home.

Central Park, East Malvern, is nothing like its namesake in New York. The latter offers a road circuit of six miles, and almost limitless variation in both terrain and topography within its borders. Landy's Central Park was far more limited in scope. A stock-standard park in a stock-standard middle-class suburb of Melbourne, an oval (now John Landy Oval) occupies its northern end, while a greenhouse is the biggest feature at the southern end. A gravel path of around 600 metres runs around the oval. A spirit level would detect some rise and fall, but it is pretty well pancake flat.

For Landy, however, Central Park's paramount virtue is that it *was* central. His family home was just across the road at the southern end of the park. Within a few minutes of finishing study, he could be changed, across the road, and running. "I lived right opposite ... and that was a huge advantage, I make no bones about that. I didn't have any travelling to do whatsoever, just walk across the road and I was in business."

Perry and his Williamstown teammates trained at Newport Oval, and other places, including Melbourne's Tan Track, where Cerutty would hold a stop-watch on them as they ran repeats up the 500-metres long Anderson Street hill. Occasionally, Landy would join the "Cerutty gang" at Percy's flat in Domain Road near the Botanic Gardens for a lecture on some topic or another. Once or twice, he did "long runs" from the Williamstown clubrooms.

Overwhelmingly, though, it was Central Park. "I just trained entirely at home. I had to try and get through my university course. I don't think I ever ran away from my home more than once or twice a month, and even that I doubt. I was tied up in university studies and when I decided to have a go at running rather than footy, I thought the best way to achieve it was to use what I had, which was the Park."

The park and the local streets became Landy's training venues. As Cerutty undoubtedly knew, and Landy and the other athletes at that time came to realise, it did not matter much what they did for training, as long as they did it. "I did train very consistently," says Landy. "I'd run around the streets at night, say three times a week. The rest of the time I'd run around the gravel track." His 600-metre repetitions owed as much to the perimeter of the track as any scientific training notion. "I'd do a bit of PT [physical training] — not much, physical exercises, gymnastics, stretching — but I had to work it in with doing the university course. I caught the train probably about 8am from Caulfield, be back at 5pm and have a meal. I used to do about three hours' study a night, so nearly all my training was done late at night, which people found very hard to understand, but it worked."

If Landy's parents found this strange, they kept it to themselves. "I was very fortunate. I had very supportive parents. Not that they were into athletics as such, but they were very supportive of anything their kids did."

This sort of outdoor training was possible in the milder, southern hemisphere winter. Of course, it would hardly have been possible in the northern hemisphere. "We had an 'all-year-round' climate. I never had a tracksuit. I ran in a jumper, a pair of shorts and sandshoes; that's all I used, and I ran countless miles around a gravel path. People in Canada, or the UK, or Europe, couldn't do that — it was very much more difficult. There weren't indoor training facilities overseas then, so a country like Australia had a big advantage."

Around Australia, it was a similar story. Whether it was Perry, Warren, Dave Stephens, Neil Robbins and others at Williamstown; Landy at Central Park; Plummer, Power and their Western Suburbs teammates at Concord in Sydney; Albie Thomas at Kogarah; or Al Lawrence and his crew at Botany, the 1950s runners used what they had.

When Albie Thomas trained alone, he often used to imagine he had company. Distinguished company it was, too. "We had role models from overseas," recalls Thomas. "In *World Athletics* [an English magazine], you'd see pictures of Zatopek, Mimoun, Iharos and all these guys running. I can remember running up on Bexley Oval and I'd try to mimic someone. I could picture myself mimicking Bannister or Ibbotson. Up and running tall and going, and you had that picture in your mind. It was their technique you were copying."

Williamstown was probably the strongest running club in

Australasia. Yet its facilities were nothing flash. Geoff Warren remembers a "dirty, dusty, stinkin' old" piece of fabric on the floor. "We called it a gym mat," says Warren, "but it was a terrible thing. It had a horizontal bar above it and that was our one gymnastic thing." Warren also recalls pack runs from the various homes of John Pottage, another Cerutty gang member, in Melbourne's semi-rural outer eastern suburbs. "We used to go to his house once a week, first at Croydon and then at Ringwood, and go out and run on the hills of Warrandyte. To us they were huge runs, probably 16 miles. His wife would put on a big spread."

Sydney's Botany boys "used to train at a funny little grass track" recalls Warren. "You'd scorch around the track. It had a lamppost or two in the way where the track had to deviate around them." The Newport Oval, too, had its idiosyncrasies. It was an Australian Rules oval. "In the summer it baked pretty hard and was worn down flat" Warren says. "In winter, it was wet and slippery. One side went alongside an old quarry, there was a bit of a dip, you had to get out of there and fight up the other side."

If training varied, and facilities in all cases were far from what they are today, the athletes of the 1950s had one strong asset — their clubs. "The basis of our development was interclub," says Albie Thomas. "We all ran competition, went out and ran for our club."

Nor were they selective about when they competed. You started with the first round of interclub and finished with the club finals, which came after the state and national titles — if your club made the finals, that is. In Victoria, for instance, there was much media discussion one year on the impact of Geelong Guild's being relegated from the top grade of competition. Would this mean Macmillan and Landy would have their preparation for international competition compromised?

The two premier milers in the country belonged to the same club (Geelong Guild), went to the same university (Melbourne) and were both coached by Cerutty (though they did not train together). As he chased Olympic selection, Landy competed against Macmillan at club, university, inter-varsity, state and national level. The two university races in May 1951 were the first of a series of races featuring the pair. Almost invariably, it was Landy who would set the pace, Macmillan who would win the race. Spectators paying attention only to the finish of the mile perhaps unkindly dubbed Landy "Macmillan's tail-light", a reference to the number of times he finished right on his rival's "tail".

As the 1951–52 Victorian interclub season got started, Landy was keen to get after the Olympic qualifying time. The Australian Olympic Federation had set a mile standard of 4:10.0 for selection in the team to Helsinki, or 3:53.0 for 1500. After a couple of lead-ups, Landy ran a personal best for the mile of 4:14.6 at Olympic Park on 10 November.

Melbourne's evening paper, *The Herald*, reported on the race in its Monday edition two days later. The paper had caught up with Landy's training routine, too. "Victorian amateur athlete John Landy had a midnight run as his final trial for the mile at Olympic Park last Saturday — in which he set a new Australian record." Noting that Landy had been swotting for his university exams, the report commented: "He left his books just before midnight and ran the two miles to Malvern Railway Station and back. Then he went to bed at about 1am. It is nothing unusual for Landy to study for five hours at night and then go for a training run." More modestly, Landy insists he did no more than four hours study.

The following week, Landy showed that his winter work had made him faster, as well as stronger. He reeled off a personal best 1:55.7 half mile, then told *The Age*'s Bruce Welch he expected "to build up his condition by training with Macmillan, Perry, [Terry] Sullivan [a promising young Victorian] and other pupils of Percy Cerutty over the holidays".

The training camp to which Landy was referring was the one that turned out to be his one and only visit to Portsea. He arrived late on the Friday night, slept outside in his sleeping bag through heavy rain and was photographed training with Macmillan on Portsea Oval under Cerutty's watchful eye.

A few weeks before that, Landy, Macmillan and Perry met in what was billed afterwards, if not before, as Australia's "mile of the century" (Ben Kerville, *The Sporting Globe*, 28 November 1951). It was run, Kerville said in the follow-up article, "with no preliminaries, no last-minute instructions and no ballyhoo". The race, four days earlier at Olympic Park, saw Macmillan break Backhouse's national record and Alford's all-comers' mark and Landy beat the Olympic qualifying time for 1500 metres. Though Macmillan was at pains to say each of them was running his own race, it did have some appearance of cooperation.

Perry led through the first quarter-mile in 61.3, and Landy at 880 (2:05.2) and three-quarters (3:09.6). Then Landy took off, forcing the pace all the way to the 1500 metres mark, which he reached in 3:52.8, two tenths of a second under the Olympic standard. Shortly afterwards, Landy was reduced to a virtual jog as Macmillan won in 4:08.9 (4:09.0 for record purposes under the rules of the day) by 35 yards from Perry with an exhausted Landy another 15 yards back.

"Macmillan owes much of his success today to the brilliant Landy," wrote Kerville in his race-day report, "who ran a very sound race tactically by wresting the initiative from early pacemaker Perry, and forced Macmillan to run a very fast last lap." Kerville wrote that Landy had "had it" by the 1500 mark, a suggestion with which Landy concurs. "Three fifty-three was the time, I think," says Landy, "and I ran 3:52.8. I ran to 1500 and I just went 'bong', I was absolutely finished and Don just took off. I beat him to 1500 and he just took off and ran 4:08.9 and I just jogged, which I was criticised for, but I was absolutely stuffed. It was the only thing that got me to Helsinki, the only time I broke the qualifying time. So I got into the Helsinki team by one-fifth of a second."

Little things *can* make a big difference. Australian distance great Steve Moneghetti has a similar story about making his first team, the 1986 Commonwealth Games team. Moneghetti ran under the selection standard by less than a second in the Victorian 10,000 metres championships; Adam Hoyle, a contemporary of Moneghetti's and his superior as a junior, finished second, missing the standard by a couple of tenths. Moneghetti went to Edinburgh, ran fifth in the 10,000, then took the vacant spot in the marathon and won a bronze medal. He was away. Hoyle kept running without ever making a major championship team.

The criticism of Landy's run was not in his own imagination. For one of the few times in his career, he was heckled at Olympic Park, albeit by a few only. As another report of the race told it: "Landy was undeservedly heckled by a section of the crowd for pulling up after passing [the 1500]. He made no excuses and said: 'I set out for the 1500 standard and I got it. Why should they abuse me for pulling up?'"

"The aim was to get in the Olympic team in the 1500 metres," Landy says now. "Prior to Christmas in 1951, I aimed at that particular race and I just got it by the skin of my teeth." Objective achieved, but would it be enough?

Not even the new record holder escaped criticism, though in Macmillan's case it was self-criticism. He told Ken Moses in *The Argus*: "I did the wrong thing last night and went to a dance, instead of relaxing for the event. I had to do the right thing today and break that record to make amends to my trainer Percy Cerutty." Moses also revealed that Macmillan "chewed grass throughout the journey to keep his mouth fresh". Whatever he was doing, it certainly was not chewing the cud.

Landy's racing against Macmillan revealed his competitiveness, a trait sometimes overlooked later in his career. The racing between

Landy and Macmillan continued throughout the 1951–52 season. If Landy was the tail-light at the finish, he was the head-light showing the way for most of the races. "I tended to set the pace so Don had a bit of a ride. He was the better runner at that stage; I came second to him at 800 and 1500 by margins varying from a second down to half a second and maybe less. I did beat him finally, when I least expected to."

More of that a little later, but first Landy had a couple of cracks at running 4:10.0 on his own. In January, he ran a mile against Perry at Olympic Park while Macmillan was in Sydney winning the 880 and mile double at the NSW championships, beating Power and Plummer in both races. Landy took the lead early, ran 60 seconds for the first lap then 2:02.0 for 880. At the bell he was 60 yards clear and he won in 4:11.0, two seconds outside the mile standard. "It is bad luck that with Helsinki coming off that I should strike a runner like Macmillan," Landy said at the time, "as I don't expect there will be enough finance to send us both away." He was wrong about selection, but correct in his judgement on the finance, at least from official funds.

Finally Landy did beat Macmillan, a performance which may have had as much influence on the final Olympic selection as his earlier qualifying time. After Macmillan had won the national title in Brisbane, clearly beating Landy and Perry, a competition described as an Olympic Trials meeting was held at the Sydney Sports Ground. "I adopted a different tactic," says Landy. "I ran very slowly, back in the field, and I jumped the field and won the race which was the first time I'd ever done that. I won the race and beat Macmillan." Landy won narrowly, with both he and Macmillan timed at 4:13.6. According to a report in the Sydney *Sunday Telegraph*, Macmillan had looked "a certain winner" 20 yards before the tape. *The Age* reported that with his win Landy "probably forced consideration as an Olympic Games distance runner".

"The next week, I ran the Victorian championship and I very nearly did the same thing again, but I got blocked running through and didn't succeed," Landy says. He "failed" by inches only, again both of them running the same time of 4:13.4. Perry was third in 4:14.0 and the last lap was run in under 59 seconds.

Assuming he would not be selected, Landy called his season to an end. He took a break but when the team was announced, his name was in it, along with Macmillan, Perry and marathoner Bob Prentice. Joining Prentice in the marathon was Claude Smeal, an army captain on active service in the Korean War.

Landy was on a tractor on the family farm in Gippsland when he heard the news about selection. He had to catch up on training. He had to somehow raise the funds. But he *was* an Olympian.

5

Helsinki — An Ingénue Abroad

The two young men stare, bemused, into the window of a butcher's shop. On the other side of the glass, two cats stare insouciantly back, not at them, but past them, both aware of the men and seemingly indifferent to them at the same time. "Chops & Steaks" reads the sign in the middle of the window; "Sausages" and "Chops & Steaks" strip signs run along its bottom border. The cats — one black and white, the other tabby — sitting on an empty meat tray with a row of empty trays adjacent and behind, are the only remotely edible things in sight.

It is London's Petticoat Lane in the summer of 1952. Our two young travellers are Don Macmillan and John Landy, en route to Helsinki with the Australian Olympic Games athletics team.

The photo is highly symbolic, an image reflecting some of the factors that gave Australian sport an edge in the post-war era — two healthy young athletes from a country that had been largely untouched by the war, that had abundant food supplies and a climate that allowed year-round training finding themselves in a country that had been ravaged and in which rationing still had a further two years to run.

Rationing, brought in as a wartime austerity measure in 1940, and maintained in peacetime in a Europe struggling to house and feed a flood of refugees, was a further two years away from its official end. Tea, for example, remained rationed until October, 1952. The impact of rationing had lessened, however.

Ray Weinberg, who took the photo, had also been a member

of the 1948 London Olympic team. "We had to take our own food then," he says. Weinberg remembers that the Australians had been meaning to visit Petticoat Lane and its famous market but had not had the opportunity. "We decided this was the day to meander down and take a look." It was a Saturday afternoon, and the shops were closed. "I guess they didn't open on days when the market did." As he recalls it, it was the presence of the two cats that prompted him to get Macmillan and Landy to pose for the picture.

The 1952 Olympic team was an inexperienced one, however. Weinberg, a hurdler, and sprinter John Treloar, like Weinberg a member of the 1948 team, were "the authorities on everything," he says, "because we'd been away before".

The middle- and long-distance runners were no exception to the "innocents abroad" rule. Landy had to apply for his first passport to take the trip. Macmillan had twice been to New Zealand, but no further and marathoner Bob Prentice was also a member of the 1950 Auckland Empire Games team. As ever, Les Perry had travelled wider horizons — his wartime service had taken him to Papua New Guinea and the islands. He had been in the Auckland team, too. Percy Cerutty had journeyed to London, too, the locals regarding him with every bit as much bemusement as Landy and Macmillan did the butcher's shop cats.

The story of how war-weary Europe looked on countries such as the USA and Australia with fondness and admiration is well known. Sport formed a great part of the post-war revival and the English both longed for new heroes of their own — a hunger that would soon feed into Roger Bannister's quest for the four-minute mile — and admired sportsmen and women from abroad. Some sportspeople, like Australian Test cricket player Keith Miller, who had served in the Air Force, had played their part in coming to Britain's aid during the war, so were doubly acclaimed.

Whatever the reason, Australian sportsmen and women were

well received in post-war England. If a certain old-world weariness informed part of this attitude towards those at the height of their sporting powers, how much more would they admire a middle-aged man exhibiting all the energy and potential of youth?

A lot more, as it turned out. Percy Cerutty hit London like a tornado, so it would seem. A fit, handsome, 57-year-old man whose habitual track attire consisted of a pair of white shorts, running shoes and nothing else, had an instant and galvanising impact in England. Bill Rutherford, a columnist for the *Sunday People*, was as smitten as anyone. After watching the Australians train and Cerutty perform, he wrote that the Australian coach was "as full of life as a six-year-old, in bare feet, dressed only in a pair of trunks and as brown as a Red Indian, he took turns at sprinting with the sprinters, and tirelessly tagging along with the long-distance men".

Successive Australian team managers found Cerutty a difficult man to handle on international trips, but Cerutty balanced that somewhat by positive contributions, a fact usually acknowledged by the very same managers who had to kick him out of Villages from Helsinki to Rome. In that era, coaches were not part of the team structure as they are now, not even the all-conquering swimming team. They paid their own way, earning what money they could, perhaps by contributing newspaper columns, as Cerutty did in subsequent years.

But their advice was invaluable to the athletes they coached. Managing nervous psyches is never an easy task and, as creatures of routine, athletes for the most part appreciate having familiar faces around.

Cerutty, with his flair for self-promotion, often provided a lightning rod to draw attention away from highly-strung athletes. It was just that he so often went over the top. When the athletes travelled to Ireland for competition, he entertained the audience during a boring speech at an official reception by his antics behind a partition, the act coming crashing down, literally, with the collapse of the boxes he had piled one atop the other as a platform. Then, at a big meeting before a capacity crowd at the White City Stadium, Cerutty jogged around the track and infield, refusing all attempts to persuade him to stop for an inordinately long time. It raised a laugh, but it also wore thin.

For John Landy, the Olympic campaign had started the minute he got off the tractor at the family farm. He had come a long way very quickly. In an article previewing the national championships, Bruce Welch had written in *The Age*: "Landy may miss [selection], as he needs another two years to consolidate his form."

Whether he was reflecting the views of Cerutty, the views of the selectors, or his own, Welch's comment was perceptive. Landy *was* to make to make a far greater impact in two years time. But the Olympics were *now*. Landy had to get back into training, and he had to find a way to raise the funds to finance his trip.

When the Olympic team was announced, the selectors were required to rank the 16 athletes. Landy, a marginal selection given that Macmillan was running his events, was ranked last. The athlete ranked one ahead of him, hurdler Peter Gardner, a finalist in London four years earlier and a 1950 Empire Games gold medallist, quit the sport in disgust at his lowly ranking.

The ranking of athletes and the funding of the team was a matter of huge controversy, athletes being ranked against each other and against other sports. Swimming manager and later Australian Olympic Federation president, Syd Grange, commented that he had never encountered a method of funding better designed to spread disharmony at all levels of the Olympic movement (*Sydney Morning Herald*, 20 May 1952, as cited by Harry Gordon, *Australia and the Olympic Games*). Marjorie Jackson was ranked first, so she had no problems; however, some of her relay teammates were low on the ranking list. The way funds were distributed, money raised specifically on an athlete's behalf could not go to that athlete until all those ranked higher were covered. So the women's relay, a medal favourite, was allocated funds only after every individual ranked above it was covered.

In any case, the rankings caused no end of controversy. Having been leaked a fairly accurate version of the gradings before the selections were announced, Welch was well placed to comment on the team. "The grading of Macmillan [who was fourth] seems to be more on potential than times, as Reed and Curotta [fifth and seventh] both have brighter hopes," he wrote on 25 February 1952. Again, Gardner's treatment, especially against fellow-hurdler Weinberg (ranked third), seemed especially harsh. "Peter Gardner has smashed the 110 metres standard more times than even Weinberg, but has been placed 15th." Finally, "the placing of Gardner and Landy below NSW sprinters John Treloar and Edwin Carr is laughable". Ultimately, the Olympic results would vindicate some of the rankings and invalidate others.

Landy was in a dilemma over funding. He did not want to call on his family as the primary source. In the end, a combination of the people of Geelong, his club and his family ensured he got away. "I was helped by the people of Geelong, the Geelong Guild because I was a club member, a couple of Melbourne businessmen, and my father helped too, so I got enough funds [to] go. But it was a very different system to what it is now." Quite — the only time an Olympic team member would go to the dogs now, as Jackson did to raise money for her relay teammates, would be on a promotional appearance.

"Percy got no money as a coach, nothing at all," Landy remembers, before relating some of the escapades that 1952-style security allowed people to get away with. "He wasn't really an official coach but he had a uniform made with 'head coach' on it, which made him superior to everybody else in the eyes of the Finnish officials.

"All sorts of con tricks were performed. One was to have a blazer with a kangaroo and emu on it. One Australian [tourist] had been to the '48 Olympics as an official and he just took the pocket off that and put it on another blazer and was walking around [the Olympic village]."

Once the financial side was taken care of, Landy had to address his state of readiness. He had had only one solid winter's training behind him anyway and had taken a break from training after the national titles, assuming he would not be selected. He had not exactly been bone idle, but he had not been training properly, either. "I sort of had a 'fire up'. I got off the tractor and started training. I had about five weeks' training. I had knocked off in March, had about two months off, and started again."

Landy flew out of Melbourne with most of his teammates on 10 June 1952. It was a very different trip then, even if it was in the most modern airliner in the Qantas fleet, the Constellation. It took three days to get to London, with two overnight stopovers. The Kangaroo Route was aptly named, the plane departing from Sydney and touching down in Darwin, Jakarta, Singapore, Calcutta, Karachi, Beirut and Rome before ending its journey in London. In Singapore, the Australians stayed at Raffles Hotel (where else?). When they crossed the equator, they were issued with a special certificate commemorating the transit from southern to northern hemisphere.

The Australian team arrived in London just a few days before the British Amateur Athletic Association championships, in which many of them were scheduled to compete. Interestingly, current-day views on the matter would indicate this was precisely the *worst* time to compete after a long trip. Four days is right in the middle of the period of recovery from jet lag and adjustment to the time change. Nevertheless, Landy made a grand first impression. In his first run, he equalled his previous best mile time, 4:11.0. "I ran second to Bill

Nankeville two or three days after getting off the plane, in the British Mile championship," Landy recalls.

Ben Kerville, of *The Sporting Globe*, wrote for the Melbourne sports paper that, "as usual, Landy adopted front-running tactics". They very nearly paid off, too, Nankeville only catching the young Australian in the last 50 yards of the race.

Despite some criticism, athletics team management had decided that they would travel from their London base to several competitions, thereby breaking the monotony of being in one location the whole time. Next stop was Belfast, capital of Northern Ireland. This time it was an outright personal best for Landy. "I had a good run, 4:10 or something like that." Welch reported that "Landy had to run most of the distance on his own, as opposition was too weak".

The mile was a handicap race, a common practice in England then and a means of giving the better runner some competition. Landy gave opponents starts of up to 80 yards, but still he won by almost a full lap of the track. Still, he was earning high praise. British Olympic starter Fred Halford commented he had not seen a runner over the last 15 years with such relaxation, smoothness and style (as John Landy) and that the young Australian would prove one of the most promising runners in the world when he gained further international experience.

Landy found some opposition, on paper anyway, waiting for him in his next race, a two miles event in Middlesborough. The north-east of England has always been a nursery for distance running, its countryside ideal for harrier events and the competitive streak of its inhabitants suited to most sports.

Yorkshireman Len Eyre was Landy's main opponent. He had been selected for the 1500 in Helsinki. In 1950, he had won the Empire Games three miles and finished second in the mile, and had won four Yorkshire mile championships from 1948 to 1951. Landy won by 75 yards in 8:54.0, a British Empire record. He told Welch he should have broken 8:50.0. Gunder Hägg's unofficial world record was 8:42.0.

It was a great run on a grass track, but then officials lobbed a hand grenade Landy's way. The track was not certified. "They took the time off me because the track had to be surveyed or something like that," Landy says. It actually turned out to be *long*, to the tune of three feet each lap. "John Landy became the third fastest two-miler ever, and finally proved his low grading for the Olympic team was a bad error," Bruce Welch reported.

The prospect of running the 5000 metres in Helsinki now started to cloud matters. Many good judges had encouraged Landy to believe he could run well at the longer distance and after Middlesborough he looked as if he was moving towards agreeing with them. Welch's report said Landy was "now likely to switch to the Olympic 5000 metres in preference to the 1500 metres". Landy told Welch that he might be too inexperienced for the faster-run 1500 but would be happy to tackle even Zatopek in the longer event.

Even before this, Landy had been considering the longer Olympic race. He was being nudged in that direction from a number of sides. A report in the Melbourne *Herald* summed up the case for the longer race. "Landy's fast mile at Belfast impressed, but it is felt he is better suited over the long distance," the story ran. "The more powerful finishing runs of the British milers, Bannister and Nankeville, give them the edge [on Landy] in the 1500 metres."

Five days later, however, Landy suffered a slightly demoralising defeat in a 5000 at White City, going down to England's number two runner, Alan Parker. "The 35,000 crowd had their biggest thrill when Alan Parker of Barrow won the 5000 metres for England," it was reported. "Landy had led for most of the way and put on a spurt at the bell. Parker ... 300 yards from the finish ... began a dramatic sprint. In 80 yards he had made up eight on Landy and passed him."

It was Landy's "down" run of the tour and, maybe, a sign that he was running out of fitness off his limited training base, both in the two months immediately past, and overall.

Others in the team were showing form, though there were injury concerns. Ray Weinberg had fallen in a stormwater drain in Singapore, injuring his knee. Fortunately, help was at hand thanks to Weinberg's own initiative. As a result of his experience in 1948, he had convinced team management of the need for some sort of medical back-up on such a trip. Now, he was grateful for the healing hands of masseur, George Saunders. Maurice Curotta, another of the team with 1948 experience, was also having problems. He had injured his hamstring in a race at the end of May in the US, where he was attending college.

Don Macmillan was the subject of varying reports. Like Landy, he won praise on arrival, a reporter noting he was "moving effortlessly and appreciating the perfect surfaces here". The reporter continued: "Those who saw him at the Empire Games in Auckland say he has been transformed from an ungainly, styleless runner of 1950, to a smooth running machine now." The same report quoted Cerutty predicting, "this man will get down to close to four minutes one day". Less than a fortnight later, however, Welch included an injury update in his report from Middlesborough saying that "the problem men are [discus thrower Ian] Reed and Macmillan who have lost confidence, and [sprinter John] Treloar who is unable to shake off a leg muscle injury".

A week later again, Macmillan ran an Irish all-comers record for 1000 yards at an international meeting in Dublin. He ran 2:12.4 after going through 880 in 1:55.0. "I am now satisfied with my form. This run will sharpen me up and be of value." Ultimately, Macmillan and Treloar would both be finalists in Helsinki, injuries and loss of confidence notwithstanding.

Les Perry had had some niggling injuries, too, but he ran a

personal best 29:18.4 for fourth in the British Amateur Athletics Association six miles and just over 14 minutes for three miles in Belfast and was clearly moving into top form.

The women sprinters were in grand form and justifying their position as medal favourites. Marjorie Jackson had run well throughout the tour. Fund raising at the Wentworth Park dogs aside, her year had gone smoothly. The one other hiccup in Australia had been when she and her parents had been involved in a car crash on the way to New South Wales titles at the Sydney Sports Ground. In another drama, Jackson was briefly hospitalised. Australian Associated Press (AAP) reported that on 8 July 1952, she was taken to Charing Cross hospital for X-rays after complaining of pains in her side. "Jackson went through her normal routine training at Motspur Park today, although handicapped slightly by a strapped-up side," the report continued. Team manager Miss Gwen Bull was then quoted as saying: "We were concerned about Marjorie yesterday, but we are no longer worried. X-ray pictures are negative and the pain has disappeared."

It was thought the sprint star had slightly damaged cartilage between the lower ribs on her right side. She had been surrounded by photographers when she appeared on the Motspur Park track; this may well have been one occasion when an athlete wished Cerutty had been there as a distraction.

The relay squad had practised changeovers the previous day at White City. "The baton-changing practice … was a failure," according to AAP. "The girls are running in their best form, but lack of cooperation in the changeovers is losing them yards. All were upset at the end of practice. With no coach available to instruct them, the girls did not have a clue as to how to make their changeovers effective." Even an equal world-record performance the previous Saturday had not inspired confidence, the AAP report said, before concluding: "Unless the changeover flaw is overcome it could rob

Australia of what appears to be a certain Olympic victory." The report turned out to be sadly prophetic, as Australia dropped the baton in the Olympic final. By 1956, when there was still no satisfactory coaching of the relay, Shirley Strickland virtually took over the role as relay coach and the team won.

Strickland herself was in excellent form, though her prospects were tempered by the reality that she would be meeting the hero of the 1948 London Games — Fanny Blankers-Koen of the Netherlands — in sprints and hurdles in Helsinki. Late in the Australian season, Strickland had pulled off an impressive two-state double. In Launceston she ran 24.3 for 220 yards on Saturday, then flew to Melbourne where she ran 11.5 for 100 metres and 11.2 for the 80 metres hurdles on the Sunday. The 100 metres time was an equal world record and the other two were Australian records, but none were acceptable for record purposes because of following wind. Nevertheless, Bruce Welch reported in *The Age* that Strickland "was amazed by her times as she had not been training hard. She danced on Saturday night and flew to Melbourne at 6am yesterday [Sunday] morning." More dancing, please, Shirley.

Cerutty was also making his views known through the usual channels. He expressed his concerns about the arrangements in London to Joe Galli. The diet and accommodation were his main worries and he was sure Australia's likely opposition would not have contemplated a similar set-up. "We can be sure that Continental countries (particularly Sweden, Germany and Soviet Russia) will have their athletes training hard, and under iron discipline in the weeks before the Games start," wrote Galli. "This is the only way to produce results, which Cerutty could get, had really national support been given him." Referring, no doubt, to the good performances of Landy, Macmillan and Perry, Galli noted: "Only Cerutty-trained men have shown improved form." Finally, from the man himself, came: "My men are the only fit members of the team. The others are under-conditioned — and they know it now. But it is too late to make any appreciable difference at this stage."

Whether it was the diet, the accommodation, or — most likely — the looming reality of major world competition and the desire just to get to Helsinki, the air of tension in the Australian camp was palpable. One report had it that "unusual mannerisms and slight displays of temper … has [sic] become a daily feature of the team's routine. Tension is most noticeable among the women athletes. Most are easily upset." Possibly this was just after relay practice — but the one exception was Jackson. "Marjorie is in top form," the report continued, "and appears unconcerned that within a few days she will clash with the world's most famous woman athlete, Fanny Blankers-Koen."

Whether it was having a mitigating effect on the tension, or perhaps even contributing to it, the team manager, New South Wales solicitor and athletics official Keith Donald, had cancelled all remaining competitions after Middlesborough and announced the team was "going into smoke". Donald told *The Herald*: "I plan to take the team to live near Motspur Park, near Surrey, in caravans and train around the clock." Other Olympic contenders were getting to know too much about the Australians, he said. "Britain's Olympic people have seen more than they should have of our stars. Miler John Landy is attracting particular attention as he ran their champion, Nankeville, a gruelling race at White City when he was only four days off the plane."

Even in closed camp, the debate about whether Landy should run the 1500, the 5000, or both, continued. His poor run against Parker tipped the balance. A few days later, a report appeared saying: "John Landy has decided to revert to his former decision and to set himself for the 1500 metres at Helsinki." The report cited the Parker race as the catalyst for the change of mind and added that Landy "has not trained this week". On the day the team arrived in Helsinki,

Ron Carter filed a story for *The Argus*, writing: "John Landy will be withdrawn from the Olympic 5000 metres … his coach Percy Cerutty announced today." Another story said that Landy may still run the heats of the 5000, which were scheduled for two days before the 1500 heats. Ultimately, he ran both heats, but the indecision must have imposed a cost.

Just before the team left London for Helsinki, it had reached its full complement with the arrival of marathoner Claude Smeal. Army captain Claude Smeal's story is fascinating. New South Wales state marathon champion the previous year, he had been on service in Korea, continuing to run in an area behind his own lines where snipers were not unknown. A special marathon "trial" had been set up for him near Seoul, and Smeal had run 2:44:05. Although this was outside the standard, reports of it generated public backing and also the support of media magnate Frank Packer. Smeal was added to the team.

The Japanese were apparently as enamoured of the marathon then as they are now. They were certainly at the forefront of marathon technology. AAP reported that Smeal "will use a special type of shoe [in Helsinki] used by Japanese marathon runners. These have rubber-treated soles and weigh only a few ounces."

Landy's impressive tour had certainly raised expectations. On the eve of the Games, athletics team manager Keith Donald warned of the difficulty of winning any medals, much less gold medals, and said: "The only members of the athletics team likely to excel are Marjorie Jackson, Shirley Strickland, the women's relay team, Ray Weinberg, John Treloar, Morris Curotta and John Landy." (*The Age*, 19 July 1952.) Donald expressed disappointment in others, including Macmillan, and hoped that Les Perry "will improve further".

And so to Helsinki. The Finnish capital had been chosen to host the Games of 1940, which were cancelled because of the war. After London, Helsinki was an obvious choice.

If Helsinki lost one Games because of "hot" war, its second-chance Games of 1952 took place in the context of the Cold War between the Soviet bloc and the USA and its allies. The politics could not but intrude. The Korean War, one of several proxy battles between the main cold war protagonists, was still being fought. Cold War symbolism abounded. The Soviet Union had not competed in 1948, at which time the International Olympic Committee still recognised Russia, rather than the USSR, as the national Olympic committee. Its price for coming to Helsinki was the demand for a separate village for Soviet bloc athletes. Ostensibly it was for security purposes, which it was, though more likely to keep the athletes securely *inside* the village, rather than allowing them to wander freely (and, perhaps, defect).

Claude Smeal had come straight from active service in Korea to run the marathon for Australia. Mal Whitfield, the American defending champion in the 800 metres, had served as an airman in the Korean conflict in between Games. He would win again in Helsinki, in the same winning time as London, proving neither he nor the Cold War had moved far in four years.

Most symbolic of all would be the shock victory by Horace Ashenfelter of the USA in the 3000 metres steeplechase. Ashenfelter was an FBI agent, as was US 10,000 metres representative Fred Wilt. The favourite for the steeple was the Soviet runner Vladimir Kazantsev, who had set a world record in the lead-up to the Games. However, Ashenfelter had improved his previous best by over 15 seconds in the heats. He and Kazantsev shared the lead late in the race before the latter charged to the lead at the last bend. The final water jump proved decisive: Kazantsev made a hash of it, Ashenfelter, on his inside, took control again, dashing clear to win in a new world record. Ashenfelter had improved no less than 21 seconds at the Games! Inevitably, his win was presented in a Cold War context with headlines about FBI men running down Russians. It was a good story, and for once it fit the facts.

(Things are not always what they seem where security is concerned. A personal story here: two-time Olympic representative Chris Wardlaw and I went to Japan to run the famous Fukuoka marathon in 1978. Two of the invited runners were from the Soviet Union — 1978 European champion Leonid Moseyev and silver medallist Nikolai Penzin. These two "gun" runners were always accompanied by a thickset fellow we immediately dubbed "the KGB agent". The nickname seemed to be confirmed when we would see him accompanying the other two on training runs. He had a lumbering gait and invariably wore no-name running shoes and black socks.

Next time I saw him was in the race, when it became clear that he was, in fact, an athlete. As I approached the turnaround point near 22 kilometres, he was coming back past me in the opposite direction, right on the heels of the leading pack. He finished just outside the top ten in a time of 2:13:00.0. A KGB record, we reckoned.)

Security was an issue in the arrangement of the Helsinki Olympic Village (or, more accurately, villages). It is common for Olympic hosts to have more than one village; practicalities mean that some sports need to be accommodated closer to far-flung competition venues than the main village. Ballarat, the rowing venue for the 1956 Melbourne Olympics, had its own separate Olympic Village. So it was in Helsinki, but with its own Cold War overlay. The Soviet Union, which had not accepted its invitation to compete in 1948, accepted so late this time that there was no other option other than to house the USSR athletes separately. The Soviets, and their eastern bloc allies, were housed at Otaniemi, eight kilometres west of the city centre, well away from the main village at Kapyla, near the main stadium. Female competitors were housed separately again, the eastern bloc women in a separate building within the Otaniemi village, the rest, including the Australians, at a nurses' training college in the city centre.

Despite the complicated logistics, everything was done to make life comfortable. A report in *The Argus* on the Australians' arrival mentions that they were all fit, though tired from the ten-hour plane journey via Copenhagen and Stockholm. The athletes had tucked into a meal of reindeer steak on their first night in the Village and were entertained by a Finnish jazz band, a Swedish soubrette and a team of three female acrobats. Congenial the entertainment may have been, but the arrangements complicated matters for two of the Australians: Les Perry and Percy Cerutty were determined to meet Emil Zatopek.

Zatopek was the world's greatest distance runner. He had won the 10,000 metres at the 1948 Games and finished second in the 5000. Until a month before the Games, he had been undefeated at either distance for 72 races over almost a full four years; he would remain undefeated at the 10,000 for six years. He raced prolifically and won almost every time, sometimes by grinding opponents into the cinders, other times with a withering sprint.

A tale by Geoff Warren reveals how the Australians idolised the great Czech athlete: "We tried to emulate his training. I'd heard that Zatopek did these massive numbers of 400-metre repetitions, up to 30 and 40 on a night with 200 between, at racing pace, in army boots. I thought, 'that's for me'. I dug out a pair of army boots; they were slightly tight for me, but I persevered. I took the skin off my ankles, but I tried to out-Zatopek Zatopek. I'd do 30, 40 or 50×400, until I was doing a marathon of them, starting after work and finishing around midnight, in these heavy boots, slipping in the mud around Newport Oval. Once or twice a week I'd try to add a few more, thinking 'I don't know if Emil ever did this many, but it must be good for me.'"

Later, perhaps when Perry came back from Helsinki, Warren found out that the army boots Zatopek wore were not the leather ones of the parade ground, but parachute boots, made of rubber and canvas, and were "much better than anyone else was wearing for running at the time". Warren said in 2006: "It was a big revelation, and it gave me a laugh at myself. I don't think it did any lasting harm — except a bit of scarring around the ankles where the boots took the skin off."

So it was clear why the Australians wanted to catch up with Zatopek. Cerutty, however, had already spent his first four hours in Helsinki looking for another quarry, Finnish running great Paavo Nurmi. Perry beat him to Zatopek, donning his Australian tracksuit top and jogging boldly through the gates of the "closed" Otaniemi village. The Australian Prime Minister, Robert Menzies, had twice recently failed to ban the Communist Party — one time by legislation overturned in the courts, the other by referendum. Perhaps the guards at Otaniemi thought Perry's a fraternal visit from one socialist comrade to another! Whatever the case, they discerned no security threat.

Perry was directed to the track, introduced himself to Zatopek and was soon running, and chatting, with the great man. Zatopek was fluent in several languages, including English. (Years later, at a press conference at the first world championships in Helsinki, where Zatopek was an honoured guest, he apologised to a media conference that he could not answer questions in Finnish. But at least he knew enough to deliver his apology in the local tongue!) Zatopek insisted Perry join him for dinner and entertainment. Where the Australians at Kapyla had jazz and acrobatics, at Otaniemi it was the Bolshoi Ballet. Perry returned at midnight, raving to the others about his day. He and Zatopek remained lifelong friends.

Cerutty went to Zatopek the following day. He, too, was lavishly looked after but accepted the offer of overnight accommodation — in Zatopek's own bed. The great man said he had a sleeping bag and would doss down outside. An incident was narrowly averted when Cerutty was found in Zatopek's bunk by Czech team officials with their gold medal hope nowhere to be seen, but Zatopek's charm carried the day.

Landy also met Zatopek — there is a picture of the two of them shaking hands at the training track with Cerutty looking on — but he did not have any significant conversation with him, as Perry and Cerutty did. The brief meeting occurred at the Eläintarha track, the old Zoological Gardens stadium used as the warm-up track for the Olympics. The stadium, with its beautiful old wooden stands and buildings, had relevant history, too. It was here that Nurmi had set world records for 1500 and 5000 metres an hour apart at the 1924 Finnish championships, demonstrating to obdurate Finnish officials that he was quite capable of doing the double at the Paris Olympic Games, when both events would be on the same day. They relented, and selected Nurmi for both events. He won both in Paris, again setting world records.

Landy, whose study of entomology was based on observation, watched some of Zatopek's training sessions, which were as extraordinary in the manner they were conducted as in their content. "[Zatopek] was like the Pied Piper," says Landy. "He was running with all these blokes following. He was infinitely patient, wanting to help people. He was a terrific personality. I just joined in running with him. I did more of it by observation; I watched how he ran. The sort of thing I got out of it was that he didn't make a feature of the 400s he ran supposedly fast, [but] the ones in between were pretty quick, too. There was more of an emphasis on recovery, narrowing the time of recovery."

Landy also noticed some technical features of Zatopek's running, some of which he had already observed of other Europeans. For all his emphasis on how athletes should run like certain animals, Cerutty gave virtually no direct advice on technique. "I was very impressed and trying to work out why they ran with this high arm action," Landy says. "I twigged to the fact that it came more [from] the way that they landed with their feet. Their arms were following. These were things that didn't come out of Cerutty's training at all and that I applied when I came back."

Before Landy, or any of the others, got back, there was an Olympics to run. Helsinki was a watershed for Australian Olympic performances, kicking off, as it did, the post-war boom that — a flat spot through the 1970s excepted — has continued uninterrupted to this day. Australia won six gold among a tally of eleven medals, and had a further nine top-six placings. Consistent with the way the team was ranked and selected, results were analysed one sport against another. Athletics did well, contributing three of the gold medals through Marjorie Jackson (100 and 200 metres) and Shirley Strickland (80 metres hurdles) and a bronze from Strickland (100 metres).

There was also the one that got away. The mixed omens for the women's relay — equalling the world record before the Games, breaking it in the heats, but also some demoralising changeover sessions — were decided unequivocally on the bad side, Jackson dropping the baton a few strides after the final changeover with third-leg runner Winsome Cripps had been apparently completed. As Bruce Welch reported in *The Age*, "Winsome Cripps was in the lead when she reached Miss Jackson, Australia's last runner. All that seemed to be needed was for Miss Jackson to take the baton and run for the tape. Marjorie Jackson appeared to take the baton all right, but suddenly faltered and the baton was on the ground. She recovered well, but the lead had been lost." Amazingly, the baton bounced back off the track into Jackson's hands and the Australians completed the race, undisqualified, in fifth place.

The relay was won by the American quartet, breaking Australia's world record. "The four coloured girls running for the United States brought off the biggest upset of the whole Olympic Games," Welch wrote. Two of the "coloured girls" — Mae Faggs and Barbara Jones — were from Tennessee State University and coached by Ed Temple.

(The Tigerbelles, as the TSU women's team was known, would eventually produce 15 Olympic gold medals for the USA. Coach and team members were pioneers for female Afro-American athletes.) Frustratingly, the Australians defeated the Americans a week later at the British Empire versus USA match in London. "The arena hushed as Miss Cripps approached Marjorie Jackson to make the final change, but Miss Jackson made no mistake and crossed the line five yards ahead," read the wire service report of that race — the wrong race to win.

When Winsome Cripps arrived back in Melbourne on Saturday 9 August, *The Sporting Globe* carried her account of the dramatic final change in Helsinki. "[It] all happened in a split second. Marjorie had taken the baton from me and I had run on for three or four strides," said Cripps. The Australians were in the inside lane of the track. "As you know, she [Marjorie] carries her hands low, and on the fourth stride her hand brushed my knee and the baton fell."

Overwhelmingly, however, these were the Games of Zatopek. The Czech runner was already a hero to the Finns, having run great races previously in Helsinki and Turku. The Finns loved their distance running and were big enough to embrace a non-Finn who excelled at it. Despite a struggle with influenza earlier in the year, which was compounded by trying to get back to hard training too soon, Zatopek was favoured for the 10,000 coming into the Games. But only one of a panel of five athletics experts picked him to win the 5000. Even fewer knew that the marathon featured in his plans.

He won all three, for an unprecedented Olympic distance treble. The track double at 5000 and 10,000 metres has been regularly contested, and several times won, throughout Olympic history. Few add the marathon, however. The only runner to have a chance at the treble since is Finland's Lasse Viren, who won the 5000 and 10,000 (each for the second time) in Montreal in 1976, and finished fifth in the marathon.

The 10,000 was run as a straight final on the first day of competition. Among the 70,000 spectators crammed into the stadium were Nurmi and Hannes Kolehmainen, the two men who had begun Finland's reign as a world distance power with their Olympic victories in an earlier era. Perry, bubbling over with nervous energy, led at a fast pace for the first couple of laps before sinking back into the pack. He hung with the leaders beyond halfway before deciding there was little point running himself to exhaustion with his main event, the 5000 metres, coming up. He dropped out after 20 of the 25 laps. By 7000 metres, only Alain Mimoun of France could stick with Zatopek's pace, but with three laps to go even he had to let go. Zatopek strode remorselessly on to win the first of his three Helsinki gold medals.

In the 5000 final four days later, Zatopek somewhat perversely relied on his sprint. Herbert Schade of Germany led for almost the entire first 4000 metres at a pace that started at world record schedule but slowed progressively. At the bell, the German runner led from Chris Chataway of Britain, Mimoun and Zatopek. Chataway made the first move, taking the race on with 300 metres to run. He led onto and around the bend before a bizarre confluence of moves left him sprawling on the track and Zatopek sprinting away to victory.

Athletics World, the influential English athletics magazine, described the dramatic final lap thus: "Just past the crown of the bend Zatopek made a decisive attack just as Mimoun was passing Schade, who in turn was fighting it out with Chataway. Suddenly the vast crowd, who were already in an uproar, let out a bellow, for the Englishman lay sprawled across the concrete curb. Brushed perhaps, but not barged, he was tired enough to trip over a blade of grass. Zatopek … stormed up the straight to complete his last lap in a prodigious 57.9 seconds, and so to win by five yards." Zatopek, noted for his relentless tempo and his surging, had won with a final sprint, covering the last lap at a pace close to his maximum speed for 400 metres.

Finally came the marathon that, contrary to legend, Zatopek had been considering for perhaps as long as a year. Certainly, his name was among the entries lodged with Olympic officials a month before the Games. Another tale of Zatopek's marathon debut is almost certainly true. He probably *did* ask Jim Peters, the British runner who had set several world bests in the marathon, whether the pace just before the halfway mark was too fast. Peters supposedly muttered back that it was too slow, a reply Zatopek chewed on for a little while before reluctantly increasing the tempo. Zatopek won his first marathon in Olympic record time of 2:23:04.

Perry, who began the Games by leading Zatopek and everyone else in the 10,000 metres, was the best performed of the Australian middle and long-distance men. His run in the 10,000 was something of a disaster at face value. He had gone to the Games to finish races, not drop out of them. Yet his initial failure had a positive side to it. Not only was it in line with Perry's knack of producing the magnificent failure, as in the 1948 national 5000 metres when he keeled over while leading in oppressive heat, but it was also a learning experience.

Perry ran the 5000 heats two days later in entirely different fashion. Unlike in the 10,000, a straight final, he had heats first and was fortunate enough to draw Zatopek. Having dispelled any lingering self-doubts about his own state of readiness with his gold medal, Zatopek was at his expansive best. As Bob Phillips describes it in *Za-to-pek! Za-to-pek! Za-to-pek! The Life and Times of the World's Greatest Distance Runner* (The Parrs Wood Press, 2002), Zatopek remonstrated with Aleksandr Anufriyev of the Soviet Union for setting off too fast, chatted with Chataway and encouraged others, including the American Curt Stone and Perry, to keep up. In the final lap, with Anufriyev, Bertil Albertsson of Sweden, Perry and Chataway the only runners still with him, Zatopek held up five fingers, reminding them that was the number to qualify automatically, so there was no need for a dramatic and energy-sapping battle to the finish.

Perry was an Olympic finalist. He finished sixth in the final, the highest placing obtained by an Australian in an Olympic 5000 metres until then and not substantially bettered in the event at either Olympic level or, since 1983, world championships level, until Craig Mottram won a bronze medal at the 2005 world championships in … Helsinki, where else?

Macmillan had run on day one as well, going through the heats of the 800 comfortably enough. The next day's semi-finals were another matter. "Don Macmillan was badly outclassed in his 800 metres semi-final. He was last away and stayed there," Welch reported starkly in *The Age*.

Macmillan's main mission was the 1500, however. Another 1500 contender, Patrick El Mabrouk of France, had won his 800 heat and then simply scratched from the semi-finals, presumably to save himself for the heats of the longer race. Macmillan ran, and finished a tailed-off last in his semi, in 1:58.4. Given his subsequent form in the 1500, it appears Welch's judgement was wrong and that the Australian was simply conserving energy, though in a more obvious manner than El Mabrouk.

The 1500 heats were on 24 July. Controversially, the Olympic schedule had been amended, with the addition of a semi-final round, a change that Roger Bannister was certain ended his chance of winning the gold medal. In any case, Macmillan was comfortably through his heat in fourth place. El Mabrouk proved there was nothing wrong with him by winning heat four, albeit in the second-slowest winning time of the six heats. The semi-finals would be harder, but Macmillan qualified in third place (six to go through) in the first semi-final, making him Australia's first Olympic 1500 finalist since "Tickle" Whyte in 1928 and only the second since Flack in 1896.

Now, on the eve of the final, the biggest race of Macmillan's life, Cerutty agreed to a bizarre plan. Professor Frank Cotton, of the Department of Physiology at Sydney University, was the pioneer of sports science in Australia and was attached to the Olympic team as a science advisor. Forbes Carlile, who had worked in Cotton's laboratories and was to become one of Australia's best-ever swimming coaches, had taken up modern pentathlon and made the Helsinki team. Cotton convinced Cerutty, and Cerutty in turn convinced Macmillan, that running around to warm up was a waste of precious energy. The swimmers warmed up in a warm bath, he said, and it worked. How would it work for runners? Well, you would wrap up in two cotton tracksuits, a towel worn around the head, turban-fashion to prevent heat loss, until the body temperature had reached 101 degrees Fahrenheit and the pulse rate around 115. Then he would be ready.

Somehow, Cerutty and Macmillan allowed themselves to be convinced that this bizarre routine might transfer from the controlled environment of the pool to the uncontrolled one of the warm-up track. More incredibly, they would make the change the day of an Olympic final. It did not work. Macmillan was almost dehydrated as he went to the starting line. Josy Barthel of Luxembourg won in a boilover result in 3:45.2; Macmillan, who had simply boiled over, was ninth, running with the winner and second-placed Bob McMillen of the US for most of the race but lacking the energy to go with them when they moved forward to medal-winning positions. Roger Bannister, his routine broken in a less drastic and avoidable manner, finished fourth. He was a chance in the straight, but could not maintain his run.

"Don ran extraordinarily well," said John Landy of Macmillan's performance. "Percy had this idea from Prof. Cotton that you had to be very warm. So he conned Don into being wrapped up in tracksuits and towels and being carried into the ground. Despite all that, Don got up and ran ninth, which wasn't bad, in the final." From this remove, the plan seems so bizarre and radical that you wonder how either man was convinced of the need to try it. Perhaps, more than anything else, it spoke of the inexperience of this particular group of pioneers and maybe a lack of confidence on Macmillan's side.

Landy's Helsinki Olympics began with the 5000 metres heats. The dilemma over which event he should run had come to a surely unsatisfactory conclusion. The heats of the 5000 were on two days before the heats of the 1500; the final on the same day as the 1500 heats. If Landy had made the final of the 5000 — admittedly a tall order by that stage — what would he have done? Probably run it, but it is hard to conceive he would not have been better off with the indecision resolved before the Olympic heats.

Landy was drawn in the first heat of the 5000 metres. The first five in each heat were to go through. Even with a superb run for his state of training, Landy would have struggled. His heat included Alain Mimoun, defending champion Gaston Reiff of Belgium and Britain's Gordon Pirie.

In fact, Landy did not run well. Mimoun won in 14:19.0; Landy was tenth in 14:56.4. Alan Parker, who had caught Landy in the last lap of a 5000 metres in London a couple of weeks earlier, ran 14:18.2 for second in the second heat, qualifying comfortably for the final. Thirteenth, and second last, in this heat was a young American named Wes Santee. The 1500 shaped a little better, but not enough for Landy to get through his heat. The first four were to go through, and Landy finished fifth in 3:57.0. On the result of the final, two days later, it was a loaded heat. It was won by El Mabrouk (fifth in the final), from (finals silver medallist) McMillen and Bannister (fourth in the final).

"We went well in England, but I didn't run particularly well in Helsinki," says Landy, looking back. "You had to be a bit lucky; the first three in my heat got in the first five in the final, so you had to be a bit lucky. On the other hand, I didn't run particularly well. I was so far behind in the 5000 it wasn't funny, but you had to have the training to do it." By now, he was coming to the realisation that he didn't have that training — not yet, anyway.

Now, years later, Landy believes his short build-up might have been the explanation for his performances. He had been running seriously for fewer than two years at the end of the 1951–52 season; it was hardly the time to take a break from training, certainly not the sort of extended one Landy took. His assumption that he would not make the Helsinki team was wrong and he had to build up quickly again off a limited base. "When I got to Helsinki I think I might have been starting to, on a very short build-up, starting to fold a bit," says Landy. "Anyway, I didn't run very impressively there."

On the final day of athletics competition, Bob Prentice and Claude Smeal finished well back in the marathon. Prentice finished 37th in 2:43:14; nor was there a fairy-tale result for Smeal after his preparation behind the lines in Korea. He was 45th in 2:52:23.

After the Games, several members of the Australian team, including John Landy, travelled back to London to compete for the British Empire team against the USA. The athletics had been on first in Helsinki and the match actually took place on the Monday after the Games concluded — Bank Holiday Monday, as it turned out. Hard as it is to imagine any other event going up against the Olympics these days, in the pre-worldwide television age, this was not all that unusual. Indeed, Empire versus USA matches were a tradition that survived into the era of the Commonwealth Games. Gerald Backhouse had run for the Empire against the USA in 1936, part of a 4×880 yards relay that chased the Americans home in world record time.

Landy was also part of a relay team — this time a four times one mile. The relay was notable for the fact that Landy and Roger Bannister ran for the Empire and Wes Santee for the US. This was the one and only time the three men who would soon spearhead the chase for the four-minute mile ran the same race. "None of the three remembered much of each other, not a conversation, nor an impression of one another's abilities," wrote Neal Bascomb (*The Perfect Mile*, Collins Willow, 2004).

Not a lasting one, maybe, but Landy got more than a fleeting look at Santee. As luck would have it, they were both on the same leg, the third. The Americans had a lead, which Santee quickly built on. But then Landy cut it down in the last 440 yards and they changed over virtually together. The USA went on to win.

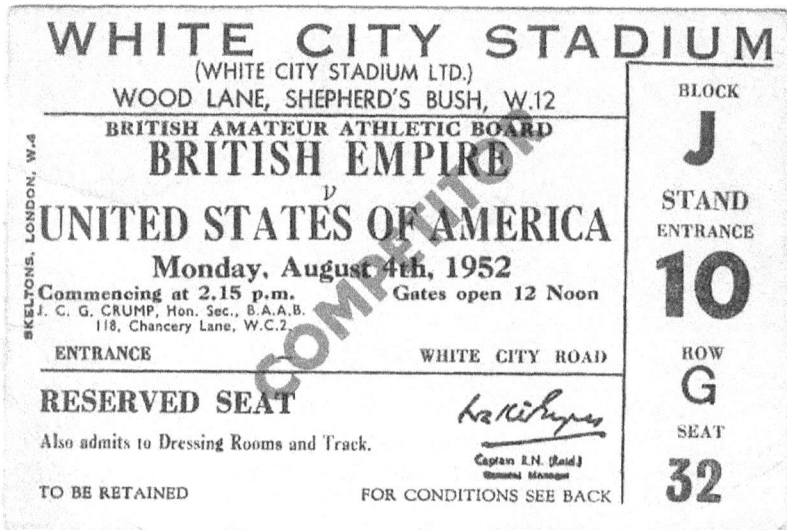

John Landy's competitor's ticket to the British Empire v USA match in London immediately after the Helsinki Olympic athletics. The match staged a 4×1 mile relay, the only time John Landy, Roger Bannister and Wes Santee ever ran the same race.

"Australian John Landy displayed his best form for several weeks in running the third leg of the four miles relay," said one reporter. "Landy gained 25 yards on his American opponent, Wes Santee, who clocked 4:11.8 for the mile." If the estimated gain is no more than broadly correct, Landy probably ran quicker than his recorded time of 4:09.9. In that case, it would have been his fastest mile to that date.

Landy also raced in Glasgow. "I ran third in a three-quarters of a mile race behind Arthur Wint [of Jamaica, the Helsinki 800 metres silver medallist]."

Cerutty, Les Perry and Don Macmillan headed off from Helsinki to take part in some meetings on the European circuit. The athletics circuit then was nothing like the professional business it is today; it was not hard to turn a handy profit from legitimate payments for travel expenses and daily allowances. Not hard for others, that is, but the Australians, in their naïvety, were happy to front up for the cost of their travel, room and a bed. Not surprisingly, they were popular with the promoters.

Landy had come straight back home after the Empire–USA match to catch up on his neglected studies. As Winsome Cripps related the story of the relay disaster, Landy gave reporters on hand to greet the team a frank assessment of his own performance in Helsinki. "I was not fast enough. You have to see them over there to realise what they are doing. As for Zatopek, well he was out of this world."

Despite the success of the Australian team in Helsinki, and the athletics team's winning half the six gold medals, the overall performance was not greeted with unadulterated praise. "We were castigated by some of the press when we came back," says Landy. "The critics said we never should have been selected, that sort of thing. [It] probably gave me a lot of incentive to try and redeem the situation. I thought we were judged a bit harshly."

Bruce Welch, in *The Age*, outlined some of the criticisms, though he aimed no barbs at the Cerutty-trained distance contingent. He instanced the treatment of sprinter Cripps and relay runner Verna Johnston, who was given a low ranking, despite the relay's obvious medal potential. He declared it a cynical ploy to take advantage of the women's federation's ability to raise funds. "This meant federation funds would first have to go to male athletes graded above her, though their performances were poor by comparison with world marks. Obviously, the AAU [Australian Athletic Union] knew the women's supporters would make sure the girls got to Helsinki." Welch also championed the rower and cyclist, Mockridge and Cox. Cox only got to the Games, he said, through the generosity of his workmates and his mother, a sole parent, who took out a mortgage on the family home (*Australia at the Olympic Games*, Harry Gordon, 1994).

The distance runners had enjoyed modest success, but to John Landy, the trip to the Helsinki Games had shown how far behind Australia was in some matters and exposed him and his teammates to what the top athletes were doing. In later life, Landy was called on to write several reports on the state of athletics, and sport in general, in Australia. He also was one of those who lobbied for the establishment of some sort of institutional support for Australian athletes. He showed those same analytical skills in appraising the national performance in Helsinki. "It brought home to me the fact that we were a long way behind," says Landy. "I came back feeling a little bit depressed that our standards were nowhere near them. This was before Frank Cotton and Forbes Carlile were really doing anything in swimming. In athletics, we were carried by Marjorie Jackson and the girls. They were the ones who were dominant. We were nowhere in boxing; in cycling we had [Russell] Mockridge and [Lionel] Cox, but not much else. Generally speaking I came back from Helsinki with the idea that we had a hell of a lot of work to do in training, but also in our competition; we were at a disadvantage from that point of view.

"We had to do something to improve, and we did improve in 1956 — partly because it was our home ground, but also because of the revolution in swimming; we were dominant against the Americans. Our athletics team improved again — even though 'Marj' retired [after the 1954 Empire Games] — we had people bobbing up in all events. In athletics it was more the discovery of Betty Cuthbert and Marlene Mathews, in addition to Strickland. 'Chilla' Porter came along, Hec Hogan had just started in '52 [when he just missed the team], and he came up."

Nonetheless, Australia did still enjoy those natural advantages of year-round climate, an abundant diet and a healthy lifestyle. "We had advantages, even though we didn't have good coaching in many sports. In athletics we weren't too bad [but] we didn't have competition and had to overcome our isolation. Most people didn't compete outside Australia except at Olympic and Commonwealth Games. Competition was not like [it was] in Europe or North America."

Soon, Landy would show that none of that really mattered, provided the drive and ambition were there. And he would inspire a generation to follow.

6

The World Takes Notice

Harsh condemnation of athletes adjudged to have failed at an Olympic Games is not only a present-day phenomenon. True, it may be more prevalent in a time of government-funded teams, when politicians or media can turn on athletes and demand an explanation as to why x dollars of funding did not lead to y number of medals. But it existed in John Landy's day, too. Each of Landy, Wes Santee and Roger Bannister was judged to have failed at the 1952 Helsinki Olympic Games. It was a harsh judgement, particularly on Bannister — he *had* come fourth, after all — but it was passed, nonetheless. Driving it, in Bannister's case, was the fact that he had had both the most private and, paradoxically, also the most scrutinised, preparation of the three.

First, it is necessary to wind back to November 1947, the year before the 1948 London Olympic Games. Roger Bannister, then just a few months short of his 19th birthday, was offered funding and support as a "possible" selection for the Games. As Bannister relates (*Four-Minute Mile*): "The 'possibles' were to receive assistance ranging from special coaching organised by the Amateur Athletics Association (AAA), to food parcels given by the Dominions to supplement their limited rations."

Bannister refused the offer, reasoning that his best chance at Olympic glory would be four years later in 1952. That decision, as he tells it, attracted "considerable publicity" and some criticism. Nevertheless, Bannister already had a plan for his 1952 Olympic campaign. When he followed that plan, he also attracted criticism. He decided to run only half miles in 1950, and ranked sixth in the world. In 1951, he was the year's fastest miler and ranked number one.

Bannister raced hardly at all in the lead-up to the 1952 Games. He did not defend his mile title at the AAA championships (the race in which Bill Nankeville defeated Landy) and he staked everything on winning with "one supreme explosive effort on 26 July 1952 in the Olympic final at Helsinki".

Bannister was totally thrown by the addition of a semi-final round in the 1500 at the Games. Perhaps he had earned the right to do things his way, but from this distance it hardly seems surprising people did not understand. And it is only a short step from not understanding to criticism. (Even the Queen expressed some puzzlement. When presenting Bannister the Cup for his 880 yards victory at the AAA titles, Bannister writes that she inquired whether it was not more usual for him to run the mile.) Nevertheless, Bannister had run his heart out for Britain in Helsinki and been far from disgraced. Partly, he paid the price for a lack of success for the whole team. The most colourful turn of phrase came from a journalist who complained: "I felt like suing British athletics for breach of promise."

Wes Santee, by comparison, escaped with the least amount of public criticism. As a student at Kansas University, he was insulated to a large degree. He also had the consolation that he had been selected for the wrong event. He had finished second in the 5000 metres at the US Trials, guaranteeing him a place in the team, then he had been prevented from running the 1500, in which he insisted he had a better chance. Officials believed that, at 19, he was too young to run both, so must run the event for which he first qualified.

But Santee was badly wounded by his Olympic experience. He missed the support of his college coach, Bill Easton, and his Kansas teammates. He was embarrassed by his failure in the heats. Acting on a well-meaning piece of advice from Fred Wilt, Santee had stuck close to "the German guy", Herbert Schade. What neither Wilt nor Santee knew — until 3000 metres into the race — was that Schade wanted to put some doubt into the minds of the other gold medal favourites with a fast heat. He went through 3000 metres in 8:23.0. Santee was a couple of seconds behind and 19 seconds under his previous best time for the distance. His last five laps were not pretty. As a result, Wes Santee, too, burned with ambition to show the world that he was better than the athlete who had run the heats of the wrong event in Helsinki.

When John Landy got back to Australia, nothing had changed, yet everything had changed. He absorbed the post-Olympic criticism. He went back to his study. He went back to his routine of university, home and training. But if Melbourne University had not changed, if home was just as welcoming and supportive, and training still almost invariably involved slipping across the road to Central Park and running around in the dark, Landy's attitude had changed dramatically.

The Greek philosopher Heraclitus once said that no man can step into the same river twice, for neither the man nor the river remain the same. John Landy was not stepping into the same Central Park post-Helsinki as he had been before the Games. Central Park may not have changed that much but Landy certainly had. "I came back with some ideas and I put them into practice," Landy says. Partly, the changes Landy implemented were to do with style and technique. Having observed Zatopek and other European runners, he believed they ran far more on their heels than the Australians. This could be put down to footwear: most Australians ran in spikes designed for sprinters running on grass tracks in the big professional sprint meetings. Even into the early 1950s, there were specialists churning out hand-made spikes for athletes, but nothing designed for middle-distance runners.

Landy says the question of running shoes "was crazy". Referring to pictures of him running early in his career, he noted his "very low arm carriage". His observation of the European runners in Helsinki revealed a different style of running and he asked why. "Everything here came out of this professional grass sprinting approach," says Landy. "The shoes had this big clump of long spikes on the front and absolutely no heel. You carried your hands way down and were pushed up on your tippy-toes. You can't run like [Europeans] if you're on your toes." Les Perry's fall in the 1948 three-mile title might have been explained by the spikes athletes wore then, as much as exhaustion, Landy thinks. "He was tremendously determined and would push himself beyond the point of no return, [but with] these long spikes, it was easy to trip up. I think his foot came close to ground and he tripped over."

At that stage, however, they were the only spikes to be had and athletes went to great lengths to obtain them. Landy recalls Hope Sweeney, one of the most noted manufacturers of running shoes in Melbourne, as "a really good bloke, but the greatest procrastinator". That procrastination almost led to an athlete going to the 1936 Berlin Olympics without his spikes. "Alf Watson was in the hurdles in the team to go to Berlin," says Landy. "In those days they were going by boat. The gangway was up, the streamers were up, and Sweeney came down to the pier and threw the spikes up to Watson as the boat moved out." In any case, one of the things Landy did before leaving his Helsinki teammates behind to return to Melbourne was to implore Perry to bring him back a pair of the spikes worn by the Europeans.

Footwear aside, Landy was impressed by the Europeans' attitude and fitness, as exemplified by Zatopek. On his return to Melbourne, he had described the triple Olympic champion as "out of this world". But he did not necessarily believe that others, including perhaps himself, were permanently locked out of that world. Hard work was the key to entering the world inhabited by Emil Zatopek, and Landy now embraced hard work.

Landy had flirted with the idea of retirement to focus on study and career, but he rejected it. Even so, his aims, when he repeats them over 50 years later, seem modest. "I set myself the goal when I came back to break Don Macmillan's [Australian] record [4:09.0]. I reckoned that I had a limited future in athletics."

After Helsinki, Macmillan had stayed on in Europe to study in London, leaving the Australian middle-distance field open for Landy to conquer. He could win the national title. "Don had elected to stay away, so I reckoned my chances of doing that were reasonably good — but I didn't see myself running better than 4:07.0, or 4:06.0 at the absolute outside." He would, of course, do much better, and conquer fields far broader than Australia.

Landy stepped up his training. He also re-doubled his commitment. By the time 1952 turned to 1953, he would not have missed a day of training since returning from the Games. All that running was being done with a modified style. As he took note of what Zatopek and the others were doing at the Eläintarha track and in the Helsinki Olympic stadium, Landy came to the conclusion that his running action was actually *restricting* him.

An end of year article in *The Argus* (*1952: Australia's Finest Year of Sport*, a magazine produced by the newspaper) summed up Landy's thinking: "His arm action was too low and loose, he was landing too high on the balls of the feet ... and imposing too great a strain on his thigh and calf muscles. He was getting a 90 percent return for 100 percent effort. To do better, he found he had to relax by distributing his weight and the strain more evenly throughout the body." Eventually, the article continued, Landy found the answer. "Now, with each stride, he comes down from just behind the ball on to the flat of the foot in the rocking action of a curved blotting pad. By doing so, he finds he releases tension from the thigh and calf muscles, and allows the knee to flex with each stride in an infinitesimal moment of relaxation."

That, the article proclaimed, was "the secret". That, and not missing a day in almost five months. Cerutty used to tell his runners, "You might run faster than me, but you won't run harder." Landy could truthfully say at this stage, "You might train harder," (and that would be doubtful, anyway), "but you won't train more often."

Landy raced as soon as the Australian domestic season got under way late in October, 1952. Like most Australian (and British) athletes of the day, he ran for a club — in his case, Geelong Guild, the club of Alex Hillhouse and Bill Ramsay — but he was also anxious to test the improvement he was sure must be there. He was in the midst of his university exams, but still the times came. On 25 October, Landy ran a mile in 4:17.0 "despite heavy rain and a sodden track", according to the report in *The Age*. Steve Hayward, the athletics writer for the evening paper, *The Herald*, saw a little more in Landy's performance. "[Landy] showed a smoother, better-balanced style than when he last raced in Victoria. He finished with a brilliant burst."

Landy had come a long way since. Indeed, his progress from the previous year was remarkable. In his first interclub race of the pre-Olympic season he had chased MacMillan home. Macmillan ran 4:17.0; Landy was a second behind. The run "naturally tired him", Landy had said. The same time a year later was no more than a pipe-opener.

The next week, Landy really started to show the results of his hard and consistent training. He smashed Perry's Australian residential record for three miles by 16.4 seconds, running 14 minutes exactly (the equivalent for the slightly longer 5000 metres would be 14:28.0. Perry's Olympic final 5000 time was 14:23.0). Landy ran 4:34.0 for the first mile and 4:43.0 for each of the last two. His performances and style changes were being noticed. "Lift your arms and break a record. Seems silly, doesn't it," said the *Sporting Globe*'s correspondent. "Yet John Landy's higher arm carriage had a direct influence on his record-breaking three-mile run at Olympic

Park on Saturday." The report also noted how "effortlessly did his immaculate white spikes glide along the brick-red track". These were the European shoes, with a built-up heel, brought back by Les Perry.

Landy continued his "another run, another record" progress the next Saturday, running 5:23.6 for 2000 metres. Perry, having delivered the "go-faster shoes" to Landy, was powerless to catch them. He finished over 40 metres behind in 5:30.0. Ray Weinberg joined in the record-breaking that day, running 14.3 seconds in the 110 metres hurdles. Reports noted he was "more than a stone over his normal racing weight. Two hurdles which he jumped before the start of the race were the first he had tried since his return [from Helsinki], either in racing or in training." Both record races were held as invitation events during the Victorian schoolboys' championships. The kids must have been duly impressed by the Olympians.

Landy now backed off — a little. Perhaps it was reports that Josy Barthel, the tough little Luxembourg athlete who had been the surprise winner of the Helsinki Olympic final, had been invited to race in Australia. On 17 November, Landy ran a mile in 4:14.8 — slightly faster than his first of the season, but he had backed off. For a start, he had left the white spikes at home. He ran three fairly even 64-second laps, then came home in 61.3. Landy did not intend running a "good" mile until just before Christmas, Ken Moses reported. He would be waiting for Barthel "if he comes".

Landy vowed to himself after Helsinki that he would never stand on a starting line again wondering whether he was the fittest man in the race — he *would* be the fittest man on the line. He told Moses: "I am out to build up my stamina … It was stamina that beat me when I was away at the Games, and I do not want it to happen again."

Now Landy ran a two miles race at Malvern Cricket Ground. The grass track at the home of Malvern Harriers, where Cerutty had "come down to have a run" almost exactly ten years earlier, was circular, with no straights. It was also wet on the evening of 18

November 1952. Landy ran 9:08.2, beating Perry and Australian cross-country champion Neil Robbins comfortably. It was another Australian residential record, though considerably slower than the 8:54.0 he had run in Middlesborough in the lead-up to the Games.

Now Landy was ready to talk about the style changes. "I learned a lot in Europe," he told Ben Kerville of *The Sporting Globe* (19 November 1952). "Over there all of the really good distance runners put the whole of their foot to the ground." After explaining how this prevented the leg muscles from becoming over-tense, Landy offered Kerville and his readers a practical test of the efficacy of the European style. "Try standing on your toes and feel the tension in your calf and thigh muscles. You'll see what I mean."

Four days later, Landy ran an 880 in 1:56.7 before having a week off racing. He had competed six times since starting back, setting national records for three miles, 2000 metres and two miles, running a relaxed first-up mile in the same time as had left him "tired" a year earlier and now running a quick half mile. His stamina was there; his speed was there. He was ready for something special.

First, however, let us back-track a little to Belgium's Gaston Reiff. Unlike Landy, Reiff was closer to the end of his career than the start. He was a runner of some brilliance, some accomplishments and some versatility. He was also one who often unaccountably failed to live up to expectations.

Reiff's greatest career achievement was his gold medal in the 5000 metres at the 1948 London Olympic Games. It was a medal that owed as much to the extravagance of Emil Zatopek's tactics as the talents of the winner. Having won the 10,000 metres, Zatopek engaged in what the official report of the Games called an "unnecessary duel" with Erik Ahlden of Sweden in the heats of the 5000 metres the very next day.

As the Official Report of the 1948 Olympic Games says: "Though the best part of 100 yards ahead of the rest of the field, and qualifying with ease, they elected to stage a spirited battle, much to the delight of the crowd. How far this battle affected their running in the final two days later it is impossible to say."

Certainly, it is open to speculation whether or not it might have made a stride's difference in the final, held two days after the heats. From the official report of that race: "By half distance the race had resolved into a four-sided contest [between Zatopek, Reiff, Ahlden and Wim Slijkhuis of the Netherlands]. With four laps to go Reiff suddenly jumped his rivals, running a lap in 67.8 seconds, over two seconds faster than the immediately previous one. Zatopek seemed out of the race and it was Slijkhuis, some 20 yards behind Reiff, who was in second position at the bell. With Reiff almost exhausted 300 yards from home, Zatopek started one of those now-familiar rushes. With unbelievable speed, he closed the gap between himself and Slijkhuis and then, as the tape got ever nearer and nearer, he charged after Reiff.

As the report described: "With perhaps twenty yards to go the Czech was practically on level terms and Reiff, with an agonised glance over his shoulder, produced a small amount of unexpended energy, sufficient to take him over the finishing line a bare yard ahead [14:07.6 to 14:07.8]. Despite the adverse conditions [a wet and muddy track], both men beat the previous Olympic record."

Reiff went on to set world records at 2000 metres a month after the '48 Games and 3000 metres (the first man to break eight minutes) the following year. But he stepped off the track with 500 metres to run while defending his Olympic title in the 1952 final.

Bob Phillips, the British journalist and statistician, observed that "the nerves of Reiff had failed him again". He also noted: "Reiff was one of the finest runners of his generation and was to set marvellous world records of 5:07.0 for 2000 metres a month later (post-London Olympic Games) and 7:58.8 for 3000 metres the following year. Against the clock, and at these intermediate distances, he was in his element. Usually in the major championships, he failed to match expectations ... " (*Za-to-pek! Za-to-pek! Za-to-pek!*, Bob Phillips.)

Reiff's versatility extended down to the mile and 1500 metres. After the devastation of the Helsinki final, he turned his attention to the shorter distances. He went to Gavle, the Swedish town where he had run his 3000 metres world record three years earlier. Later, Cordner Nelson and Roberto Quercetani wrote in their middle-distance history, *The Milers (Tafnews Press 1985)*: "Six days after the Olympic 1500 ... Reiff, who had dropped out of the Olympic 5000, followed a pacemaker through the 440 in 61.0 and the 880 in 2:02. Then he pushed the pace hard to get away from a fast field and he passed three quarters in 3:03.8. Even at that pace [Ollie] Aberg challenged on the last turn, but Reiff held him off. In the homestretch [Ingvar] Ericsson made a run at Reiff while the Swedish crowd roared, but the strong Belgian stayed ahead for a close victory." Reiff ran 4.03.4, a fifth of a second ahead of Ericsson, 4.03.6. Aberg was third in 4.04.2. It was the fastest mile since 1945. Only Hägg and Andersson had ever run faster than Reiff and Ericsson.

Nelson and Quercetani saw it as marking a watershed. "This race, along with the Olympics, proved beyond question that 1952 was a turning point in the history of mile racing. Harder training, especially of the interval type, was changing all concepts of how fast a mile could be run."

Reiff wasn't done with the mile just yet. After a couple more races, including breaking Hägg's world record for two miles with 8:40.2 in Paris on 26 August 1952, he came to Antwerp for another mile on 13 September. His opponents included Don Macmillan, who had been touring and competing around Europe with Cerutty and Perry. "Macmillan, who had run 4:08.8 three days before, pushed the pace sensationally (59.5, 2:00.2, 3:02.3)," goes the report in *The Milers*. "While Macmillan faded to 4:12.0, Reiff passed 1500 metres in 3:47.6, then finished fast in 4:02.8."

Faster again, but for one reason or another, Reiff's two runs barely registered beyond the world of athletics insiders. "That was almost lost," says John Landy. "He ran 4:02 and got very little publicity." Landy suggests the reason was because Reiff was in his 30s (he was just short of 32 years old) and supposedly a 5000/10,000 metres runner. "They didn't take it seriously and it was close to the end of the season. But quite frankly that was one of the efforts to go very close, perhaps one of the first," says Landy.

Did it open the window on the four-minute mile? Not so much as if Bannister had done it, Landy says, adding that Bannister was seen as the athlete "most likely to do something in Europe". In addition to this, Bannister had his tight-knit group of supporters dedicated to claiming the glory of the first sub-four minute mile for Britain and, for added motivation, his conviction that he had been "robbed" of his chance of victory in Helsinki by the late addition of a semi-final round.

So if a balding, almost 32-year-old Belgian, with a dodgy temperament and better known as a long-distance specialist, could not re-ignite the public debate about a four-minute mile, who could?

What about a 22-year-old Australian who had been running seriously no more than two years, whose best mile time was 4:10.0, whose hobby was chasing butterflies, whose training consisted mainly of running laps of the park opposite his home late at night, who had been inspired by Zatopek and had observed the world's best runners, notebook and pen to hand, like he might a rare specimen?

John Landy rested on the last weekend in November, 1952. He did not run in the interclub mile that day, preferring to save himself for another crack at the three miles the next week. Melbourne was experiencing its normal capricious late spring-early summer weather. The following week's athletics was washed out by torrential rain, which flooded the track and jumping pits at Olympic Park.

Landy was "very frustrated. I got on the train at Caulfield and it was pouring with rain. The meeting was cancelled. I was due to run a three-mile and have a shot at the Australian record, which I'm pretty sure I would have broken. I was pretty pent-up about that, so the next week I took it out on the mile."

On 12 December, Steve Hayward previewed the following day's athletics with the prediction that Olympian John Landy was out for "a hard run" in the mile. Landy had said publicly that he wanted to have a crack at Macmillan's record that day. But not everyone was convinced. *The Sun* reported on the morning of the race: "John Landy, who ran 4:16.8 on November 29, will be out to improve on that time. But it is doubtful if his form is good enough to beat the national record of 4:09.0 set up in November 1951 by Don Macmillan." Little was right in this report. Landy had not run on 29 November (much less run 4:16.8), his form was good, and the record did go. (Strangely, the same paper had reported three days earlier that Landy was after Macmillan's record in the race. Looks like the Saturday reporter did not bother reading the story of his Wednesday counterpart.)

On the eve of the race, Landy went to a social gathering of Helsinki Olympians at marathoner Bob Prentice's place. It wasn't a big night, though he shared a couple of beers with his teammates. Les Perry, who was also running the mile the next day, agreed to help with the pace as long as he could.

"I got home late," says Landy. "The next day I had to work at the Titles Office in Melbourne [Landy had a vacation job there]. We had to work on Saturday mornings. I got up late and had to catch the train in a hurry, so I didn't have any breakfast." Landy worked till 12:30pm and then set off through town to Olympic Park. Ernest Hillier's chocolate shop was a Melbourne institution, its chocolate nut sundaes a feature. The impact of the aromas wafting out of Ernest Hillier's had the same impact on the famished Landy as the siren song did on Ulysses's sailors. "I thought, 'I've got to have one'.

So I had a chocolate nut sundae, but that wasn't enough so I had two meat pies."

Fuelled in equal parts by ambition, meat pies and a chocolate nut sundae, Landy warmed up for the interclub mile. He lost track of the time and was alerted by another runner, Frank Dooley, to the fact that his race had been called. Dooley had won the APS 880 and mile for Xavier in 1949, a year after Landy's APS mile win. "[Frank] said, 'you're going to miss the race,' so I roared over and I got in the second row of the mile. There were about 25 [competitors] in it."

It's hard to say what Landy's real expectations were. He says to this day that his aim was merely to break Macmillan's national record. That was only 4:08.9, though, and Landy had run 4:14.6 easily and been in record-breaking form at other distances. His own best was 4:10.0, which he had matched in the Empire versus USA relay before coming home and doing the best training of his life. Another sign that something bigger than just the Australian record might have been in the offing was noted by Ben Kerville in *The Sporting Globe* the week after the race. "His mother, 'for once', as she puts it, went down to see him," Kerville wrote.

Whatever his private ambitions, Landy stood on the second row of the start line, a 4:10.0 miler aiming at something a second or so faster. Perry led off the line, but within 300 metres Landy had shot to the front, for good. "I thought, 'I'm going pretty easily.' I heard a couple of [lap] times like 59 seconds and 2:01 and I thought, 'This is real easy.' Then they said 3:03 [at the bell] and I thought, 'No, there's got to be something wrong.'"

Landy powered through the final 440 yards in 59 seconds. Now he was not the only one who thought something *might* be wrong. The timekeepers went into a huddle, unable to believe the time shown on their watches without some form of validation. "Nobody would speak to me," Landy remembers. "Len McRae came over and said, 'You've run 4:03.' I said, 'That's impossible.'

All the timekeepers were huddled around. I was dead scared something was wrong."

If Landy was feeling ominous rumblings, they may well have been emanating from his stomach, rather than any negative vibrations. It was still not two hours since he had wolfed down the pies and the sundae. Within moments, however, the officials had come to the only logical conclusion possible. Watches that had been right an hour before the race and would still be right an hour later could not somehow have been wrong during the race. Not all of them, not all at once. Nor could a track that was surveyed at 440 yards suddenly have shrunk (if anything, the recent soakings it had absorbed might have bloated it!). It was re-surveyed anyway, and found to be spot on.

John Landy, who had never broken 4:10.0 before, had run 4:02.1. For record purposes, it was rounded up to 4:02.2, but it scarcely mattered. For the second time in a few months, a miler had run the fastest time since the days of Hägg and Andersson. This time, though, rather than a grand runner at the end of his career, it was by a promising novice at the start of his.

Mostly, what Landy remembers now about the run was how easy it seemed. Running into the unknown often is. Repeating the performance, much less bettering it, was where the pressure would come in. He recalls a feeling of "careless rapture", even today.

Tom Roberts, one of John Landy's friends and a man who would run in the first sub-four minute mile in Australia in 1956, recalls that no news photograph was taken of the finish of this historic race. The story ran big, but it was not front-page news. *The Herald* and *The Sporting Globe* had Saturday night editions, *The Sun*, *The Argus* and *The Age* came out the following Monday morning. *The Herald* and its stable-mate, *The Globe*, both found space to cut a one-paragraph report into their front pages. Under the heading "Record Smasher", the former reported that Landy "just missed breaking the world record", a forerunner of many such reports. Steve Hayward's story ran on an inside back page, along with a posed picture of Landy taking off his spikes. *The Globe* stuck rigidly to the facts in its one-paragraph front page pointer, saying Landy had run "4:02.1 for the mile". Ben Kerville's report was on page 14 inside.

Of the Monday papers, the broadsheets gave greater prominence to Landy's feat. Bruce Welch's report was the back-page lead in *The Age*, under the heading, "Landy Top Miler in World Today". *The Argus* ran two reports from Ken Moses, one on page three with a picture, the other on the front page of the sports section. The *Argus* picture, while captioned as depicting Landy taking the lead early in the race, seemed to be of another race. It seems strange that if a photographer was there for the paper he would not have taken a photo at the finish. *The Sun* had athletics on the front page, but it was an article reporting that dual Olympic sprint gold medallist Marjorie Jackson had won the Helms Award for best sportsman or woman in Oceania. Its report on the Landy race was deep inside the sports section.

The reaction was swift as news of Landy's time flashed round the world. Bannister, who had finished ahead of Landy in their Olympic heat and then seen him run in the Empire versus USA match, wrote in *Four-Minute Mile*: "I could hardly believe the improvement from the runner I had known in Helsinki."

Landy had revived talk of the four-minute mile, too. For the first time since the Hägg–Andersson rivalry was at its peak, the magic mark seemed inevitable again. Four laps, four minutes — it could be done. Here was an athlete, not quite 23 years old, fired up by his experience at the Olympics and imbued with a new sense of exploring his limits. A four-minute mile might be within those limits.

If Gaston Reiff had sparked excitement among insiders, Landy's run fanned that spark into a conflagration that would soon rage all around the world. Ben Kerville, writing in *The Sporting Globe* on the night of the race (13 December 1952), quoted Percy Cerutty, who had just arrived back in Melbourne from his extended Helsinki trip. "Landy is certain to break four minutes for the mile, particularly if he is given reasonable pace, as has been provided for Hägg and other famous milers in making their best run," said Cerutty. He also made other, more personal, remarks that would prompt Landy to sever their relationship.

The papers two days later had some time to assess. Acclaiming Landy the "top miler in the world today", *The Age* quoted Landy as saying the Olympic Park track was "not as fast as it could have been". *The Age* also noted that "it was a personal triumph as he had coached himself for this attempt since his mentor Percy Cerutty only recently returned after seeing the Helsinki Games".

On the matter of credit, Landy stuck steadfastly to the agreement he had reached with the other members of the Cerutty gang who had become disillusioned as a result of the Games' trip. He gave the coach his due, and more. "Most of the credit must go to Perce," he told Ken Moses in *The Argus*. "I have trained to his methods. A lot of people are against them, but had it not been for him I would not have got anywhere near my time today. Only hard work gets results. Perce has been telling us that all the time, and our trip to the Games confirmed what he said."

Moses also included in his story the claim that Landy had been talked out of retirement by Cerutty only a couple of weeks earlier. Even on the surface, it seems curious. Cerutty had only just arrived back in Melbourne, so when would he have talked with Landy? And why would a man who had just run national records for three different distances, and had come back from Helsinki fired with ambition, be talking retirement anyway? Sims does not mention it in *Why Die*, nor does it appear in any other report. It was plain wrong.

Writing in that night's *Herald,* Steve Hayward commented how

Landy had doubled his training. "He has followed the Zatopek plan of running many [repetitions] of 440 yards or 600 yards at training sessions." Two days later, in the mid-week edition of *The Sporting Globe*, Kerville wrote a follow-up. It began by praising Landy's willingness to learn from the best in Helsinki. "In Landy's case … he went to the Olympic Games with his eyes and ears wide open and picked up every snippet of information he could learn about the art of running."

Kerville also spoke to Landy's mother, who had come along to watch the run. She said it was "for once", but clearly she had been listening attentively to her son on athletics. "I went with my fingers crossed," said Elva Landy, "hoping that John would 'crack' the Australian 4:09 record by not too miserable a margin. I was stunned when they announced his time.

"We've been hearing from John about this wonderful Gunder Hägg for so long. I've often wondered just how he managed to make such fast time. It just didn't register that John had run somewhere within reach of Hägg."

Yet not all the reaction was favourable — understandably so. The runner the world had seen in Helsinki was not a four-minute mile candidate, not even based on his impact in Britain before and after the Games. So the improvement was regarded sceptically by some.

Arthur Daley, a sports columnist for *The New York Times*, made certain Australians would remember him with cynicism for years to come. Noting Landy's lack of credentials, Daley fulminated: "This sceptic finds himself extremely reluctant to accept on face value the recent news from Australia that an unknown named John Landy had run a mile in 4:02.1. No matter what anyone says, unknowns just do not run miles that fast … Gunder the Wunder [Hägg] ripped off a dozen or so miles at 4:06.0 before he got down to his magic figures. Never in the history of foot racing have strangers come up from nowhere to shatter or approach marks. They always bore credentials first, a background of other high-class performances."

Daley went on to disparage Australian timekeepers, or at least the quality of those who would time interclub races. He also — wrongly — speculated that Landy had probably run on a grass track. "Landy's clocking makes a fellow pause. He just doesn't have the credentials," he said, before thundering to a conclusion. "It would be nice to hear that Landy's 4:02.1 is a completely legitimate performance. For the present, though, please pass the salt."

Australian columnists returned serve. No doubt it was darkly muttered into pots of beer in Australian pubs that the Americans had killed Australia's champion racehorse Phar Lap (who died in mysterious circumstances after winning his first race in the USA) and now they were out to get John Landy. Anyway, Landy soon backed up his great run with other great runs. Daley was gracious enough to recant, or smart enough to recant graciously — whatever. Time wounds all heels, as one wise humourist once observed.

(History gave *The New York Times* smarty-pants a more fitting comeuppance than the most witty shaft aimed his way back then possibly could have: the shifty, ducking and diving "entrepreneur" played superbly by George Cole in the British comedy series, *Minder*, was named none other than Arthur Daley. Who these days could take anything written by Arthur Daley seriously?)

Time Magazine, then, as now, one of the most prestigious news magazines in the world, more than balanced up the reaction from America. In an end-of-the-year piece on 29 December 1952, the magazine reported in glowing terms how Landy had re-opened the possibility of a four-minute mile. "The dream of a four-minute mile, once considered a physical impossibility, seemed a bit closer to reality last week," *Time*'s correspondent wrote. "An Australian agricultural student named John Landy, who had never beaten 4:10.0 in his life, suddenly raced through the most sparkling mile performance since Gunder (The Wonder) Hägg's world record 4:01.4 in 1945." Describing Landy as an "amateur entomologist who developed his leg muscles chasing specimens", the article detailed the changes he had made since Helsinki and their impact. It also (wrongly) repeats the story that "Despite his progress, it took the most persuasive efforts of this track coach [Cerutty] to convince Landy that he had a real chance for the record." *Time* concluded with a quote from Landy saying he wanted to break Hägg's record "right away. The boys in Europe are getting closer to it now, and they're almost certain to crack four minutes during their next track season."

The specialist athletics press was taking note of developments in Australia, too, and the reasons behind them. Cordner Nelson, co-author with Roberto Quercetani of *The Milers* and co-founder with his brother Bert of the authoritative US magazine *Track & Field News*, told Joe Galli that US coaches "frankly do not believe in European ideas for distance training and their runners show it. The value of the new training methods has been proved in Australia, where a willing group have lifted their usually low standards to among the world's best in only two years."

Landy's local profile was given a huge boost. The issue of *The Sporting Globe* carrying Kerville's follow-up article also contained its poll for the paper's Athlete of the Year. Not surprisingly, Jackson won, followed by tennis player Frank Sedgman, Olympic gold medal cyclist Russell Mockridge, world champion boxer Jimmy Carruthers, gold medal swimmer John Davies and top professional track cyclist Sid Patterson. John Landy came in at seventh, ahead of golfers Norman Von Nida and Peter Thomson. On the strength of just one run — albeit the fastest mile in the world for over seven years — he had been ranked above such as Olympic hurdles gold medallist and 100 metres bronze medallist Shirley Strickland; finalists in Ken Doubleday, Ray Weinberg, John Treloar and Les Perry; and Don Macmillan, who had vastly out-performed him in Helsinki.

Nor was *Time* the only magazine to include Landy in its year-ender. Confirming *The Sporting Globe* athlete of the year rankings, an *Argus* publication called "1952 Australia's Finest Year Of Sport" included Landy's profile with those of Jackson, Strickland, Perry, Winsome Cripps and Treloar.

Again, only the 4:02.1 could have possibly elevated Landy to such company. Considerable improvement on the Olympic tour, allied with failure at the Games, could not have done so. "Landy couldn't reach the Helsinki 1500 metres final. Now he's THE FASTEST MILER IN THE WORLD," the heading on *The Argus* profile read. The profile continued: "While most Australians struggled to grasp the significance of that run, the news snowballed abroad." The magazine put Landy in the most esteemed company possible. "Landy became the most freely discussed athlete since the famous Czech, Emil Zatopek, won three gold medals at the Helsinki Olympiad."

From Olympic disappointment to being spoken of in the same breath as the world's greatest distance runner was one hell of a transition. The article also gave a potted version of the philosophy of hard work Landy had absorbed from Cerutty first, and then refined in Europe watching Zatopek and the others. "Provided an athlete has the natural ability to run, his future success must depend on the amount of hard work he is prepared to put into his training, Landy says."

Less surprisingly, Melbourne University's student newspaper, *Farrago*, named John Landy its sportsman of the year. It, too, went with the Zatopek parallel, proclaiming: "Sportsman of the Year: Our Zatopek — John Landy"

One other aspect of the reaction to Landy's run was to cause the irreparable rupture of his relationship with Percy Cerutty. The coach, who had just got back from Europe after an extended trip, and was distracted by the break-up of his first marriage, had not got to Olympic Park in time to see Landy's run. Rushing to the ground from his nearby flat, Cerutty quickly realised something big had happened. He was told that Landy had run 4:02.1. At virtually the same time that Landy was staying on message in acknowledging Cerutty's part in his run, Cerutty unleashed a broadside against him.

As described by Graem Sims in *Why Die?*, Cerutty launched a tirade. Who knows what his motivation was. Was he deluding himself that his words might motivate Landy when they inevitably got back to him? If that was the case then the coach surely did not choose his words wisely. Was he simply trying to catch up with a situation that had got away from him? Landy was going somewhere and Cerutty faced being left behind. "Here's a bloke who's come home like a whipped dog from the Olympics — couldn't qualify for a final in 4:14.0," Cerutty raved. "And then he comes back and does this! After all the effort to get the money together to get him over there, he's bloody well wasted the fare."

Cerutty was probably not taking much in at all as he delivered this rant, certainly not the fact that John Landy's parents were sitting no more than ten metres away and could hear his every word. Not surprisingly, they were deeply offended and moved quietly away as soon as they could. But they told John of the outburst later, and he severed all contact with the coach from that point on. (John Landy still does not comment on Cerutty publicly, but he confirms the account given by Sims is an accurate one.)

Geoff Warren believes that Cerutty's attitude to family and parents would never have sat well with Landy. Cerutty wanted his athletes to stand on their own feet and be independent of their parents, especially their fathers. "That wouldn't have gone down too well with John," Warren says. "John's Dad was a wonderful guy, such a friendly, encouraging guy. I could tell what it meant to John. Sure John also went through an adolescent time but he thought a lot of his father and his family, and I suspect this aspect of Perce would have made him step back a bit."

Through his sympathetic contacts in the press, Cerutty gave the impression for a long time after the split that he still coached Landy.

It comes through in article after article. Landy probably unwittingly added to the impression by never coming out and denying it. He preferred not to comment rather than to add fuel to this particular fire. Given Cerutty's ability to court controversy, who can say speaking up would have ended matters once and for all? Landy does not elaborate on the reasons behind the split but he confirms that after the break, "I took no notice of his written communications and in fact had nothing to do with him."

Landy was as keen as anyone else to confirm his massive breakthrough. Athletics history is full of characters who have one great performance, on that one day when everything goes right, and then spend the rest of their careers fruitlessly trying to replicate it. Of course, it was always unlikely that 13 December 1952 was such a day or Olympic Park, with its cinder track exposed to the elements and its burnt-out grandstand still not repaired, was such a venue. Everything can go right anywhere, anytime, but it was unlikely to have done so on this day, at this venue.

Three days after his mile race, John Landy lined up at Malvern Cricket Ground for a 1500 metres. The grass track with no straights was not conducive to fast times, but Landy ran 3:49.0 to break Macmillan's Australian record. He had gone through the 1000 metres in a fast 2:31.4, close to the pace that would be required for a four-minute mile.

Landy had run 3:52.8 to qualify for the Olympic team. In a tactical heat at Helsinki, he had run 3:57.0. Although his run at Malvern was not as fast as the equivalent in his mile, it was not that far away. He had moved to another level.

Within a few more weeks, Landy would run 4:02 again. One thing he would never do again, however, was duplicate the feeling of that first run. In itself, this is not that uncommon: breakthrough performances often seem effortless. Only with hindsight does the athlete remember the hard work that went into it; and after the »

Olympic Park

Melbourne's Olympic Park has a long and varied history. At one stage, as a promoter searched desperately for ways to make the venue pay, ostrich racing was tried. It did not last.

Dick Lean, the son of John Wren's promoter of the same name, told the story to John Cain, former Victorian premier, in *On with the Show, a glimpse behind the scenes of entertainment in Australia* (John Cain, Prowling Tiger Press, 1998). "We had lighting over the whole arena. Anyway, they get these ostriches out there; they've got the place full. Maybe the ostriches looked up and saw the moon there and reckoned it was time they were in bed. So they just squat. The promoters eventually got desperate and they got a sheep dog out and tried to sool him on to the ostriches. I think one ostrich got up and took a peck at the dog, and it bolted. So, they've got to give the money back. The show just didn't happen. Lee Corneau [the South African entrepreneur who had brought the birds into Australia] disappeared and left his ostriches behind."

Amazing indeed, though the shock of the unknown John Landy running 4:02.1 for the mile could scarcely have been greater had one of those reluctant ostriches done so.

From John Landy's time to the present day, Olympic Park has been Melbourne's main athletics and football (soccer) venue. But in a long and colourful history, it has also hosted motorcycling, Australian Rules football, women's cricket, greyhound racing, tennis, hockey, rugby and American football. Most of the more exotic ventures were initiated during the time Wren's company, Melbourne Carnivals, had a long-term lease. The company built a massive concrete track, sloped at an angle of 46 degrees at the top, on the east side of the main oval. Known as the Motordrome, it had room for a football ground within its basin. The Motordrome opened in November 1924, before an estimated crowd of 35,000 with visiting American riders being pitted against Australian stars Ron Hipwell and Charlie Disney. (From *Of ostriches and athletes*, an article by Marc Fiddian that appeared in The Malvern Caulfied Progress on 16 January 1991.) The use of the area as a staging ground for US Army vehicles during World War II effectively invalidated this lease and the land reverted to its original purpose as a home for amateur sport.

Not that all was smooth sailing. Olympic Park was caught up in the politics swirling round the choice of venue for the 1956 Olympic Games, which were awarded to Melbourne in 1949. Development of the ground stalled pending final decisions, and the immediate post-war years saw endless complaints by the Victorian Amateur Athletic Association (VAAA) about the facilities and the administration of the ground by the Olympic Park Trust. In October 1948, for instance, delegates to the VAAA Council criticised the trustees for using the association's hurdles in kennel shows without permission. The delegates instructed the Council to "lock the hurdles up" when not in use and sell those surplus to requirements.

Less than a week later, Ron Aitken, the man who in 1946 had moved the original Victorian Olympic Council motion that Melbourne apply to host the 1956 Games, said the 1948–49 Victorian titles would be moved to the St Kilda Cricket Ground. Olympic Park had been ruled out because of lack of sanitation and other facilities.

This brought the predictable political response: the government promised to spend money. Within weeks, it was reported that £12,000 was to be allocated for the installation of proper sewerage, new dressing rooms and strengthening of the grandstand. However, money promised is not money spent. At the first meeting of the VAAA Council for 1949, delegates demanded that the VAAA write to the trustees and demand to know when repairs were to be made. Not that the office-bearers needed much prodding. The president, Mr (later Judge) J. X. O'Driscoll, told delegates it was a disgrace that the ground should be allowed to go to wrack and ruin. The association had repeatedly complained of the lack of sanitary arrangements at the park, and would keep on complaining until conditions were remedied. The government then promised £50,000 for re-development, though none of the original money had yet been spent "because of shortage of materials".

Even when things got better, it was two steps forward, one step back. In August 1950, the trustees agreed to put down a cinder track. Within a month, delays to the beginning of the work forced the start of the interclub season to be put back three weeks. When the new tracks were officially opened in January 1951, the reaction, thank heavens, was largely positive.

Then there were arguments about other matters. At the start of the 1950–51 season, the VAAA interclub committee felt compelled to protest to trustees about the operation of a bar at the track. "It was felt the practice was not in keeping with the true ideals of amateur sport," the temperate ones wailed. The matter was raised at the next council meeting, the secretary of the interclub committee pointing out that the majority of the people at the bar were not interested in what was going on at the track. Delegates were somewhat reassured by the news that proceeds from the bar license went back into ground improvements.

In April 1951, the grandstand at Olympic Park burnt down. An incomplete clean-up aside, nothing was done and *The Argus* reported in October that athletes would have to change in old tin sheds and tents.

The lack of facilities meant meetings were more vulnerable to unfavourable weather. Tracks may be "all-weather", athletes and officials are not. *The Age* reported interclub was cancelled on the first wet day of the season; the rain itself was not the problem, only the lack of facilities meant no-one could find shelter. "The shell of the burnt-out stand was a dismal reminder of the quick work promised months ago by the Olympic Park Trust," Bruce Welch reported. "It is eight months since the stand was burnt out and two months since work was due to start."

The more things change, the more they stay the same, of course. I myself well remember training from Olympic Park in the late 1970s and early 1980s. Thieves regularly raided the change-rooms. When an attendant was placed on the gate and a training charge applied, the light fingered ones merely forked over the token entry fee and continued on their opportunistic way.

> The gates would shut promptly at seven o'clock. Sometimes we would be finished training around the surrounding parklands by then, sometimes not, and we would have to find a way in. Things only improved after we fed a story to the press that Rob de Castella, Australia's premier marathoner, was having his preparation compromised by having to climb the fence after his exhausting long runs!

» breakthrough comes the burden of expectation.

With Landy, the expectation of a four-minute mile started the moment he crossed the Olympic Park finish line in 4:02.1. At times, over the next 18 months, it would become a crushing burden indeed.

Up until now, however, it had all been simple. "I came back [from the Games] with some ideas and put them into practice." As simple as that. "If I did develop into a reasonable runner at that stage, it was what I learnt in Helsinki which was critical on top of the general ideas of Cerutty and others."

In one run, though, Landy had surpassed all expectations and re-shaped the landscape of post-war miling, shocking both himself and the world. "I had no idea I was able to do what I did. I was absolutely flabbergasted. When I ran 4:02 I thought it was way beyond my capacity, bearing in mind that the ([Olympic] 1500 a few months before had been won in the equivalent of about 4:03 to 4:04. I did it easily. I came home in 59 seconds and it was such an easy run. It would seem to anyone looking at it, 'give him a couple more runs and he'll run four minutes'. But it didn't work out that way," Landy adds ruefully.

They had all gone to Helsinki to learn. Cerutty had chased after Paavo Nurmi to learn, and he had followed Perry to Zatopek to learn. But John Landy, who had gone with his eyes and his ears open, had learned most of all. He had done it by observing, not by searching. "The big win I had was going to Helsinki," Landy says now. "Two things: first was how I changed my style — that was probably minor, but it was still important. The other one was to see how they ran these repetition laps."

Others saw how hard Zatopek trained, and he did. Landy, however, observed that as important as his fast repetitions were, they were not the key. It was the recovery that was more important and by reducing that, one got fitter. "They concentrated on recovery, it was much more methodical. I changed my running program. It took me three or four months' training after Helsinki to run 4:02.1 and I ran it dead easy. It was the best run I ever had. Bang, just like that."

The Victorian interclub program took a break over Christmas, resuming three days into the New Year of 1953. There had only been a few hundred spectators — mostly fellow-competitors — to witness Landy's 4:02.1. Already, on 3 January 1953, there were 2000 at Olympic Park to see the unexpected local hero run his next mile.

Steve Hayward reported that the track was "poor". The curator was on holidays, and it had not been watered, so the surface was rock-hard. Spikes hardly made a mark, much less penetrated the surface. Landy was suffering from a head cold. On a cool afternoon, with a strong southerly wind opposing the runners in the finishing straight, he led through 440 yards in 58.4 seconds. Perry, determined to help Landy, took over aiming to lead till the halfway point. But he could not last the whole lap and Landy was back in front at 880 yards in 1:59.4. On his own now, Landy slowed marginally to reach three-quarters of a mile in 3:01. A final lap as fast as he had produced three weeks earlier would put him right on four minutes; a second and a half slower and he might still break Hägg's world record. He was 3:44.4 at 1500 metres, still on target for the record, and possibly four minutes. But he was straining this time, not flowing effortlessly. The wind hit him head on and he crossed the line in 4:02.8.

"Australia's miracle runner, John Landy, today failed gloriously in his attempt on the four-minute mile," began Ben Kerville's report in *The Sporting Globe*. Kerville said that Landy expressed "polite disgust" at the condition of the track.

"Glorious failure" would come to be a phrase closely associated with Landy, and other contenders, until the four-minute mile was actually achieved. One thing Landy had learned already was that if he was to achieve the goal in Australia, it would have to be through his own efforts. There was no-one to stick with him, not even Macmillan, had he been around.

But he had now twice shown the world that the four-minute mile was possible, and maybe imminent, rather than some distant dream. The momentum generated by Hägg and Andersson, lost with their suspension for accepting illegal payments and, for the rest of the world, with the war, was building up again. And there was no question who was generating the drive. Just in case anyone was in doubt, especially Roger Bannister, *Athletics World* sounded the alarm bells in its first edition for 1953. "Brutal Assault on Four-Minute Mile", screamed the headline. "Landy Runs 4:02.1 & 4:02.8 Within 21 Days."

"Never since the Hägg-Andersson era of 1942–45 has the classic and impregnable 'Four Minute Mile' been so closely threatened as in the last few weeks," *Athletics World* "eye-witness correspondent" J. H. Galli wrote. "The assailant, 22 years old, 5ft 11-1/2in Australian, John M. Landy, ran a non-qualifying fifth in his 1500 metres heat at Helsinki last July in 3:57.0." And, as Roger Bannister wrote subsequently in *Four-Minute Mile*: "Wherever I went after John Landy's two races the inevitable question was broached. Was it possible for a man to run a mile in four minutes?"

Landy had shown the answer was yes. But who would be the man to do it? The Europeans, the Americans — they were all wondering the very same thing.

7

The Race is On

Nobody felt the impact of John Landy's two magnificent runs either side of the New Year of 1953 more than Wes Santee and Roger Bannister, soon to be revealed as the other main protagonists in the race for the four-minute mile. Both were failures in Helsinki, Santee an ignominious one like Landy. He was "gapped" in his heat of the 5000 metres and, much to his chagrin, had not even been allowed to bid for a place in the 1500. Bannister's was more a case of falling short of expectations — his own and those of the British public. His own feelings were magnified by the criticism of his training methods and race planning. He had done it his way, and failed. Fourth place a failure? Such is often the fate of those who aim high.

When news of Landy's break-through reached Santee at the University of Kansas and Bannister in London, each had an added source of frustration. Here was this young Australian, on the rise, and with another couple of months of his domestic season in which to reach the ultimate prize. Meanwhile, both of them had to wait for the northern hemisphere outdoor season. Bannister had no indoor competition. Santee did, but the nine, ten and eleven laps to the mile indoor board tracks, which made for great theatre, were no place to run fast times.

Like the way cyclones spin clockwise in the southern hemisphere and anti-clockwise in the northern, the feelings of Santee and Bannister in the northern hemisphere were the diametrical opposite of Landy's in Melbourne. Landy feared the Europeans were poised to break four minutes in their outdoor season if he did not achieve the feat in the southern hemisphere first; conversely, Santee and Bannister were aghast at the prospect of Landy doing a sub-four before they even had a chance to get on an outdoor track. None of them would prove to be right, in 1953, but it added to the air of tension.

In one of the many interviews and articles on John Landy that appeared at the end of 1952, Landy was quoted as saying that four minutes was just "an arbitrary standard that has popped up conveniently in front of a world record. It is just a round figure". It would soon become a figure that was "just around", easy to conceive, hard to grasp.

Four minutes may have been an arbitrary standard, but the significance of a mile in four minutes, or less, had fascinated sports fans for years. Many track fans remain fascinated. Garry Hill, long-time editor of US magazine *Track & Field News*, writes regularly and passionately about his love for the mile, at times attributing a significant part of athletics' decline to a minor sport in the world's major nation to the eclipse of the mile by the championship distance 1500 metres. "Ahh, the mile!" Hill editorialised. "You can't overstate the importance of this basic unit of measurement to the [US] public. Yet we continually shoot ourselves in the foot by not nurturing it. Track meets without miles are like baseball games without home runs, football without the forward pass, basketball without the dunks. You know — like soccer. Yet we stage them all the time. *And we don't have to."*

Once Mt Everest was conquered for the first time in May 1953, the four-minute mile came to be categorised as "the Everest of athletics". The quest even had its equivalent of George Mallory, the British climber who disappeared on an attempt on the summit of Everest, creating speculation that continues to this day that he may have conquered the world's highest mountain almost 30 years before Edmund Hillary and Tenzing Norgay. Ken Wood, a British miler who subsequently did break four minutes, always claimed that he had done a sub-four in a training "race" with two others the month before Bannister did. The claim does not stand up to rigorous analysis.

John Landy also loves the mile, recalling that the quest for the four-minute mile was accompanied by a "four-minute mile mania". He explains the attraction of the four-minute mile as coming, first and foremost, from its simplicity. "It was a simple, round figure, four minutes, popping up in front of a world record. The mile was four even laps — four laps, each one in 60 seconds. People could understand it. It was a very graspable concept."

Another factor was the build-up of times from the 1930s on. Perhaps the first authenticated use of the term "four-minute mile" was in a 1933 article in the *New York Herald Tribune* by Jesse Abramson. The article appeared at about the same time Jack Lovelock of New Zealand and Bill Bonthron of the USA both beat the world record in the same race, Lovelock winning in 4:07.6 seconds. The next year, Glenn Cunningham, Wes Santee's University of Kansas predecessor, reduced the record to 4:06.8. Lovelock won the Olympic 1500 in Berlin in 1936 from Cunningham in a world record 3:47.8, and Sydney Wooderson of Britain, injured when he ran in the Olympics, ran a 4:06.4 mile in 1937. Through the war years, the competition between Swedes Gunder Hägg and Arne Andersson progressively reduced the record to Hägg's 4:01.4.

"There was a build-up over a long period of time, interrupted by the war, which made it even more protracted," says John Landy. "When Lovelock, Bonthron, Cunningham, Wooderson and other runners in the '30s got [to] 4:06.0, that created a great deal of interest."

Some of the interested parties genuinely thought it could not be done. Brutus Hamilton, a famed University of California coach, made a list of "ultimates of human effort" in 1934, lofty goals that he thought athletes could eventually attain. His ultimate for the mile? Four minutes 1.66 seconds. Hamilton lived to see his mile prediction refuted; he also lived to coach a sub-four minute miler — Don Bowden, the first American to achieve the feat. "Brutus Hamilton told me, 'you can run it,'" Bowden said in 2004. Presumably, Hamilton had revised the charts several times by the time of Bowden's run in 1957.

Another famous US track coach was even more definite. "There will never be a four-minute mile," said Jake Weber of Fordham University. "A man's heart will never stand it, and that's all there is to it. Four minutes is absolutely a physical impossibility." (Mel Allen, with Frank Graham Jr, *It Takes Heart*, Harper and Brothers, 1959.)

"We didn't hear much about the mile during the war," John Landy says, "but in Sweden in 1945 Andersson and Hägg got it down to 4:01.6 [Andersson] and 4:01.3 [Hägg, but ratified as 4:01.4]. Europeans other than Sweden had been riven by war.

"People built up this mystique. The Americans called it the miracle mile, the magic mile; it was built up into a big thing. Then it went very flat after the war. Hägg and Andersson got ruled out as professionals and it sort of drifted away."

Reiff arrested the drift; Landy turned the tide. Just as some had doubted that it could be done, now athletes came along who were determined to do it.

Wes Santee had no doubts, or none he would own to publicly, of his ability to run a mile in under four minutes. Burning with the failure of Helsinki, he had marched in to the office of the Kansas University campus newspaper and announced he would do it. Santee attended Ashland High School in rural Kansas. His running ability there earned him the nickname "Ashland antelope". Asked to predict a future sports story, he wrote in the 1950 high school annual: "Wes Santee has recently broken the world mile record in the time of 3:58.3, and it should stand for many years to come."

Santee had a reputation for being cocky. He was certainly ahead of his time with his flair and knack for talking up his races.

At times he agreed with the "cocky" tag — it seems he was asked about it in every recorded interview — but he preferred to think of it as confidence. In a 2005 interview with the *Lawrence Journal-World*, the newspaper of the University of Kansas campus town, he explained the difference. "To me, saying I can beat you in the mile is being confident," Santee said. "To me, being cocky is me thinking I'm a better person than you. I never thought I was a better person than anyone else. I just could outrun people."

In his competitive days, Santee was more inclined to blur the distinction between cocky and confident. "I guess I'm cocky," he said in a 1953 interview. "If you don't believe in yourself, I don't see how you can expect to run. I don't think there's anyone who can beat me in the mile. I'm great, but that's only on the track. I don't think I'm better than anyone else otherwise." ("Sure I'll Run the Four-Minute Mile", interview with Bob Hurt, *Saturday Evening Post*, September 1953.)

Hurt wrote that Santee "has startled the track faithful with his remarkable feats and flabbergasted them with his air of supreme confidence. The brash young man, a sprout of the same Western Kansas wheat region which produced Glenn Cunningham, is cocky to the point of exasperation, but he can run."

On the inevitability of breaking four minutes, Santee said: "I'm as certain I can run the four-minute mile as you are that you can drive your car home. There's always the chance of an accident, but barring that, I'll do it."

Roger Bannister was as much concerned with finding the time to run the four-minute mile as with running it. He had thought to retire after the Helsinki Olympic Games, but he decided to continue both to prove to himself that his training could produce results and to rebut those unkind, and unfair, critics who had assailed him.

Bannister rejected retirement, opting to run for two more years through to the 1954 British Empire Games and the European championships. They seemed worthy goals, even if at the time he would probably have been looking at the Empire event as a warm-up for the tougher competition he could expect from his European rivals.

As he struggled to come to terms with his disappointment in Helsinki, Bannister wrote in *The Four-Minute Mile* that he "had found new meaning in the Olympic words that the important thing was not the winning but the taking part — not the conquering, but fighting well. All week I had seen the interplay of success and failure and felt no bitterness about my own race." He had also concluded that his personal outcome was "failure", especially in the light of his pre-Games training, which had been capped off by a time trial over three-quarters of a mile in 2:52.9. "I had never run at such speed before," Bannister wrote in *The Four-Minute Mile*.

And failure it was. Nor was it any use agonising publicly about what might have been. "What use was there in revealing the speed of my last time trial before the Games? I did not have second sight. How could I have foreseen the arbitrary revision of the program at the last minute — a change which made nonsense at a single stroke of a long year's training schedule." Concluding there was no "second chance" in the event of an Olympic failure, Bannister also decided there was no point discussing it. "Any attempt to explain away a disappointment is taken as an admission of failure." So he kept his counsel and made new plans.

He decided he would continue running for two more years, provided he could still keep pace with his medical studies. He already knew that his work commitments would preclude any sort of campaign for the 1956 Olympic Games in Melbourne. Just as Bannister had worked resolutely away at his goal of winning in Helsinki, so now he needed a goal to justify remaining in the sport. Part of it was vindication. "My running had become something of a crusade. It was as if I were preaching about a special attitude to running that I felt was right. It was a combination of the Greek approach that I encountered at the Olympics and of the university attitude that Oxford had taught me. I coupled this with my own love of running as one of the most perfect forms of physical expression." (*The Four-Minute Mile.*)

Gradually, over those months, Bannister's goal would crystallise around the four-minute mile. Landy's 4:02.1 and 4:02.8 ensured that the goal was back on the agenda. To deny it would be churlish. "To say, 'Four minutes is only a time' was presumptuous, unless I had an answer for the inevitable follow-up question — 'Well, if it's possible, why don't you do it?' Whether as athletes we liked it or not, the four-minute mile had become rather like Everest — a challenge to the human spirit. It was a barrier that seemed to defy all attempts to break it — an irksome reminder that man's striving might be in vain."

Each of Landy, Santee and Bannister had limitations on their ability to commit fully to the quest. For Bannister, it was the pressure of combining training and competition with his schedule at the hospital where he worked. He crammed his sessions of 10x440 yards into his lunch-break. It left him exhausted, but it was all he could fit in.

Santee, in some ways, was the least encumbered. He was a student on a sports scholarship. His course and his lecture times were fitted around his training schedule. Though he took a part-time job to earn some spending money, he was basically untroubled by the sort of demands placed on Bannister. For Santee, the pressure came in his racing program. He was on scholarship at the university, so he was expected to run for the university, as hard and as often as the competition demanded. Only during the (northern hemisphere) autumn cross-country season would he have one race a meeting. At indoor and outdoor meetings he was expected to run multiple events for "KU" (Kansas University).

As 1952 became 1953, Santee went undefeated at both 880 yards and the mile through the indoor season. As the outdoor season got under way, he ran in relays, dual meets (against other universities) and in the odd invitational, week after week. Finally, he baulked at the demanding schedule, and won some concessions from the tough Kansas coach, Bill Easton. He would run his college competitions, but some meetings would be reserved for the mile only. "Wes gave up a lot of opportunities to run the mile when he was in college," recalls Dick Wilson, a teammate of Santee's from 1950–54. "He believed he was part of the team, and that was coach Easton's philosophy."

Landy also felt the pressure of combining study and running. In his case, the restrictions were self-imposed, rather than imposed by the workload as with Bannister, but it was real pressure nonetheless. Study commitments precluded Landy from going to Europe to pursue further competition. In an early 1953 interview entitled, "He Chases Butterflies" in *Goodyear's Magazine for Men*, Landy revealed he had already refused invitations to run in London later in the year. "I couldn't possibly run in Europe. I'm doing my fourth year of agricultural science. The course has already taken far too long, and athletics mustn't interfere with it any further."

John Landy, of course, was not done when he ran 4:02.8 on 3 January 1953. Even ruling out Europe, he had another two to three months' racing coming up, with the national championships in Perth, and other opportunities. One thing this second 4:02 did force, however, was a recantation from his critics. The backlash from Arthur Daley's first column had already caused him to backtrack. Furnished with further information from the news wires and the ubiquitous Joe Galli, Daley had already written on 29 December 1952: "Maybe too much salt was taken here."

Suddenly, Australians were "earthy and realistic" rather than hicks incapable of surveying a track and operating a stop-watch. "Since there was no intention here to disparage the Landy achievement it is felt that fairness compels the presentation of supporting evidence relating to his feat," Daley wrote. Miraculously, Daley now remembered that no fewer than the first eight finishers in the Helsinki 1500 had broken Lovelock's Olympic record, and that "none had overwhelming credentials as far as competitive backgrounds were concerned". Unknowns do break records, it seems.

By now, Daley was such a fervent convert that he was oblivious to the news that Landy would not be racing in Europe in 1953, preferring to complete his studies at home. In a "Forecast for 1953" column that appeared on 4 January (thus, was written before the 4:02.8), Daley predicted that in July, "John Landy of Australia runs a mile in 3:59.9." Presumably, Landy was going to do that 3:59.9 around Central Park, an idea that may not have been as silly as it sounds!

The 4:02.8 mile had attracted the attention of another American reporter. Gayle Talbot, in Australia to cover the Davis Cup Challenge Round played in Adelaide on 29–31 December, popped in to Melbourne to take in Landy's race. Alan Trengrove, who went on to become a legendary tennis writer, reported Talbot's comments in *The Sun*: "This boy's terrific. He'd be a huge success in the States." Three years later, he would be.

It had been widely reported that several prominent athletes — Landy, Les Perry and Ray Weinberg among them — were threatening not to go to Perth for the championships because of the cost of the trans-continental trip. The same edition of *The Sun* carried a letter from an A. E. Hearn of the Melbourne suburb of Surrey Hills: "In admiration of John Landy's magnificent performance, am enclosing a £1 postal note to aid the sending of Victoria's team to Perth," Hearn wrote.

The idea that John Landy might achieve the four-minute mile any time he ran was now starting to take hold. The interstate press discovered him. Writing in *The Sun Herald*, the Fairfax Sunday paper in Sydney and New South Wales, Frank Tierney gave a list of the things Landy needed to break the world record:

- a relaxed mental outlook towards the race;
- a certain amount of nervous energy to be released;
- skilful pacing assistance;
- a level track with "life" in it;
- a temperature not more than 80°F (26.6°C);
- atmosphere free of humidity;
- no wind.

Looking at that list, you might almost comment, "No chance!" Conditions matching those criteria would be very good indeed.

In *The Sporting Globe*, Ben Kerville added a couple more:

- the first half-mile run in 1:59.0 at most, preferably a bit faster;
- three quarters of the mile to be reached in a fraction less than three minutes so that he won't have to run faster than 61 seconds for the last lap to record 4:01.0.

In this sort of atmosphere, John Landy went to Perth for the 1952–53 national championships. As most Australians know, Perth in late January is not hot — it is *stinkin'* hot. The average daily maximum temperature is 31° Celsius, and there are only two days of rainfall. Moreover, it is usually windy. Perth in summer is not the sort of environment conducive to fast middle-distance running, much less world records, much less the first sub-four minute mile. Herb Elliott and Merv Lincoln pushed each other to 3:59.6 there in 1958, the official margin between them given as "inches", and Mike Hillardt ran substantially the same time, an electronic 3:58.35, in 1987. There have been only a couple more since and the fastest 1500 metres, 3:39.65, was run by 2002 Commonwealth Games bronze medallist Youcef Abdi.

Landy continued to mine his magical vein of good form, winning the 880 yards in 1:53.6 and the mile in 4:04.2 in Perth. They were his first national titles, having finished second to Macmillan in both races the previous year. There were some sensations, including a number of disqualifications. Jim Bailey, who would come back to give Landy a fright in years to come, made Les Perry's progress hell in the mile and was disqualified after crossing the line in second place ahead of him. Two days later, he was disqualified for interfering with two competitors in the 880 heats. Lucky he did not run the 440, or four blokes would have been in trouble. A colourful character, Bailey introduced himself years later as "the most (dis)qualified runner in Australia".

Victorian Neil Robbins, another member of Les Perry's Williamstown club, was disqualified from the six miles for inadvertently taking a couple of steps on the inside line of the grass track. Robbins, the favourite, had led until caught and passed by Geoff Warren. As he tired badly in the final laps, he trod on the line.

Ben Kerville described Perry as "fuming" over the decision. "It's the most ridiculous thing I've ever heard," said Perry. "The fellow ran a good, game race and didn't deserve that treatment." Landy's memory of this incident, and the subsequent disqualification, would have repercussions on the most dramatic race in Australian athletics history, the 1956 mile championship — but more of that later.

The 1953 nationals also saw the first manifestations of the mania that would develop around the four-minute mile and its major protagonists. Landy went to Perth accompanied by Tierney and Kerville's "recipes" for how to cook a world record mile. Once there, his every move was covered by a watchful media. The paparazzi had yet to be invented, but their forerunners were in Perth, as were the antecedents of the 24-hour news channels. Everywhere Landy went, it seemed a reporter bobbed up. He was photographed boarding the bus for the airport and the flight over, and again on arrival in Perth. His pursuit of entomology — invariably characterised as his "hobby of butterfly chasing" — was a particular point of obsession.

Once he got to Perth, Landy announced his intention of "going into smoke". He disappeared into King's Park with his butterfly net. His mates went along with his desire for time alone, Les Perry telling journalist Steve Hayward that the star miler would be back "when he feels hungry". Perth's *Daily News* managed to snap a photo of Landy running along a grassy ridge above Perth Water, but that was pretty well it. The only detailed story that appeared about Landy's visit to King's Park was published in a media supplement, *The Broadcaster*, the Saturday after the championships.

Pumping up its "'scoop'", the article told how everyone had wanted Landy. "One American news weekly with a circulation of millions went so far as to commission an eastern states photographer to follow Landy to Perth and 'stick with him' to get personal pictures, including butterfly pictures." Conveniently ignoring the fact that this, presumably, was exactly what *The Broadcaster*'s own photographer was doing (though he was a hard-working local rather than a dreaded eastern stater), the report continued with a breathtaking result of its investigative reporting. "*The Broadcaster* newsmen's trip to King's Park revealed that butterfly catching is not one of Landy's methods of training — it is simply a form of relaxing." Well, I'm blowed. And, just in case anyone was still missing the point — "It is the type of thing an old lady could do for hours without feeling exhausted."

Another little paragraph detailed Landy's last supper before his mile race. "The night before John Landy made his Leederville attempt on the mile record he dined in a Perth restaurant. He ate all the usual things, including fish and vegetables. But there was one way he differed from the other diners. He poured a fair quantity of salt into a jug of water and drank the lot in the course of the evening. Salt lost through excessive sweating had to be replaced, he said."

In a more perceptive piece, a journalist under the *nom de plume* "Beverley" reported on Landy's visit to a scientific institute. A knowledge of science had helped his running, she wrote. "Firstly, it has given him an analytical approach to his studies of style and training methods. Secondly, his knowledge of human physiology — although not so complete as a medical student's — has been an

asset in understanding the stresses placed on the body in running."
Presumably, John Landy did not know Roger Bannister well enough
at this stage to have a good knowledge of his rival's interests, but
the comment on physiology could have easily been made with the
English medical student in mind!

The mile final came first, on the Saturday of the championships.
Not a minute too soon: even 1953 Perth could take only so much
of butterflies. Landy won by a l-o-n-g way in 4:04.2 and a mini-
controversy was whipped up around the failure by officials to call
Landy's lap times. "I would have appreciated knowing how the watch
was going," he said, with understatement.

The reality was that Perth had never seen running like this.
Estimates of the crowd varied — 10,000 in one report, 8000–9000 in
another. In any case, it was a huge crowd in a city with a population
of 350,000 at the time. Landy-mania, four-minute mile mania — call
it what you like — was on the rise. Everyone wanted to watch — even
the officials who were supposed to hold up the finishing tape. As Ben
Kerville reported: "[Landy's] effortless running so mesmerised some
officials that judges were still struggling to stretch the tape across
the line as he raced up the straight. Two officials, fighting to wrest
the worsted from the stick around which it had been wound, just
managed to leave Landy about four feet of tangled wool to breast as
he stormed through. Landy's impetus took tape and stick out of the
judge's hand. He deftly caught it, then held it aloft for photographers
— certainly the toughest tape anyone ever tried to break." Two days
later, Landy won the 880 yards easily in 1:53.6.

On the day in between, Professor Frank Cotton returned to the
scene with an analysis in Perth's *Sunday Times* on "Physical Factors
Which Limit Speed of Man". He outlined nine factors: one, the
primary act of will; two, the discharge of energy by the motor area;
three, the role of neuromuscular functions; four, the contractions of
muscles; five, the coordination of the contractions of muscles; six,

the activity of the muscular enzymes; seven, the action of the heart; eight, the activity of the lungs in providing oxygen and getting rid of the carbon dioxide; nine, the series of accessory glands, liver, suprarenal and so on. Cotton went on to outline "peaking" for performance, the warm-up (still giving an optimum temperature, though not suggesting the athlete get there a-la-Macmillan!) and observing that the conditions needed to be optimal. Fifty years later, it is hard to envisage the average reader — for whom this was written, remember — being interested in a similar analysis of Steve Moneghetti or Benita Johnson.

Not surprisingly, Landy was now assuming a pre-eminence among local runners. He came back from Perth tired, but improved his two-mile record to 9:01.2 (still inferior to his Middlesborough run) and then won the Victorian title in a slow 4:11.0. "I know when I've had my chips," he remarked pithily, suggesting his season might be at an end.

A week later, Les Perry took the three-mile record back off Landy, running 13:57.8 to win the Victorian title. The runner who had led the way in Victoria, in Australia and internationally in Helsinki was now, inevitably, asked whether he could have beaten Landy. Perry declined to express an opinion. "I am always satisfied to finish second to John Landy," he replied. Forget the answer, the question would not have been asked six months earlier.

Around this time, Landy encountered a drunk driver on one of his late-night runs. He was on a foggy stretch of one of his regular training runs around the streets where he lived. The car weaved towards him, then stopped, well out of harm's way. The driver wound down his window, stuck his head out and asked: "Who do you think you are? Bloody Landy?" Name recognition, even from drunks.

"I was a bit offended," Landy says, "and I said so to my father. He fell down laughing and made me take it a bit less seriously." It would not happen to Craig Mottram now, Landy agrees, because so many people are running, or walking, for exercise. "If you did it then, you were a bit of an eccentric. I used to dread running this circuit around Warrigal Road, back down High Street. If I got it wrong I'd have to go through the crowd coming out of Ashburton cinema and they'd give you billy-o. Anybody running, particularly at night, was regarded as a 'nutter'. It's almost impossible to comprehend [now]."

Maybe famous Australian tennis coach Harry Hopman had the High Street crowd in mind when he wrote in praise of Landy's dedication to training in his regular newspaper column in April that year (*The Herald*, 22 April 1953). "While you were at the pictures or square-dancing, maybe, last Saturday night, John Landy was doing a ten-mile training run around Central Park, opposite his home in East Malvern. I mention it to illustrate that the champion who can take records or championships without putting a tremendous amount of work into his sport is rare."

In another interview with Joe Galli, which appeared in the April edition of *World Sports*, Landy made his own attitude clear: "To do any good, you've got to get stuck into it." Though he gave no quote from Landy to support it, Galli wrote that Landy's story was a perfect exposition of the theories of Percy Cerutty. Landy also rationalised that it was better chasing records on his own, claiming that "serious opposition is a distraction from the intense concentration needed to maintain the pace". Maybe this was one of Cerutty's nostrums; Herb Elliott would say something remarkably similar four years later.

Landy also said that he may retire at the end of the following season (1953–54). "I don't want to carry on indefinitely. I can make no decision about the 1954 Empire Games, because my employment may not permit my going." Landy continued to run through till April–May with university and invitation races, but he did not get back to the high-points of November–January. His assessment soon after the nationals was probably right. He *had* had his chips — but it had been a pretty substantial meal.

The pendulum now swung back to Europe. Though Landy feared several runners on the continent might come through to challenge for the four-minute mile, none of them did. Perhaps it was the fact that, while the Europeans ran the mile, their main focus was the 1500. Maybe the progress made by Barthel and Reiff in the Olympic year was a peak that could not be sustained until the next generation came through.

For whatever reason, the European challenge would come from England only. And it would come from Roger Bannister only. Likewise, it would not be the Americans who had reached the Helsinki 1500 metres final — silver medallist Bob McMillen, and Warren Druetzler — who continued the push in the USA. It would be all Wes Santee. Like Landy, though, Santee was somewhat constrained by his circumstances.

Bannister was restricted by his medical studies and hospital duties; however, unlike his rivals, he was not chafing at the restrictions, not outwardly anyway. He found his time to train during the day, and filled it with training that he believed would do the job. Bannister also had the McWhirter twins scheming away in the background on his behalf and for the glory of Britain.

But just who were the McWhirter twins? Ross and Norris McWhirter were university "chums" of Bannister's at Oxford who both went on to become sports journalists. In addition to *Athletics World,* they subsequently found fame internationally for *The Guinness Book of Records*, a book they wrote and annually updated together between 1955 and 1975. Just as Joe Galli passed on all the news from his European contacts to Cerutty, so Norris and Ross McWhirter passed on all the information they gleaned on Landy and Santee to Bannister.

They also put themselves pretty much at Bannister's disposal. "The energy of the twins was boundless," he writes in *The Four-Minute Mile.* "For them nothing was too much trouble, and they accepted any challenge joyfully. After running together at Oxford as sprinters they carried their partnership into journalism, keeping me posted of the performances of my overseas rivals. They often drove me to athletics meetings, so that I arrived with no fuss, never a minute too soon or too late. Sometimes I was not sure whether it was Norris or Ross who held the watch or drove the car, but I knew that either could be relied upon."

Bannister continued to race sparingly. It suited his notion of gearing up for a limited number of supreme efforts, and also fit well with the time he was devoting to his training. Of the three protagonists, Bannister was the one with the least amount of endurance fitness, but he had been training for more years than either of his two rivals, which probably balanced the ledger somewhat.

After training through the winter months, Bannister made an enjoyable racing trip to Morocco with a couple of other British athletes. Racing in Morocco then was a far less demanding challenge than now, in the country that has produced two of the greatest middle-distance runners of the past 20 years, Said Aouita and Hicham El Guerrouj. Then, it was a pleasant interlude in a warmer climate, good for relaxing, running and sharpening oneself for the sterner challenges ahead.

Bannister's first major race of the season was the Oxford versus Amateur Athletic Association (AAA) match at the university's Iffley Road track. This was the track Bannister had re-built during his days as Oxford club president and the venue he had already marked out as his preferred one for the four-minute mile. Now, on 2 May 1953, Bannister tested himself for the first time. Stripped down to its essentials, his idea for a four-minute mile was that it had to be run at as even a pace as possible. "The miler is limited by lack of oxygen, and in order to keep his oxygen requirement to a minimum, would need to run at the slowest average speed to achieve his target of a four-minute mile — the ideal would be four even laps of 60 seconds each," he wrote (*The Four-Minute Mile*). Moreover, the time must be the primary concern, not the race. "If the time is the real object of the race, other competitors must be ignored, unless they co-operate wittingly or unwittingly, in the time schedule."

Bannister had enlisted the witting help of Chris Chataway, one of his Helsinki roommates, for the Oxford versus AAA mile. Chataway, who had fallen on the bend in the dramatic last lap of the Olympic 5000 metres final, was a miler of mediocre achievement at the time. And he was concentrating on his studies in 1953, so it suited his purpose to sacrifice himself for a friend.

Bannister's ostensible target was Sydney Wooderson's British record 4:06.4, a world record when Wooderson ran it in a handicap race in 1937. Chataway agreed to run as fast as he could for the first three quarters of a mile. He did, leading through 61.7, 62.4 (2:04.1) and 61.1 (3:05.2). A four-minute mile was out of the question, but Bannister needed only 61 seconds to beat the record.

Bannister ran 58.4 for the final lap, giving him a final time of 4:03.6, smashing Wooderson's record and confirming his credentials for the four-minute mile. "We were delighted to have done so well in a first attempt," he wrote (*The Four-Minute Mile*). "This race made me realise that the four-minute mile was not out of reach. It was only a question of time; but would someone else reach the goal first?"

In the short term, at least, "someone" could only be Wes Santee. He had run 4:02.4 at the Compton International in Los Angeles, defeating Olympic finalist Denis Johansson of Finland and Gaston Reiff and openly stated his intention of running fast in the US national collegiate championships (the NCAAs) on 27 June. As he had gone through the first 880 yards of his 4:02 even slower than Bannister had in the Oxford race, there was a very real possibility that he might break four minutes.

This would never do for the McWhirters. Bannister wanted to be the first man to break four minutes and the twins were determined that he would be. Everest had been conquered by a British-led expedition (though a New Zealander, Edmund Hillary, and a Nepalese Sherpa, Tenzing Norgay, had been the two who reached the summit on 29 May 1953) and the wave of euphoria washing over Britain had been reinforced with the coronation of Queen Elizabeth II. The four-minute mile would be the perfect final prong of a trio of British triumphs. If there was the slightest possibility of Santee's getting to this particular summit first, it must be forestalled.

So a plan was hatched that could make sense only within the walls of secrecy that surrounded it. Expose it to any scrutiny and it would have been seen to be senseless.

Santee was due to race on 29 June. The time difference between Dayton, Ohio (venue for the NCAA titles) and London would allow Bannister to get in a race on the same day but before the American. Chataway was unavailable this time, due to pressure of his exams. So the schemers and dreamers turned to another source, an Empire runner living in London. To Don Macmillan, in fact; and the Australian, though surprised at the approach, agreed to help.

The bizarre plan was for Macmillan to pace the first two and a half laps in conventional fashion. Another runner, Chris Brasher, would start the race but immediately fall back, allowing himself to be just ahead of Bannister once Macmillan pulled out. Thus he could pace Bannister over the last 660 yards despite the fact he was ostensibly being "lapped".

A meeting was found into which the race could be squeezed. The Surrey Schools meeting was set down for Motspur Park in London on the day in question. The organisers were only too pleased to slip a mile into the lunch break for one of Britain's heroes. But first, Bannister had to recover from a muscle injury, sustained when he ran the 440 yards at the Middlesex Championships "for speed". After five days rest and with the aid of therapeutic massage, he was able to resume running. Two half-miles run at four-minute mile pace convinced him that the muscle could withstand a race.

So whose idea was this bizarre event? "An enthusiastic friend," says Bannister (*The Four-Minute Mile*). The same friend suggested the need for secrecy, Bannister continues, in case his injured leg did not hold out. He was also uncertain how he was to be paced.

In *The Perfect Mile*, Neal Bascomb tells a very different story, albeit largely within the same framework. Bascomb has Bannister ringing Macmillan to ask him to "help" in the race as part of a British Empire effort to thwart Santee, outlining how the proposed pacing was to go and telling him he would be picked up by one of the McWhirters on the morning of the race.

Harold Abrahams and Jack Crump were also present, along with Philip Noel-Baker. Abrahams and Crump were the two most influential men in British athletics; Abrahams was the 100 metres champion at the legendary "Chariots of Fire" 1924 Olympic Games. From 1948 to 1968 he was honorary treasurer of the British Amateur Athletic Board, the sport's controlling body. Crump was international team manager for British teams and ran the international competition program. Noel-Baker, a former Olympian, is described by Bannister in *The Four-Minute Mile* as "one of my closest advisers". Though Abrahams was a great admirer of Bannister's and Crump had managed Bannister, Chataway and another middle-distance runner, Walter Hesketh, on the recent tour to Morocco, there seems little earthly reason for them to have attended a "paced time trial" staged at a schools' meeting. Equally, there seems no reason — other than the request that the "trial" be accommodated within the meeting program — why it was included as an invitation race. Nor, that two official timekeepers were brought in to officiate, with Norris McWhirter holding the third watch.

No other reason, that is, other than to assure that the performance counted for world record purposes. In fact, what the arrangements made for the race indicate was that the McWhirters were making sure every "i" was dotted and "t" crossed in the event Bannister should run either a British or world record, or even history's first sub-four minute mile. Why else would Abrahams and Crump be there other than to observe all was above board in this totally contrived "race"?

Despite being handicapped by a sore leg, Macmillan did the pacing duties admirably. He ran 59.6 seconds for the first lap, 60.1 for the second but then could not push all the way through the next 220 yards, as planned. By now, however, Bannister was closing on Brasher, who had run the first two laps at a snail's pace. "[Brasher] proceeded to encourage me by shouting backwards over his shoulder as he ran ahead of me, just preventing himself from being lapped," wrote Bannister (*The Four-Minute Mile*). Bannister went through three laps in 3:01.8 (third lap 62.1) before speeding up marginally, but not quite enough, to finish in 4:02.0. It was the third-fastest time ever run, behind only Hägg and Andersson.

"All things considered, it could hardly be called a race," Bannister acknowledged in *The Four-Minute Mile*. Indeed not, but one wonders what the reaction would have been if he had broken Hägg's world record, or even four minutes.

Bannister and Brasher went off for a weekend's hiking in Wales and were thus oblivious to the furore the run created. *The Times* reported that "The profound secrecy with which the project was planned and carried out … prevented all but a favoured few from being able to give an eye-witness account." Having got the peevishness about being "scooped" off his chest, the correspondent observed more relevantly: "Nor is anyone quite sure about the motive behind the secrecy." Was it simply a test of his recovery from the injury or was it to have a decent crack at running fast without having to deal with the speculation beforehand?

The overwhelming weight of evidence — especially if Abrahams and Crump were there — points to the latter conclusion. But having been present to ensure all was above board, officialdom now had to deal with the fact that instead of a world record or a sub-four minute mile, it was now faced merely with ratifying a British record, one, moreover, that the claimant already held.

No-one would be unduly deprived by a belated application of principle and, from this distance and in my personal view, this is precisely what happened. Just over a fortnight later, the BAAB met and ratified Bannister's 4:03.6 as a British all-comers' and national record. It rejected the 4:02.0, however, saying it was "compelled to take this course of action because it does not consider the event was a bona fide competition according to the rules". While recognising the public enthusiasm for records, the statement continued, "[The BAAB] does not regard individual record attempts as in the best interests of athletics as a whole". One wonders whether Abrahams and Crump dissented from this point of view or, if they did not and they were at Motspur Park, why their views were not made known on the day.

Later on the day of Bannister's 4:02.0, Wes Santee ran 4:07.2 in Dayton, Ohio to win the US national mile. The race was run in sweltering heat and he won by almost five full seconds. However, it was Santee's earlier 4:02.4 time that had provoked such panic in the Bannister camp. This was the race Santee and his coach, Bill Easton, had targeted after their agreement earlier in the year that he would deviate on occasion from the obligation of running first and foremost for Kansas. The build-up to the race turned feral when Finland's Denis Johansson suggested Santee would be a good runner when he got a bit older and wiser. "Santee is too immature to be a great miler," Johansson said, within earshot of reporters. Presumably, this means he said it *to* them.

(Johansson had also experienced the US college system when he attended Michigan's Purdue University. He had also won his semi-final at the Olympics, raising Finnish hopes, before finishing tenth in the final, one place behind Don Macmillan.)

In his *Saturday Evening Post* profile on Santee, Bob Hurt reported the young Kansan's reaction. "I was really mad. I don't mind being criticised by someone better than I am, but he's not. He's just a pop-off. I went out there with the one thought of beating Johansson. Nothing else mattered. I usually think about the prizes I'll get or the time I'll run, but not this time. I just wanted to beat Johansson, and beat him bad."

Actually, both Johansson and Reiff, the latter especially, *did* have far better credentials than the brash Santee. One was an Olympic silver medallist and world record holder; the other was an Olympic finalist and heir to one of the deepest traditions in distance running history. It was Santee who had done nothing to that point. But credentials are only what an athlete brings to the starting line. Once the gun goes off, it is what you have on the day. And Wes Santee, like John Landy, was a vastly different athlete in 1953 than the callow youth who had failed so ignominiously in Helsinki the previous year.

Even then, however, Santee was convinced he was destined for bigger things. There was his announcement on his return from Helsinki that he was going to run the four-minute mile. And during the 1952–53 winter, he took on 28 fraternity housemates in a relay — Santee running just over 13 and a half miles from Tonganoxie to Lawrence solo, his opponents doing half a mile each — and beat them by 200 yards.

In the Compton race, Reiff led through 880 yards in 2:05.2 and into the next bend. Then Santee took off, winding up the pace stride by stride. He opened a 15-metre gap to Johansson and was never threatened, winning in 4:02.4. Only Hägg, Andersson and Landy had ever run faster, and no-one off such a slow first half mile. Johansson ran 4:04.0, a personal best, but he was chastened nonetheless. Reiff, who had been nursing a foot injury, was almost another two seconds back in third place. Santee told Hurt: "I could have run that last half just as fast, even if we had run the first half in 2:03.0. That would have put me under four minutes, but those other guys would have been willing to settle for a 4:10.0."

Hägg had written to him, Santee revealed, saying that he could be the first man under four minutes but that he must hurry (referring to Bannister). "I am flabbergasted, thrilled and impressed," Santee said. "I have no more prized possession than that letter."

Following the Compton race, Johansson swallowed some humble pie. Picking up on Santee's earlier riposte, he observed: "He taught me not to pop off so much." Reiff, too, was impressed, especially by the speed of the last 700 metres. He predicted Santee would beat Bannister should they meet (they never did): "Santee runs the last five or six hundred too fast." The losers were pleasing themselves. No-one cared what they said. All the reporting after the Compton race discussed not if, but when, Wes Santee would break four minutes for the mile.

Fifteen days later, Santee was in record mode again. This time he won the national collegiate mile title in 4:03.7. Then he went on and won the national mile, on the same day as Bannister's 4:02, in 4:07.6.

Santee commented on his rivals in the *Saturday Evening Post* feature. He felt Landy was going for the record too often, but expressed respect for him. He would not be afraid to race him, however: "I don't think there's anybody I can't beat." On Bannister, Santee delivered a tart response to the manner in which the British runner raced. "I would probably have run the four-minute mile if I'd been out chasing an electric rabbit," he scoffed. "Pacing is an important thing in running. That's part of the event. The runner is supposed to do that himself. But if Bannister wants to do it the other way, more power to him."

Santee raced in Europe after the American season had finished.

Like many Americans to this day, he found it hard to race consistently straight after a long domestic season with many races. He ran no fewer than 20 races in Europe, some of which were brilliant, others not. One of the former came in Gothenburg, Sweden on 23 July when he ran 3:44.2 for 1500 metres, edging out new Swedish hope Sune Karlsson, who ran the same time.

Santee had a great range. He could run the 100 yards in 10.5, the 220 in 22.5, the 440 in 47.9 and the 880 in 1:49.9. Nor was his stamina in doubt, not if the race against the relay team of his college fraternity companions is anything to go by.

Bannister's season petered out in anti-climactic fashion, too, at least for those hungry for the four-minute mile to fall. After the controversial Motspur Park race, he ran and won the mile at the AAA championships in a moderate 4:07.0, then ran in a 4×1 mile relay that set a world record. Finally, he reduced his 880 personal best to 1:50.7 in a race against Olympic 1500 finalist Patrick El Mabrouk of France.

By September 1953, each of the main contenders had had a full season tilting at the four-minute barrier and still it remained unbreached. In chronological order, Landy had run 4:02.1, Santee 4:02.4 and Bannister 4:02.0. Viewed simply against the world record, they were all within a second of Hägg. But it wasn't the world record that was making people froth with excitement; it was the prospect of the four-minute mile being broken at last. And like the summit of Mt Everest before Tenzing and Hillary reached it, the four-minute mile might have been in sight, but it remained tantalisingly out of reach.

John Landy sums up this perception — which would build further through the coming Australian track season — about the "Everest" of athletics, which even saw some reviving of the old notion that maybe it could *not* be done. "There was this feeling that runners were getting close to [four minutes] but couldn't get there. The press kept booming it up as perhaps an impossible barrier, the 'mystical four-minute mile'. People could understand it and became interested in the many attempts to break the barrier."

People certainly were becoming interested. The Melbourne Olympic Games were just three years away as the Australian track and field season got under way in late 1953. Despite constant bickering about venues and costs — the final choice of the Melbourne Cricket Ground as the main stadium had only been decided earlier that year in the face of an ultimatum from the International Olympic Committee — the Games were not really entrenched in the public's mind at this stage.

"People didn't talk about the [1956 Olympic] Games, they talked more about the four minute mile," John Landy says. He contrasts that with the Melbourne 2006 Commonwealth Games or the Sydney 2000 Olympics, which were "never off the menu" as marketing departments pushed their cause. "That just didn't exist in the 1950s. There was a lot of bad publicity over the venues, [but] people didn't really know what the Olympic Games were going to be like. I didn't really think there was much interest until the year before the Games."

Landy was the focus of interest although, behind him, others who would become Olympic prospects were coming through. Dave Stephens, yet another runner from Perry's Williamstown club, had finished third in Landy's breakthrough mile in December 1952. He would go on to break distance world records in the run-up to Melbourne. Al Lawrence, from Sydney's Botany club, finished third across the line in the national six-mile title in Perth, behind Geoff Warren and Neil Robbins (who would be disqualified). But at this stage, it was only the mile that mattered, and only John Landy was running international-class times for the mile.

The build-up to the Australian season was peppered with reports of what Landy would do, when he would race, and who might come out to race against him. One story expressed concern that the relegation of Landy's club, Geelong Guild, to the B-grade section of interclub competition might impact on his race plans. Another story said he was planning a series of three mile races in December; yet another, appearing in a Sydney paper, suggested Bailey and rising young New South Wales half-miler Bill Butchart might be recruited as pacemakers for record mile attempts.

That Landy had almost single-handedly revived interest in athletics in his home state was illustrated in a report in *The Argus* on 21 November 1953 A weekend columnist waxed lyrical about interclub competition in terms that would make present-day administrators weep. Complete with accompanying photo, the report commenced: "No other city in the world can match Melbourne's weekly, non-stop athletic carnival. You've got to see one of these interclub meetings to believe it. It's nothing to see five events going at the same time, with each set of competitors completely oblivious to the others. But it's a spectacular sight for spectators."

On the same day, Landy kicked off his season with a 4:09.2 mile for his club in B-grade. He had not yet completed his final exams, but assured reporters that he was fitter than ever. "The only thing of which I am certain is that I have a greater capacity for punishment this season after a solid preparation," Landy said.

By now the newspapers were touting every Landy race as a potential sub-four minute mile. The Friday 4 December edition of *The Herald* gave "the treatment" to a story by Steve Hayward previewing the following day's athletics. Leading the paper on page one, the story proclaimed that "Tomorrow may be the 'M-Day' the athletics world has been awaiting for years." A panel highlighted the details in larger and bolder type:

"The place: Olympic Park

"The time: 3:10pm

"The target: The Magic 4-minute mile

"The runner: Victorian John Landy"

One more puff of hot air in that story and it would have burst. Imagine the pressure Landy was under.

Peter Banfield must have spoken to a different John Landy for his preview in *The Argus*. This Landy was only going to run his fastest time for the season and was still concentrating on a building-up program.

And the result of this race after all that? Bruce Welch reported in *The Age* on the following Monday that "meteor miler" John Landy had been held back by a strong wind to 4:09.8, actually a touch slower than his season-opener. The following day he ran an Australian record 2:25.5 for 1000 metres at Newport Oval in a Williamstown Athletics Club meeting in which Geoff Warren narrowly beat Dave Stephens and Perry over 3000 metres.

A week later, however, Landy did have a genuine "crack". There were only three other competitors in what was a special mile race at Olympic Park. Two of them — Empire Games miler, John Marks, and Perry — were determined to do what they could to help with the pace; but what help they were was in pushing, not pulling.

Landy led at the end of each lap in 58.2 and reached the half mile in 1:58.6. With a lap to go he was at 3:00.2. A tick under 60 seconds and he had four minutes in sight; a couple of ticks under 62 and he would break the world record. At 1500 in 3:44.4, both possibilities were still alive, but exhaustion and a suddenly gusty wind slowed him noticeably in the final straight. At the finish, Landy clung briefly to an official for support; a few minutes later he was physically ill. He had done all he could and come up short. His time was 4:02.0, equalling in a solo run what Bannister had achieved with artificial pacing at Motspur Park and beating by 0.4 what Santee had managed running scared against world-class opposition.

But Landy was still short of the goal. For all his harder training, it was only a tenth of a second faster than he had run at the same time in 1952. Declaring that his one remaining run for 1953 would be "for fun", Landy said: "I've done as good as I can. If I could have run faster today I would have done so, but I couldn't." Landy told *The Argus* (with feeling, one suspects): "This record-breaking business is hard. You can't do it unless you have everything in your favour, and you must have the strength. I did not have that little bit of strength today."

In further evidence of the hold Landy had on the imagination of the Australian sporting public, the race was watched by the Prime Minister, Robert Menzies, and the Minister for the Interior, Wilfred Kent Hughes, who was also the chairman of the Melbourne 1956 Olympic Organising Committee.

Writing in the mid-week edition of *The Sporting Globe* a few days later, Ben Kerville pleaded a case for lowering expectations. In an article headlined "World Mile If They Get Off John's Back", Kerville wrote that in his opinion the world record was "in the bag, provided people climb off Landy's back and discontinue demanding the impossible of him every time he competes".

In far-off London, Roger Bannister read of Landy's unsuccessful attempts in the British press. Invariably, the headline would be along the lines of "Landy fails again". Yet Landy was compiling a string of fast miles equal to anything Hägg or Andersson had ever done, and no-one had run faster than the two Swedes. "If this was failure, what was the meaning of success?" Bannister wrote (*The Four-Minute Mile*). Ironically, Landy's attempts and the terms in which they were reported would only have reinforced Bannister's thinking on the nature of his own attempts at the four-minute mile. It could not be achieved without even pacing, and even pacing could not be achieved on your own.

The following week was the last round of athletics before Christmas. Landy strolled through a mile in 4:16.2, his slowest since the start of the previous season. But the temperature was at a sweltering 100°F (37.8°C). The same week, Jamaican sprinter Herb

McKenley trained at Central Park while visiting Melbourne for professional races. He implored Landy to go overseas for at least one season. McKenley also expressed the view that Landy had the world record "in the palm of his hand. All he has to do is relax more and forget about the record. Then he will find it is his before he knows it."

Landy was not without acclaim, at least not in Australia. In the year-end round-ups for 1953 his 4:02.0 mile won honourable mentions. It was the only sporting performance to make *The Age*'s selection of the year's news highlights and *The Sporting Globe* named Landy and world champion boxer Jimmy Carruthers as its joint sportsmen of the year for 1953.

John Landy's bold racing may not have been rewarded with the first sub-four minute mile, but it did earn him the status of number one miler in the world for 1953.

8

The Final Ascent

On Thursday 11 February 1954, a man got off a train at Sydney's Central Station, jumped in a car and was whisked across town, with police motorcycle escort, to the Sydney Cricket Ground where he took his seat in the VIP enclosure to watch a much-anticipated event.

The man was Prince Philip, the Duke of Edinburgh. He was on a Royal Tour of Australia with his young wife, Queen Elizabeth II, whose coronation had been one source of British pride in June the previous year. The royal couple had returned by train from Wollongong, south of Sydney, and Philip was in a screaming hurry to get to the Cricket Ground to see not an Australia–England Test match, nor an Australia–British Lions rugby league international, but John Landy running the mile at the Australian athletics championships.

"Duke's Peak Hour Dash to See Landy" screamed the front-page headline in the following day's Melbourne *Sun*.

Such was the state of near-hysteria that now surrounded Landy's every race. For most of the past 50 years, the SCG had been used intermittently to stage state and national championships. For all that time, events — including the 1938 British Empire Games — had been run on an irregular grass track. The Empire Games, for example, had a track with a 50-yard straight and then one more or less continuous curve following the SCG fence line. The 100 yards and 120 yards hurdles were conducted on straights in the infield.

For the 1953–54 Australian track and field championships, however, a special new track had been laid out, with proper bends and straights (even if they were only 70 metres long). It was said to be the fastest grass track in Australia — this *was* Sydney, after all — but almost an inch (25.4mm) of rain had fallen in the 48 hours before the mile was held. In horse-racing parlance, the track was dead.

When the Duke expressed his interest in attending, the mile start had been re-scheduled from 5:30pm to 6pm. Despite royal patronage, however, Landy ran "only" 4:05.6, beating Jim Bailey by over 50 yards.

One newspaper report quoted a weather "expert" as saying the gusty wind and heavy track had cost Landy as much as seven seconds. "It certainly was a handicap, but hardly equivalent to seven seconds," Landy commented when the proposition was put to him. Somehow this and other reports about the conditions were conflated in the US as excuse-making by Landy. This triggered another barrage of columns suggesting that if Landy was as fast on the track as he was at making excuses, the four-minute barrier would be long gone by now. United Press columnist Oscar Fraley remarked that it seemed the only way Landy would run four minutes would be "downhill with a wind blowing behind him".

"I never made excuses," says John Landy. "Excuses were made on my behalf. I remember one US writer writing [that] 'every time he runs something goes wrong, the tracks are wrong, the wind is wrong — does the wind blow in circles down under?' I didn't make excuses but in the sense that things did go wrong a few times, I was a bit frustrated by the fact that I couldn't improve."

What the brouhaha *did* illustrate perfectly was the atmosphere building up around the four-minute mile and its three main protagonists. As with the championships in the heat of Perth the previous year, how anyone would imagine the four-minute mile being achieved in championship conditions, on a grass track with shorter-than-usual straights almost beggars belief.

Landy was quoted after the race as saying his run felt every bit as good as when he ran 4:02. It probably was, and he probably would have run it again on a good cinder track.

Wes Santee, too, was getting into the swing of things. His usual medium of competition as the calendar year opened was indoors. But he travelled to Louisiana at the end of December 1953 to run a mile outdoors at the Sugar Bowl in New Orleans. He ran 4:04.2 off his winter training, finishing with a 55-second final lap. He had another mile lined up a few weeks later, this one organised by West Coast promoter Al Franken at the Pro Bowl football game at the Los Angeles Coliseum, but an unseasonal downpour left the track waterlogged and the race was cancelled.

Then, in February, his national association threw him a hand grenade, banning Santee from international competition for the remainder of the year after an investigation into his alleged insulting of German officials after a race the previous year. He could still race in America but, like John Landy, he had no real competition in his home country and he was chasing the four-minute mile without the aid of colleagues willing to set the pace for him. Without the stimulus of top competition, it would be that much harder.

So, once again, the first, best chances to break four minutes in 1954 would fall to Landy. The increasing rank of VIPs coming to his races — the Australian Prime Minister, the Governor of Victoria, the royal consort — was merely symptomatic of the pressure he was under.

Bannister had his carefully planned approach, with limited racing and orchestrated pacing regarded as essentials, an attitude that was reinforced when he started training with Chris Chataway and Chris Brasher at lunchtimes. Brasher, who was coached by Franz Stampfl, an Austrian ex-winter sports representative who had been interned in Australia during the war, had persuaded Bannister to join them for training sessions and discussions on the four-minute mile quest. It rubbed against Bannister's ideal — that he would do it his way, or »

A matter of timing

One of the quirks of the four-minute mile, as it was run in 1954, was that it was impossible to record a time of 3:59.9. It was also possible for three timekeepers (the required minimum) to record an athlete at under four minutes, but for that athlete not to break four minutes. How so? The first part is simple. Rules at the time mandated that times in middle-distance and distance races be rounded up to the next highest one-fifth of a second. Thus Gunder Hägg's world record was rounded up from 4:01.3 to 4:01.4. John Landy's break-through time in 1952 was 4:02.1 but rounded up to an official 4:02.2.

The second anomaly follows on from the first. Three watches had to record the winner's time. If two of the three agreed, that was the official time. If all three were different, the middle time was taken as the official time. Then that time was rounded up. Hägg's three watches read 4:01.2, 4:01.3 and 4:01.3. So the official time was 4:01.3; the ratified world record time 4:01.4. Bannister's eventual sub-four had no such problem — the three watches all read 3:59.4. But Landy's 3:58.0 also suffered from the rounding-up rule. The three official watches recorded 3:57.8, 3:57.9 and 3:57.9. Time = 3:57.9. Ratified new world record equalled 3:58.0, even though no watch had him running that time.

The rounding-up rule was changed by the IAAF in Melbourne in 1956, so Herb Elliott was able to run a world record 3:54.5 in Dublin in 1958. But when Peter Snell broke that four years later, his time was the middle one recorded on the watches. One timekeeper got Snell at 3:54.2, another at 3:54.5 and the third at 3:54.4, the last of which became the official world record.

Imagine the furore had the watches at Iffley Road, Oxford, on 6 May 1954, read 3:59.8, 3:59.9 and 3:59.9. Official time: 4:00.0. Now what would the McWhirter twins have made of that?!

» not at all — but he was persuaded of the need for compromise and, despite his misgivings, soon found the arrangement both congenial and rewarding.

Landy, though, was under an immense weight of expectation. Unlike Europe, Australia was not awash with international sports stars, especially in athletics. The sport was being promoted around him — the Victorian Amateur Athletics Association staged "twilight meetings" as an innovation to give him better conditions — and he felt the pressure of delivering with every race.

"It had been building anyway," says Landy, "ever since that first 4:02.1 had alerted the whole world to the possibilities. I lost the sense of 'careless rapture'. People would just pin me down every time I ran. When I got to Perth [for the 1953 nationals] it was 'here's the four-minute mile at the Leederville Track'. That bedevilled my career, in many ways, that I had to constantly deliver these fast times. I felt obliged to do it when all the people turned up. It was very, very difficult.

"It was partly my nature, partly the lack of competition, that I wanted to run very fast times. But it was so much sold to the public on the basis of the anticipation of the first four-minute mile that it was very hard when everyone turned up to run just to win. It was very difficult to say, 'I couldn't care less, it's a lousy day'. Windy days, I'd have to go and run 4:06 or something. People could not make a distinction between winning a race and running four minutes. To them it was like the 100 metres, but unfortunately it isn't like that."

Landy was concentrating more on speed than ever before. For the first time, he varied his Central Park routine, running a measured lap on the grass oval instead of using the gravel path. And he was timing his efforts as he worked out regularly with half-miler Len McRae. There was a pay-off, both for McRae and Landy. On 16 January 1954, set up for the first 660 yards by Landy, McRae ran 1:52.1 for 880 yards to break Don Macmillan's national residential record. Behind him, Landy reduced his personal best to 1:52.8.

Landy *was* doing great things for the sport. On 21 January, the first of the twilight meetings was staged in Melbourne. A lot of distance-running people — Les Perry, Percy Cerutty and their Victorian Marathon Club fellows among them — had been working for a long time to get distance races staged in the evenings to avoid the middle of summer days with the searingly hot northerly winds. Almost 15,000 people crammed into Olympic Park. The meeting was timed to enable city workers to get down after work; it was summer holiday-time for many others. They came from everywhere. Trams from the city were jam-packed, cars and pedestrians thronged Swan Street and the roads leading to Olympic Park. "There was a football grand final atmosphere around the ground as queues grew to about 100 metres and traffic police battled to keep the long lines of cars moving into the parking areas," *The Age* reported on its front page the following day.

Caught up in the traffic jam was the star attraction. Describing his trip to Olympic Park that day, Landy recalled he went to the ground with Len McRae and Ian Ormsby. "Ian had a red Singer. The closest we could get to Olympic Park was the top of Anderson Street [on the opposite side of the Botanic Gardens, about a four-minute mile away]. We couldn't get near the entrance, so we bunked each other up and over the fence. A doctor who knew my brother saw us and said: 'Look at those larrikins climbing over the fence to see Landy run.' His son replied: 'Dad, that *is* John Landy.'

"The possibility of the four-minute mile — people got quite besotted by it," says Landy with understatement. "It was quite weird."

The officials had to throw open the gates and the crowd burst the fences, sitting on the edge of the track. Federal treasurer Arthur Fadden represented the Australian government on this particular night. Landy didn't break four minutes; he ran 4:02.4. "A great sigh of disappointment followed the announcement of his time," *The Age* reported, "but the crowd's sympathy was with Landy." Landy told one journalist: "I thought I had it."

The national titles intervened between this twilight meeting and later ones. So, too, did a Landy injury, to his left ankle. In a forerunner of what would come with his Achilles tendonitis before the Melbourne 1956 Olympic Games, the newspapers gave daily bulletins on the state of his recovery.

On 23 February, Landy again fronted up for an Olympic Park twilight meeting. He had recovered from the national titles, where he had won the mile but been sensationally beaten in the half mile, finishing sixth in a race won by Jim Bailey. This time, the weather was the problem. Melbourne basically has two summer wind-streams. When the wind blows from the north, it is hot to very hot, but the wind invariably dies down in the evening. The blustery southerly, or south-westerly, though cooler, usually keeps on blowing, as it did this night, with wind gusts of up to 20 miles per hour.

For the first time, Landy had a semblance of pacing. Len McRae led, with the aim of taking him through halfway in 1:57.0. The wind held McRae back to 1:59.0. Landy took over and reached the bell in 3:01.0. A smaller crowd of 2500 urged him on and he passed through 1500 metres in 3:45.0, but he was held back to 4:02.6 at the line. Bruce Welch in *The Age* called it "the greatest race of [Landy's] short but meteoric career". He finished almost ten seconds ahead of Bailey, with Geoff Warren third and Denis Johansson of Finland fourth.

"I felt I had broken the world record when I breasted the tape," Landy said. "I have never felt better in my life and I think I might still run the four-minute mile this summer." Johansson acclaimed Landy as "without doubt the greatest miler the world has seen. Landy's effort tonight would have returned him a time of about 3:58.0 in the conditions he would strike in Europe."

Johansson had accepted an invitation to come to Australia to race Landy. The Finn, a finalist in the 1500 metres in Helsinki, would be competing out of season, but he came anyway. He came because he had an ulterior motive: he wanted Landy to come to Europe, using Johansson's Turku club as his base for an assault on the four-minute mile. US sprinter Mel Patton was also in Australia for a world (professional) sprint championship. He was trying to convince the Australian star to come to the west coast of the USA to race against Santee at the Compton Invitational in early June and to compete in other meetings.

It was a dilemma for Landy who, publicly at least, had been undecided until late 1953 as to whether he would even go on to the 1954 Empire Games in Vancouver. Had he achieved either a sub-four minute mile or the world record, he may not have. Gradually, though, he had become convinced that he should continue. He realised that if he was ever going to devote a year to running, 1954 was it. He had completed his degree at the end of 1953 and he had a job lined up teaching at his old school. "I was doing part-time work in the titles office. I had a clear go, I had my degree and the idea was I could come back and teach. I'd spoken to Geelong Grammar and they were keen for me to go to Timbertop, so I virtually had a year to concentrate on running."

Despite his disappointing results in Australia, Johansson was making progress on his real mission — to get Landy to Finland. As he had shown in the lead-up to his race against Santee the previous year, he was a match for the American in any war of words. Where that attitude had rubbed Santee the wrong way, Landy saw beyond it. "He was one of these people that make outrageous statements, [such as] he'd beat me, Santee, or anybody. He came out here, he was out of shape, and he was so far behind it wasn't funny. I got to like him. He was combative, very outspoken, but he had a lot of good traits. When he saw that I was a good runner, he said: 'Look, if you came to Finland, without any question, you'd run 3:58.' He said, 'When

I go back I'm going to get you an invitation for you to run for my club. I'll organise that and you can have that as the build-up to your run in Vancouver.' That seemed to me to be a very sensible thing to do because I'd get the competition ... [I'd] get really fit coming into Vancouver."

The US deal offered by Patton, on the other hand, meant he would travel to the west coast, race, then come home again. "The Americans were very keen to get me to go to Compton Relays and the Fresno Relays," says Landy. "Run against Santee and not much more — it didn't seem to me that I'd get anything near the sort of deal I got in Finland [where] conditions would be better and also that I would have three months' conditioning and racing."

With that decided, Landy completed his Australian season. A third Melbourne twilight meeting did not recreate the magic of the first two, Landy reportedly despairing of the windy conditions when he arrived at the track and running "only" 4:05.9. Bruce Welch reported Landy as being "disconsolate, but far from exhausted", so it is a fair bet that the pressure of chasing the record, on his own and often in unfavourable conditions, had got to him as much as the conditions themselves.

In any case, the weather can't have been all *that* bad as Geoff Warren won the three miles in 13:55.8, upstaging Landy by taking two seconds off Les Perry's national record. "Apart from some of Landy's mile efforts," wrote Peter Banfield in *The Argus*, "Warren's performance was one of the greatest seen at the track."

Then, virtually on the eve of his departure from Australia, Landy ran his sixth 4:02 mile, this time in truly bizarre circumstances. He had accepted an invitation to run at the Easter Fair at Bendigo, 150 kilometres north of Melbourne. Bendigo had a fast grass track (unlike Sydney, which only boasted one). The mile was held on Easter Monday, 19 April, the last day of a carnival that included cycling and professional races. Len McRae would again set the pace

Help them to represent Australia at the Empire Games!

LOCAL STAR DISTANCE RUNNERS

Block courtesy "Argus"

GEOFF. WARREN

1950

Vic. Junior 880 yds. Champion

1951

Vic. Junior 5 Miles Cross-Country Champ.

1953

Aust. 6 Miles Champion Vic. 5 Miles Cross-Country Champion

1954

Victorian & Australian 3 Miles Champion and Record Holder

NEIL ROBBINS

1952

Victorian 5 Miles Cross-Country Champion; 10 Miles Cross - Country Champion; 15 Miles Cross-Country Champion.

1954

Victorian & Australian 6 Miles Record Holder.

THE FASTEST - EVER AUSTRALIANS AT THEIR DISTANCES . . . BUT STILL REQUIRED TO FIND £520 FOR THEIR FARES AND EXPENSES.

CAN YOU HELP THEM REACH VANCOUVER WITH A DONATION LARGE OR SMALL?

WILLIAMSTOWN AMATEUR ATHLETIC CLUB
Hon. Sec.: A. FINLAYSON,
121 North Rd., Newport
Hon. Treas.: R. WATERS,
40 Collingwood Rd., Newport

ENSIGN PRESS PRINT. 3-3 VICTORIA STREET FOOTSCRAY

Being picked in the team was only half the battle. The poster seeks funds towards the £520 Geoff Warren and Neil Robbins had to raise to go to Vancouver for the Empire Games.

and Jim Bailey came down from Sydney for the race. McRae raced through the first 880 in 1:59.0, then pulled out. Landy followed, a stride or so behind in an estimated 1:59.3, but he had a problem. His Australian Rules Football background had returned to haunt him. In the early stages of the race, one of the spikes on his right shoe had pierced a discarded stop from a football boot.

These stops, made from thin layers of leather, were nailed into the leather soles of the boot. Affixed to the boot with one or two "whacks" from a hammer, they would be commonly dislodged and strewn all over the ground during the winter football season. This one — still in John Landy's possession to this day — was pierced clean through Landy's spikes and remained attached. It cannot have caused excruciating pain, as Landy would have been unable to continue; but, at the very least, it must have had an unbalancing effect, as he would have been aware of it every time his right foot hit the ground.

The Easter Fair crowd, estimated at 20,000, urged Landy through the final lap with cries of "Go, Landy — go!" He passed 1500 in 3:46.4, two seconds slower than in his 4:02.0 mile the previous December, but flew home to record 4:02.6. "I think I reached my peak when I ran 4:02.0 last December," Landy said, "and it looks now that I cannot get under that time. This is a wonderful track, and if I could have done it, this was the place."

Again, though, it was not to be and John Landy set off for Europe nine days later with no fewer than six of the nine 4:02 miles run in the previous 18 months to his name, but without the world record. His last training run at Central Park was 12x440 yards in an average of 59.4 seconds. Up-and-coming miler Tom Worrell trained with him, doing four in 63 seconds. "These felt very fast," wrote Worrell in his diary. They were. Landy told a farewell dinner at Melbourne's Danish Club, "I sincerely hope and expect to run at least one-tenth, and possibly one second, better than I have done out here in Australia."

Translated from athlete-speak, this most likely meant he was certain that better conditions and competition would enable him to run a personal best, that he was fairly sure it would get him under the world record, and that he hoped it would get him under four minutes. Landy would be right on all three counts.

On 28 April, John Landy left Melbourne for Turku. He travelled via Sydney, Singapore (where, the following day, he did a session of 12x300 metres averaging 37.5 seconds!), Calcutta, Karachi, Beirut, London and Stockholm. He had time for a two mile jog and a few strides in the Swedish capital before flying on to Turku. (On the day Landy arrived in Turku, he went for a three or four mile jog, but the notable fact in his diary entry is that he wore a tracksuit, something he rarely had to do in Central Park!)

After the failure of his repeated attempts to break the four-minute mile in Australia, Landy had travelled to Europe with the feeling that the next best chances would fall to Santee and Bannister. This boding was borne out, of course. He had been in Finland only a few days when Bannister broke four minutes.

Looking for the earliest possible opportunity to capitalise on his winter training, and conscious of the likelihood that Landy or Santee might beat him to the landmark, Bannister chose the annual match between Oxford University and the Amateur Athletic Association for a crack at the historic four-minute mile barrier. The match was held at the university's Iffley Road track on 6 May 1954. Bannister travelled up from London, Franz Stampfl coincidentally taking the same train, with a wary eye on the windy and stormy weather. Right up until the last, the wind threatened to thwart any record hopes, but the flag of St George on a nearby church-tower dropped as if by arrangement minutes before the race got under way. The two Chrises — Brasher and Chataway — did a superb job of pacing Bannister through the first three and a half laps before Bannister sprinted clear and ran into history.

The result and time were conveyed in Norris McWhirter's immortal announcement: "Ladies and gentlemen, here is the result of Event Number Nine, the One Mile: First, number 41, R. G. Bannister, Amateur Athletic Association, and formerly of Exeter and Merton Colleges, Oxford, with a time which is a new meeting and track record, and which, subject to ratification, will be a new English native, British national, British All-Comers, European, British Empire and World record. The time was three ..."

In fact, it was 3:59.4, but the rest of the announcement was never heard because of the jubilant roar of the crowd. Like everything else about the race, the announcement was rehearsed; McWhirter perfected his phrasing and intonations in the bath the night before the race.

Bannister had done it and, with the press being given the tip the day before by Norris McWhirter, the result flashed around the world in not much more time than it had taken him to run the race. Questions about the legitimacy of the race, and the artificial pacing, were for another day. By the end of 1954, Bannister would put to rest any lingering doubts about his competitive ability.

Bannister came back down to London that night, to celebrate and also to conduct a range of interviews. Everyone wanted to talk to the man who had done the impossible — and done it for Britain. In one interview, he gave an insight into the pressure he, at least, felt to get there first. "It had become fairly urgent for me to have a shot," Bannister said. "Landy and Wes Santee were getting close. And we did particularly want someone in this country to do it."

Santee *had* been getting close. Big crowds normally attended the major US outdoor collegiate meetings and there were 23,000 at the Kansas Relays in mid-April to see Santee run 4:03.1 on a cinder track made soft and soggy by heavy rains. "[Santee] was physically and mentally ready," his Kansas teammate Dick Wilson said. "It was windy and cold, just blowing too hard. They even put tarps up to block the wind."

The relays were just 18 days before Bannister's break-through. Santee had other mile races lined up, in California, where he might expect better conditions. Sure he might run four minutes, but he would not be the first now. "I absolutely thought I was going to be the first one," Santee later said. "I don't think there's any question that if we had run a paced race like Bannister, we would have broken it."

At the end of May, Santee ran in Kansas City. University of Kansas teammates paced him through the first three laps in 3:02.0. He came home in 59.3 for a 4:01.3, the same recorded time as Hagg's world record. He had surpassed Landy, and only Bannister was now faster. A week later, on 6 June, Santee ran in the Compton Invitational in the first of the two meetings Mel Patton had worked so hard to persuade Landy to run. Santee was in front with a lap and a half to go. With 220 yards left, he was at 3:28.7, just under two seconds faster than Bannister had been at Oxford. But Santee had already been in front for one full lap, whereas at the corresponding stage Bannister had just burst past Chris Chataway to lead for the first time. Santee went through 1500 metres in an official world record 3:42.8, but he started to tie up in the straight, running 4:00.6. "Wes has a tendency to tie up in cold weather," his coach, Bill Easton said (it was windy and 17.2°C). "Considering the weather conditions, that was probably the greatest mile ever run."

Finally, on 13 June, Santee ran the second of the Landy-less West Coast meetings, the Coliseum Relays in Los Angeles. Josy Barthel, the Olympic 1500 champion, was by now studying at Harvard. He offered to set the pace for Santee, leading him until 300 metres to go. Again Santee could not quite do it — this time he ran 4:00.7.

Had Landy run, would both he and Santee be sub-four minute milers by this stage? As both were natural racers, they most probably would have been, but it was academic. More certain was that, with his ban from international competition, the Coliseum meeting was effectively the end of Santee's season.

Landy had arrived in Turku to a welcome "almost as big as [the welcome given to] the president of Iceland", according to contemporary reports. He had hardly settled into his hotel when Bannister ran 3:59.4.

Bannister described Landy as "the unluckiest man in athletics" (reported in *The Herald*, 7 May 1954), presumably referring to his repeated solo efforts over the previous two years, with neither pacing, nor competition, on tracks that were, by world standards, inferior. "I can't assess the conditions in Australia," Bannister continued, "but I'm sure John hasn't been fully tested." Bannister also said that "the essence" of athletics was racing against opponents, not the clock.

Landy's reaction has been variously reported as disappointment, devastation, deliverance and inspiration. It was all of these, in part. With the preponderance of fast times in the previous 18 months to his name, he had hoped he would be the one to break the world record, if not four minutes. In a pre-departure interview (with Peter Banfield of *The Argus*), Landy said he would like to break the record and told him how. "I would be happiest in an arena by myself with three or four timekeepers and other officials as my only spectators. I don't want the adulation of a cheering crowd, but I do want to do it." To a greater or lesser extent, this would have been true of Bannister or Santee as well, and of any athlete before or since. Athletes expecting to run for the adulation of cheering crowds face sad disillusionment.

"They went after it," Landy says of the Oxford race. "They saw it as a British achievement. People thought I was going to be eating my heart out, but I thought if he can do that, the logic was that, since I'd been much more consistent, why wouldn't I be able to do that? I didn't say that, but that's what I felt.

"It wasn't very good conditions when they ran, but the point was he [Bannister] did it and that got it out of the road. He was the immortal, and I wasn't. But that freed me up to run whatever I could. To some extent it was a relief. I didn't have to worry because it's [four minutes] been done, so what's next?"

The feeling that, somehow or other, Landy had been "robbed" would have been one Australians could readily identify with. Here was the Aussie battler, chasing four minutes on his own in race after race, the most help he ever got — and this not until 1954 — taking him only as far as 880 yards, and along comes a "Pommy" to pip him at the post. And doing so, moreover, in a highly-orchestrated attempt with not one, but two pacemakers taking him to the point at which he launched his final sprint. Tom Roberts, a friend of Landy's, was in a dissection class at Melbourne University when he heard the news that Bannister had broken four minutes. He remembers his reaction — "I couldn't believe it. I thought: 'How *dare* he!'"

Funnily enough, Landy did not train the day of the Oxford race. In *The Perfect Mile*, Neal Bascomb speculates that perhaps Landy wanted first to see how Bannister ran. More likely, it was because he had scheduled a day off. He had several more days off before his first race in Turku on 31 May. "I didn't do any pulverising sort of training," says Landy. "I kept my condition by 'quality' training and by racing. I really relied on the condition I came in from Australia. I did do some interesting time trials ..."

Landy still has his original training diary from the period, the details of which were published in *Athletics World* (those McWhirters again!). Among his training, Landy did 10x440 yards at an average of 57.6, probably faster than anything Bannister had done for one of his key sessions. Landy also ran an 800 metres in 1:51.4 and, the next day, 12x440 in 58.6. Early in June, Landy ran 300 metres in 37 seconds and 400 in 49.7. "So, I was very sharp," he says. "I ran 23.3 for 200 metres."

So with Bannister already "the immortal" first man to better four minutes, Landy had his first race over a mile at Turku on the »

4.01.6 — 31/5

laey/hair jog 1/6

2/6   10 x 400m @ 62.5 & 7x300 @ 4.56

3. 7 x 300 m @ 41.7

4

5   2.58.8/1200m/& 1.58 (800m)
    1.58.5, 2.01,   1.58.4
6   — laey hair jog
7
8   — 4.01.6

9   — Lan jog
10 — 1 x 300m @ 42.4 & Lan jog
11 —   3. 46.4 !!

12

13

14 — Lan jog
15 — Lan jog & stride
16 — 8 steady laps
    7 x 400m @ 62 appx
    2000m in 5.12.6

17 — ½ hr jog & 6 x 300 m
                          42.5

"I kept my condition by 'quality' training and by racing." John Landy's training diary from the days leading up to his world record mile in Turku, 1954.

Turku

Turku's athletic heritage is not apparent to the visitor at first glance. There is nothing to distinguish the city from many other Finnish cities and towns. It is pleasing to the eye — a river flows through it and a few kilometres out of town there is good running to be had. Unlike, say, Lasse Viren's village of Myrskylä in central Finland, there are no forests criss-crossed by kilometres of dirt roads and trails right on the edge of town.

The wooden stands and pavilions evident in photos of the many great races at Turku stadium have long since disappeared. It is a modern facility that has more recently hosted European under-age and veterans' championships; the only nod to the old is two weatherboard buildings within its surroundings.

Once inside the Turun Urheiluliitto clubrooms (for Turku Sports Association members), a nondescript wooden building on the corner of two city streets, everything changes. Tradition reaches out from walls lined with honour boards and trophy display cases. Pride of place is a montage depicting the career of "Paavo Nurmi, Legendary King of Runners". Nurmi, winner of nine Olympic gold medals and a world record setter on 22 occasions, was a member of Turun Urheiluliitto, as were other Flying Finns Albin Stenroos (winner, 1924 Olympic marathon); Hannes Kolehmainen (winner, 1920 Olympic marathon); Harri Larva (1500 winner, 1928 Olympic Games); and, in more modern times, Pekka Päivärinta (1973 world cross-country champion).

When a visitor to the Turun Urheiluliitto asked to look at contemporary newspaper cuttings of Landy's 1954 stay, he was mistakenly handed a bulky file. The cuttings turned out to be from 1957, when Turun Urheiluliitto member Olavi Salsola broke the world record for 1500 metres, defeating fellow Finns Olavi Salonen and Olavi Vuorisalo in a race that would inevitably be dubbed "the race of the three Olavis". This was not intended to be a subtle reminder that there was a lot more to the history of Turun Urheiluliitto than its brief association with John Landy and the four-minute mile — but it certainly served as one!

A short walk from the club rooms takes the visitor to the family home in which Nurmi grew up. His father died when Nurmi was twelve and he had to work to help support the family. His mother rented out one of the two rooms in their apartment in the row of wooden houses, and the family of six slept in the remaining large room. Running must have given Nurmi welcome solitude.

Nurmi made a (relative) fortune out of his running, especially on a tour of the US after the 1924 Paris Olympics where he famously won the 1500 and 5000 metres with less than an hour between the two finals. He invested in a small shop in Helsinki, ostensibly selling men's ties. Like Jack Wren's betting shop in Melbourne, however, Nurmi's modest shop was also a front for investment in other businesses. His interests in construction (mainly housing) and shipping reputedly made him an enormously wealthy man.

But he was a Turku man, the greatest of the many fine runners to come from the Turun Urheiluliitto club.

» last day of May, 1954. In front of 10,000 spectators, lured to the Turku stadium by posters with banners reading "Come and See the World Record Broken", Landy stood on the starting line opposed by Johansson and two other Finns, Olavi Vuorisalo and Urho Vaharanta.

Vaharanta bolted from the line, but he couldn't hold an overly eager Landy up for long. "I don't know why I did it, but I ran 1.55.8 for the first 880," he recalls. "I finished up blowing up and I ran 4:01.6." In his first race on a European cinders track, Landy found the surface gave him *too* much back, contributing to his suicidal pace. Still, he was no longer stuck at 4:02, even if he was now third-fastest ever (Santee had already run his 4:01.3).

"I got too confident," Landy said in 2004. "I ran 1:55 for the first half mile. Boy, did I slow down! If I'd run that race more evenly I would probably have run four minutes then. But I was very positive about my capacity to run faster than I had in Australia." Landy told the press after the race: "I'm not a four-minute miler yet, but I soon will be." It was his most confident public comment ever.

Part of the deal with Landy's trip was that he would race in Sweden as well as Finland. Turun Urheiluliitto organised the races for him. He just ran, which he did not mind at all. "They farmed me out to other clubs' races. They obviously made money out of my presence in Finland. They farmed me out to clubs including Stockholm and Gothenburg."

Eight days after his first race, Landy again ran 4:01.6, this time in Stockholm's beautiful old Olympic stadium. It was cold — 8°C and wet. Sune Karlsson, the emerging Swedish athlete who had run the year's fastest 1500 metres in 1953, was supposed to provide the opposition, but it was early in his season.

While in Stockholm, Landy visited the Royal College of Physical Education where he was tested on a treadmill by pioneer exercise physiologist, Professor Per-Olof Åstrand. Professor Åstrand was already involved with the Swedish winter Olympic team and had tested a number of elite athletes. Though not as sophisticated as today's equipment, the physiology laboratories measured the same parameters then as now. At the instigation of one of the Swedish papers, Professor Åstrand got John Landy to run on one of his treadmills. "John volunteered and after warming up he ran on the treadmill, at a speed of 20 kmh and one degree uphill and we measured his peak oxygen uptake," Professor Åstrand recalled in 2006.

Not surprisingly, Landy returned impressive results. His peak heart rate was 194 beats per minute and his maximal oxygen uptake was 76.6 millilitres of oxygen per kilogram of bodyweight per minute. Professor Åstrand says the results were among the best recorded to that time. In the following months and years he would exhort the

Swedish national cross-country skiers he tested: "Your goal must be to beat John Landy's 76.6."

Like many an Australian in years to come, Landy was finding out there was nothing magical about racing in Europe. The culture might be more supportive, the tracks better, the competition better, but you still have to run the times for yourself. "The Finns and Swedes were early on in their season. I found myself winning pretty easily, almost as easily as in Australia. Nobody challenged me at all. I was leading most of the way, but I was running so easily that I thought 'who's going to beat me anyway'."

But something was obviously building. Landy ran 3:46.4 winning a 1500 in Helsinki on 11 June. Five days later, at Imatra (near the Finnish border with the Soviet Union), he would have had KGB men peeking over the Iron Curtain in wonder with a warm-up of 7×400 metres in 62 seconds, followed by a 2000 metres in 5:12.6. Now Landy returned to Turku. On Friday, 18 June, he ran his 37-second 300 metres and 49.7 for 400. Next day, he did a 1200 metre time trial in 2:58.8. With a day's rest, he was ready for something special to mark 21 June, Midsummer Day in the northern hemisphere.

For over 18 months, John Landy had pursued the perfect mile. It had been a solitary pursuit, for the most part, but he did not mind. He personified the adage coined by John Masefield, "That the effort failed was not against it. Much that is most splendid in history failed." There was as much merit in the pursuit of excellence as in its attainment. Now, on 21 June 1954, both elements came together in one unforgettable performance. For so long, Landy had chased records — personal, national and world records — with no hint of competition. This night, at the Turku stadium, he faced competition in the shape of Chris Chataway.

Chataway was keen to run against Landy, to measure himself against the Australian. Bannister was in two minds: he knew that this would give Landy an excellent chance to take the world record off him, but he also realised that there was no way he could ask Chataway not to take such an opportunity. Bannister wrote in *The Four-Minute Mile* that "at the time, quite humanly I think, I was a little upset" at the possibility that Chataway could help Landy.

Chataway's role in the Turku mile was the antithesis of his part in Bannister's record. One of the essential elements of pacemaking is that the beneficiary of the pacemaker's efforts knows that the runner leading him represents no competitive threat. The pacemaker is there to help, not to compete for the win. (This, incidentally, is the difference between organised pacemaking and pace *sharing*, where athletes of roughly equal ability may agree to share the leading to ensure the pace is fast.) In Turku, Chataway wanted to race John Landy. He may not have had a realistic chance of defeating the Australian, but he would do his darndest.

At 7pm on Monday 21 June 1954, the runners were called to the line for the mile. Landy had worn number one race bib in his first mile race at Turku; this time he wore number two. Chataway wore number one.

From the gun, Antti Kallio bolted into the lead. Against Landy's wishes, a pacemaker had been inserted into the field. It scarce mattered, for Kallio lasted no longer than Len McRae and other well-meaning Australian friends of Landy's. He led at 440 yards in 58 seconds. By 700 metres, Landy had taken up his familiar role of front-runner. He passed 880 yards in 1:58.0, Chataway clinging resolutely to his heels. The pace showed no sign of dropping as he raced through three-quarters of a mile in an estimated 2:57.2.

Now, at the point at which time had so often slipped away, Landy had competition. Landy's competitiveness is often overlooked, comparatively ignored against other qualities such as his front-running and his sportsmanship. His tactical sense, too, was under-developed, as even he admits, through race after race run in the leading position. Landy's will-to-win, however, was obvious from the manner in which he had raced against Don Macmillan throughout 1951–52 in his attempts to qualify for Olympic selection. And that facet of his make-up was under threat now. "When I ran against Chataway, it was different," Landy explains. "He was the only one that pushed me. In the end, I did beat him by 40 metres but he hung on until 300 to go and I didn't know whether he was going to find something extra. He didn't."

Landy raced through 1500 metres in 3:41.8, taking a full second off Santee's recent world record. Would he now tie up, as Santee had in Compton and he himself so often had in Australia?

Landy pushed through to the tape. Initially, there was confusion. Timekeepers conferred in a huddle, just as they had at Olympic Park 18 months earlier when Landy had run 4:02. Back then, Australian officials could not quite believe their watches; this time, Landy could not understand the animated chatter of the Finns. But Chataway and Johansson soon put any doubts out of his mind.

Landy had run 3:57.9 (ratified as 3:58.0), leaping his own four-minute barrier by 3.7 seconds, breaking Bannister's 46-day-old world record by 1.4 seconds. And he had done it in the manner he wished, with no real assistance beyond the stimulus of competition and his own curiosity about where his limits lay.

Johansson and Chataway seized hold off Landy's hands and more or less coerced him into a lap of honour. He was hoisted onto the shoulders of cheering Finns and tossed jubilantly into the air. Almost before Landy had come down again, the celebrations started in Australia. His run was front-page news in every paper.

"Landy, the Miracle Miler" read the *Melbourne Herald* headline. "3.58 — and 'I can do better.'" The story ran with file pictures of Landy and Chris Chataway, and a tricked up shot of a stop-watch reading 3:58.0. Another *Herald* report stated that Landy was not distressed after his record run, while family reaction appeared under a head of "John's Mother Is Thrilled." A picture showed Elva Landy on the phone. It was ringing off the hook, but it took several days before she was able to get a call through to her son.

"He's The World's Fastest Miler," the next morning's *Sun* fairly screamed. Being a news-pictorial, it had to have photos, so the feature article was illustrated with an electric-eye strip of Landy's running style, a picture of him catching butterflies, and a mock-up with Landy's image superimposed on a photo of a mile along Melbourne's Elizabeth Street from the Flinders Street station. "Exact Mile from Flinders Street Finishes Here," read a pointer, with the caption sub-headed "City Council official measurement."

"Landy's Achievement Builds National Pride," ran the heading for *The Age*'s editorial. "It is an achievement for us all," the editorial opined, "because it is no mere brilliant fluke, such as in our weaker moments we are apt to take pride in. It is the calculated result of long and dogged perseverance." The editorial detailed Landy's efforts since December 1952. "He has met with every kind of frustration — adverse weather, faulty time-keeping and the lack of a colleague fast enough to pace him. Through it all he has stuck to his self-imposed task, well aware that his goal was not likely to be reached in weeks or months. This willingness to take a task seriously is not generally supposed to be in the Australian tradition," the editorial continued in gentle rebuke to the national character.

Elsewhere, Australians celebrated in more traditional manner. At the McKinnon Hotel, in a Melbourne suburb not too far away from Landy's home, the publican displayed a more familiar — and popular — reaction to Australian achievement. "Keith Lynch called for silence in his bar Tuesday evening, said a few words about its being a great day for Australia — and asked the boys to drink, at his expense, Landy's health," reported a column in *The Age*.

Telegrams poured in to Landy's Turku hotel, including messages of congratulations from Roger Bannister and Wes Santee. The American, more publicly peeved than Landy at the manner of

Bannister's sub-four, also wished the Australian "good luck in the race against Bannister next month". The Australian Prime Minister sent a message, as did his deputy, several state premiers and the Lord Mayors of Melbourne and Geelong. An Australian flag was flown from the top of Melbourne Town Hall, a special flag: it was the one flown at the 1952 Helsinki Olympic Village and had been signed by every member of that team. Family and friends added their congratulations, one of the former referring to celebrations at "Sixty C. P. R." (60 Central Park Road, the Landy family home).

In London, *The Express* put a brave face on the world record's passing from an Englishman to an Australian: "Landy keeps prize in the Empire." By the weekend, the Australian reaction had broadened. Several Sunday newspapers ran profile stories on Landy, including one in *The Sunday Telegraph* in which his sister, Sue, noted pithily that, as a young boy, John "couldn't run a message" and that she could beat him any time she pleased. *The Telegraph* also returned to erstwhile Landy critics. Oscar Fraley, the US columnist who had suggested Landy would need to run downhill with a tailwind all the way to break four minutes, told the paper: "I am sitting here in my new sackcloth suit combing the ashes out of my hair." Arthur Daley, of "pass the salt" fame, said: "I have been chewing salt by the ton since then." Daley attempted to explain his initial cynicism: "My reaction was that of most people here. We're not used to comets rocketing around mile tracks in Australia at those speeds."

There was now a brilliant denouement building to the four-minute mile story. The only two men to have broken four minutes were due to meet once, and once only. That encounter would be at the British Empire Games in Vancouver. Unfortunately, this final act of the four-minute mile did not, could not, involve Wes Santee. As a result of some unpleasantries almost 200 years earlier, America did not belong to the British Commonwealth. American promoters were falling over themselves to get Bannister, Landy and Santee into a race, but there was never any prospect of Santee running the Empire race. (As noted, Santee's chances of breaking four minutes in 1954 were already ebbing away. He had to do his reserve training with the US Marines, a previously flexible arrangement that, due to frequently having been put off in the past, had now become inflexible.)

It did not change the complexion of the Bannister–Landy encounter. As Landy noted in an interview marking the 50th anniversary of the first sub-four minute mile, the pair complemented each other. "There was a wonderful symmetry. The phenomenally fortuitous thing was that one guy did it [broke four minutes], then 46 days later another guy knocked quite a bit off that time, and they were destined to meet." Furthermore, "One guy was a front-runner determined to run as fast as he could, and the other guy was a guy who would sit. The chance of that kind of thing happening again was very difficult, but there was an inevitability to it."

The media were onto it immediately. Then, as now, the British Empire (now Commonwealth) Games were a big thing to Australians. With the clash of the only two men in the world to have broken four minutes for the mile, it was a big thing to the rest of the world, too. It was as if, having conquered Everest, Hillary and Tenzing had squared off for the world heavyweight title.

Landy continued his Scandinavian tour and training. A few days after his sub-four, he took a shot at the world two-mile record. He missed by two seconds, running 8:42 "in an absolute gale" in Pori, on the west coast of Finland. A few days later, Landy ran 2:20.9 for 1000 metres in Levi, a ski resort in the Lapland region. Turun Urheiluliitto was working him hard! "It was one of the best races I ran. It was a 300-metre track and it was very windy," says Landy. "I had an aim in running that. I knew Bannister would be trying to convince me that I couldn't withstand his finish. The world record then was 2:20.4 [held by the Danish 800/1500 runner Audun Boysen]. I thought if I break that, it will cause them some concern, but it didn't work out that way."

The game-playing concerned how the mile would be run in Vancouver. John Landy accepted that he almost inevitably would lead. Bannister, both from his own side and also on the advice of Stampfl and others, wanted to ensure that happened. Comments were "dropped to journalists". Stampfl, a calculating man, was quoted saying that if Landy let the race develop into a sit-and-kick affair, Bannister would destroy him.

"[They were] trying to ensure I would have to lead," says Landy. "Bannister ran a 4:07 mile [at the AAA championships in London], in which he ran a 53-second last lap, as much as to say 'you try any tactical games and I will win'. In anticipation that he would do that I was hell-bent on breaking the 1000 record in Levi, which was held by Boysen. I reckon I would have got it under reasonable conditions on a 400 metres track, but I didn't get it. My aim was to create the idea that 'Hey, he is faster than we think.' When it got to talking about the race I'd say I didn't think the time would be very fast. This was a bit of game playing. In other words, I may not be leading fast from the front in Vancouver. But right from the start I knew I would have to lead."

Landy was still trying to suggest otherwise as late as his arrival in Canada. He travelled there with his father, Gordon, who had met up with his son in London. The mile clash had lifted the Empire Games out of the publicity doldrums. John Landy gave a press conference at Montreal, en route across the country. "I will be out to win the race, not break the clock," Landy warned. "Often in these so-called 'miles of the century' two fast runners will watch each other carefully and take it easily while a third man wins the race." Well and good, but in Empire terms, it was hard to think who the "third man" might be. The next best miler was young New Zealander Murray Halberg, who had broken through to 4:04.4 during the southern hemisphere season.

The build-up to the race continued to gain momentum. Landy arrived in Vancouver to what was described as a "film star welcome", *The Sun* reporting that "bobbysoxers, autograph-hunters and dozens of news, radio and cameramen swept aside Vancouver's mayor, Fred C. Hume and his official party". A police motor-cycle escort was required to get Landy's car clear of the airport logjam and, in a Keystone Kops touch of hilarity, it was held up on the point of leaving when it was realised that the other four Australians on the flight — fencers John Fethers and Rod Steele, boxer Tony Madigan and Geoff Warren — were wandering around the terminal building uncollected.

Once at the Village, there was a press conference. Landy told the media he was amazed at the attention the race was generating. Bannister's strongest weapon, he told the press, was his "strong finish". Dismayed at the level of attention, Landy stayed outside the Village for a couple of nights, but was ordered back in by team management.

The two main protagonists followed a pattern in Vancouver similar to their different approaches to the four-minute mile. Landy, the man who had borne the hopes of a nation and pulled thousands through the gates to watch him race week in, week out, trained largely in public, though he did vary the times to limit his exposure. Bannister, who raced sparingly and believed himself capable of only two or three "peak" efforts in a season, sought the privacy of a local golf club, training with Chataway or Brasher in relative solitude. Landy's training times were reported like the track work of a Melbourne Cup fancy. Landy looked in superb physical shape, often training in shorts and shoes only. Bannister was photographed miserably huddled under a blanket, nursing a cold. When the heat draw came out, the fact that the top two men had not been drawn against each other was reported as if it were amazing. It would have been truly amazing had they clashed, as there were only two heats.

Both qualified comfortably in third place, Landy finishing virtually abreast of the first two, Bannister trailing a few yards behind Halberg and Canadian runner Rich Ferguson.

Landy told the press: "I feel I will have to run my best ever race to win, as I'm running against at least two men of equal calibre or even better." Still trying to low-key his tactics, he added that he thought the final would be run in 4:02 or 4:03. Bannister expected something "towards four minutes".

Landy felt the world was owed a great race and, just like he had felt obliged to deliver four-minute mile attempts to Australian spectators, regardless of the track condition, regardless of the weather, so he now owed the world a great race in this highly-anticipated meeting. The stadium was sold out, with 35,000 crammed in. Another 100 million watched on television throughout the USA and Canada. Millions more, including Australians, listened on radio. They were all willing for something memorable.

So, Landy opted to set the pace. If he managed to create a big enough gap between himself and his rival, Bannister would effectively be setting his own pace. But, as John Landy might put it himself, it did not work out that way. It was a failure, but if ever that heading "Magnificent Failure", which had appeared over so many unavailing four-minute mile attempts over the preceding two years, applied, it did in Vancouver.

Briefly, Landy led at 440 yards, at 880, at 1320 and, indeed, until around 100 yards to go. Then Bannister put into practice the tactic Stampfl had advised at their final meeting just before he left for Canada. He kicked just once, but he kicked decisively, gaining the upper hand and holding it to the line.

Typically, Bannister looked all in as soon as he crossed the line. Landy looked the fitter and the fresher, but he was on the wrong end of a 3:58.8 to 3:59.6 loss. The only sub-four minute milers in history had met and, thanks to John Landy, both had broken four minutes.

"I knew one of us had to crack," John Landy said straight after the race, "and in the end I was the one." Of his front-running tactics, he said: "Someone had to make the pace — and I was the mug."

In fact, there was no mug. Bannister ran half a second quicker than he had at Oxford; Landy ran sub-four. It was the greatest mile championship ever run, and remains among the greatest ever. Landy made it so. But it was notable for three reasons: the tactics, the look and, as it subsequently emerged, Landy's cut foot.

First, the tactics. Fifty years later, John Landy says he does not dwell on "what if". "No, not at all: I gave it my best shot. I wasn't good enough on the day, the way the race was run. It's very hard to win a race like that the way it was run, mind you."

Basically, Landy had two choices. It was more or less pre-ordained he would lead. The only question was did he lead from the gun or pick up the pace after the first lap, or lap and a half? He had had plenty of advice — not just the publicly revealed letter from Cerutty, which he did not read — that it would be better to wait. Denis Johansson thought so; Don Macmillan thought so. Waiting entailed the risk that someone else might take the race over. It might have been a minor risk, but it would have complicated things. Going hard from the start, however, reduced the tactical possibilities. Bannister would either be able to keep up, or he wouldn't. And, as he had run the three-quarters of a mile time trials in 2:52, it seemed likely Bannister would be able to keep up, unless his nerve failed. He had certainly rehearsed following the pace.

Picking up the pace from an intermediate point is the most effective way of running the kick out of a kicker, effectively making the pursuer run gradually faster and faster so that he cannot launch a sprint. But in a two-man race, it, too, has its limitations and dangers. "It was a huge risk. I could have lost the world record — a whole lot of things, but I added it all up, I thought that's the way I run. I'll take him on and try to run him into the ground. But I didn't succeed."

That Landy did not succeed may just have been because Bannister ran the race of his life. That, certainly, was the view of Wes Santee, who was "thrilled" as he watched on television at the NBC studios in New York. "It was a magnificent race … this was really a dream race. Landy did exactly what I expected him to do, but the Englishman finished better than I thought he could. Bannister was magnificent — but so was Landy."

Landy's tactics made the race, not that he takes it as much consolation. "You don't get votes for that. They don't give you a prize for trying. You've got to win it."

Second, the look, which came coming off the final bend. With around 100 yards to run, Landy glanced inside over his left shoulder, just as Bannister burst past on his outside. It was an action of no great significance, but its timing made it appear crucial. So, too, did Landy's comments beginning with his post-race remark that "one of us had to crack". The look over the shoulder was interpreted to be the moment when Landy, in effect, "cracked" and acknowledged he had no hope of winning.

In fact, as film of the race shows, Landy had checked Bannister's position in the third lap, too. And he had done so, as he did in the last lap, by glancing to his inside. "The look" had no tactical significance; had Landy been going to win at that stage, he still would have. Nor did it cost him victory. It was just a look.

Third, the cut. The story is well known. In the middle of the night after the mile heats, Landy, always a restless sleeper, went for a walk or jog. He was barefoot. During the walk, he trod on a discarded photographer's flash-bulb, cutting his right foot in two places.

The deeper cut — between the ball of the foot and the heel — was stitched and dressed. Landy made the doctors promise to keep it secret but, like the blood from the gash, the story leaked out through a Canadian pressman who turned up for a pre-arranged interview. Like the medics, he was sworn to secrecy; but he decided to publish the story once the race was run and done. »

Racing or Pacing?

John Landy and Roger Bannister were opposites in so many ways, but especially in their attitudes to how a four-minute mile could be run.

Landy saw his running as something he wanted to do well and, like everything he wanted to excel in, he wanted to be in control of his own performance. Applied to his numerous world record attempts, what this meant was that he refused offers of organised pacing and deplored its use. He was, and is, too much the gentleman to seek to impose this view on others, but he stands resolutely by it himself. "I had a very strong view about that," he said in an interview marking the 50th anniversary of the first sub-four minute mile. "In Australia it wasn't accepted. I asked people not to pace [races]. I wanted to run the race myself, I wanted to control it, I wanted to do it myself. I didn't see it as a team thing at all."

Landy says he has "no problems" with the artificial nature of the 6 May 1954 race at Oxford. It was similar to what Bannister had done the previous year, although Landy does not see a significant difference between the 4:02.0, which was disallowed, and the 3:59.4, which was ratified. "I accepted the umpire's decision. He still did it; you can't wind it back. It's a fact. I've never looked back on it. It wasn't the way I would have run it, or ever did run. I saw it as a different thing."

If Landy didn't try to run fast, no-one else would do it for him. The fact no-one could run with him in Australia reinforced his innate view on pacing. But he did need someone who would "make me run. I think that was what was lacking." Landy found that person in Turku in Chris Chataway, even though Chataway was never going to beat him.

Bannister was from the opposite end of the spectrum. A natural kicker, he believed it was not possible to run four minutes for the mile without pacing assistance. His physiological studies reinforced the view that if he wanted to break four minutes, someone else must be responsible for getting him well into the final lap at the required pace.

Before their climactic meeting in Vancouver, Bannister's two fastest miles were both set up with pacing every bit as blatant as seen on the international circuit these days. When Bannister ran 4:02.0 at the hastily arranged race at the Surrey Schools in 1953, Don Macmillan took him through two-and-a-half laps and then Chris Brasher, who had jogged off the line, picked up the pace as Bannister came up to lap him. That "record" was disallowed, so in the fateful Oxford race a year later, Brasher took the first two laps, then Chris Chataway the next lap and into the back straight. It was just as blatant an arrangement — neither man was there for any other purpose than to ensure Bannister ran the required pace — but it stayed the right side of the line.

The other runners in what was supposed to be a bona fide race were also apprised of the plan and warned not to thwart it. Tom Hulatt, the English northern counties champion who finished a distant third, said in an interview in 1988: "It was the most memorable race I ever ran and I remember all the details. I knew the record attempt was on because Bannister asked me to keep out of his way on the first two laps." (*The Sunday Express*, 12 June 1988.)

"One might ask what the difference between those two events was," John Landy says of the two paced miles. "Ron Clarke always maintains Oxford 1954 was illegal. I took the attitude that it was the umpire's decision to say whether it was within the rules; whatever they came up with I wasn't going to argue. I never have and never will. It was a bloody good performance." What happened in Oxford was also tolerated because it was seen as a necessary part of achieving a goal that had defied the world's best milers for the previous 20 years. It was even voted the number one moment in sport in the 20th century in millennium polls.

One man who has taken a different view of it is British journalist and writer Pat Butcher. In *The Perfect Distance, Ovett & Coe: The Record-Breaking Rivalry*, he describes the pacemaking as "the worst aspect" of the first sub-four minute and bemoans the fact that it has become the template for the modern paced middle-distance race. It would have been far better, Butcher argues, had the model for the modern middle-distance runner been Filbert Bayi, the Tanzanian athlete who sent goosebumps down the spines of all who saw him by leading every step of the way in his world record 1500 metres win at the 1974 Commonwealth Games.

Of course, whatever the merits of John Landy's tactics in Vancouver, one consequence was that he unwittingly set up the sort of race so familiar to Bannister: a fast, relatively even pace from the gun.

So who is right and who is wrong? Despite commendable recent moves to get away from pacemakers in some races, the international running circuit is overwhelmingly populated with athletes running races with the sole intention of setting a fast pace and none of finishing the race. It *is* a canker on the sport and one of the bitter ironies is that many of those who bemoan the prevalence of paced races are the very same people who acclaim the first sub-four as the sporting achievement of the 20th century.

It is another irony that Roger Bannister is best remembered for the first four-minute mile. Wes Santee's assertion, made straight after the Oxford race, remains absolutely true: Put either Santee or Landy in that race and they would have broken four minutes, too.

Bannister's real achievement in 1954 — and it is a great one — was to win the Empire Games mile. Taken in its contemporary context, it is easy to see why the first sub-four minute mile swamped all else then. But it is hard to see why it still does over 50 years later. Vancouver and the 1954 European championships, rather than Oxford, set the seal on Roger Bannister's career.

» When confronted by an Australian pressman once the story had broken, Landy denied it. "All I am saying is that I went to the mile start 100 per cent fit," he said. "If I can run 3:59.6 with a limp, I've got possibilities as a runner." Fifty years later, John Landy still insists the cut "didn't make the slightest difference. [There was a] lot of blood, but it didn't amount to much. Andy O'Brien [the Canadian journalist] saw it when I got out of bed. He said I would have won …"

Like most Australians, John Landy can show an earthy turn of phrase. Rarely does he display this in public. Talking about the cut foot is one of those occasions. His response to the proposition that he would have won but for the cut: "Bulls**t. A cut's a cut when you're young and fit, it doesn't mean a bloody thing."

At the time, it took several days for the full story to be revealed, and even then only after the Australian team manager, Jim Eve, had called Landy in because of all the calls he was getting from Australian and world media after the story broke. Landy's line then, as it remains, was that he did not want the cut seized on as an excuse. "The trouble is," he told journalists, "that it will probably be used as an alibi and I don't want that." Though it was painful to treat and dress the wound, and the infection caused some discomfort, Landy remains adamant to this day that "I never felt a thing during the race."

Writing for the 25th anniversary of the Vancouver race in an article Landy describes as "the most authentic account" of the contest, journalist and writer Adrian McGregor hypothesised that if Landy had revealed the injury "for the legitimate handicap it may have been" he would have been placing the importance of victory above his own performance. "Once he decided to run, no matter what his motivation, the debate ended for him. Bannister deserved no less than a fit opponent. Landy judged himself able and … sought to have others judge him accordingly."

So what is the truth? The cut certainly could have made a

difference. Anyone who has run with a gash on that part of the foot knows two things: first, you *can* run on it, but second, you *do* feel it until the endorphins, the body's natural pain-blockers, cut in. McGregor suggests that in the final stages of the race, both runners at the limit of oxygen debt, Landy must have felt some pain and was therefore like an army fighting on two fronts. But John Landy's argument is valid, too. Medicos can give an opinion, runners extrapolate from their own experiences, but only Landy *knows*. If he ran 3:59.6 with the cut, how much difference could it have made? To suggest it made *the* difference is fanciful; to wonder if it may have made any difference is not.

Landy had two aims in 1954: one was to break the world record and the other was to win the Empire Games. Bannister beat him to the first — breaking four minutes into the bargain — and beat him in the second. Bannister went on to crown a magnificent year by winning the 1500 at the European championships in Berne later in August. Landy and Don Macmillan watched from the stands. Then Bannister retired, never to race again.

Landy also contemplated retirement and says he would have given it away had he won the Empire Games race. "The most important race of my life to me was to beat Bannister in Vancouver. I don't think I would ever have run again if I'd done that," he said in 2004.

It might have been better for John Landy had he won in Vancouver, but it was to the benefit of his sport that he kept on running at all.

9

Under Big Skies at Timbertop

Al Lawrence felt like pinching himself to see if he was awake, for surely he must have been dreaming. Here he was training at the University of Vancouver track and, there, holding the stopwatch for him, was John Landy.

Before Lawrence had left Australia, in his first national team, his coach "Chicks" Hensley had advised him to observe Landy's training closely. He had followed instructions, holding a watch on some of Landy's track sessions. So John Landy, who trained in the early evening to avoid the crowds, was glad to come down to a bustling training track mid-morning to return the favour to his teammate.

Though the two were the same age — both 24 — there was a gulf between them in competition. "John was only too happy to pass on the benefits of his experience to a young, struggling runner," Lawrence recalls (… *Chew With My Mouth Shut*, Al Lawrence).

"The spectators … saw a peculiar sight indeed," Lawrence notes. "The world mile record holder — called by many the greatest runner ever — holding a stopwatch and calling out lap times to an unknown Australian 'plodder.'"

Lawrence was one of the slew of young Australians emerging in the run-up to the 1956 Melbourne Olympics. Coming through at the same time in New South Wales were distance runners Roley Guy, Bryce Mackay and Keith Ollerenshaw.

Lawrence had developed the previous year, taking out several state distance titles. Nevertheless, he was still considered a rank outsider for the Vancouver team when he lined up against the top

Victorians — Les Perry, Neil Robbins and Geoff Warren — in the six miles at the national titles. But he won from Perry and finished second to Warren in the three miles. He was selected for both distances in Vancouver and he was off on a road that would lead to an Olympic medal in Melbourne.

Throughout 1955, it would be the emerging group who would make the pace in Australia. December 1954 saw the retirement of both Bannister and Landy. "Retirement" was a rubbery concept in those far-off days. From this perspective, it seems the top athletes — especially British and Australian ones — announced their retirement after every major championships. When a 1950s athlete talked about "retirement", they often as not meant a re-assessment as to whether they could continue to fit professional training for an amateur past-time into their lifestyles for another year or more. Athletes, swimmers, tennis players usually lost another year in an income-producing job or profession if they chose to continue their sport.

So Roger Bannister decided after the disappointment of Helsinki 1952 to commit himself to two more years in the sport along with the specific goal of the four-minute mile. At the end of 1954, he had achieved everything he had wanted to achieve. The only thing Bannister did not have was the world record, but with his philosophy of being a racer first, a time-chaser second, he realised that pursuit of such transient glory was not worth the price of further delaying his medical career.

Bannister blitzed a strong field in the 1954 European championships to win easily. This time there was no John Landy to set a fierce pace, but he produced a withering 25-second final 200 metres to sprint to victory. Though he took a few more months to announce it officially, that was it. He retired.

John Landy and Don Macmillan watched the race. "He ran very well," says Landy. "He had a mission that year. He was an excellent scholar and wanted to be a top medico. That was his aim." Speaking more generally, Landy adds: "You weren't going to stay in athletics any longer than you had to."

Landy himself returned to Australia in September 1954, in not the best physical shape. It had been a non-stop grind from the moment he got back into training after the 1952 Olympics until the Empire Games final. Now, he came crashing down. He was ill in Berne, possibly as a result of the infection from his cut foot spreading.

In early December, Landy ran in a two-mile race in Geelong, finishing fifth, over 100 yards behind Les Perry. The meeting was promoted by Landy's Geelong Guild club, which had only wanted him to make an appearance, but he insisted on running. The club president urged Landy to have a complete medical check-up before racing again.

Within a week, however, Australia's top athlete had announced his "retirement". Landy announced he would not be running again in the 1954–55 season and that his participation in the 1956 Olympics would be "pretty doubtful". His exact meaning was not clear: in a glass-half-full, glass-half-empty kind of judgement, some reports emphasised the doubt, others suggested he "might" try to get fit again for Melbourne.

Ron Carter, who had covered the Olympics for *The Argus* and would soon join *The Age* (where he was the Olympics writer for almost 40 years), noted Bannister's retirement and Landy's doubtful future and asked: "What does the four-minute mile do to athletes?" It was a fair question, too; what do you climb after you've scaled the Mt Everest of athletics?

Landy was quoted by Steve Hayward in *The Herald*: "The position is, if I could not get fit I would not attempt to race again," but added a little later, "If I can find the time for training to get 100 percent fit, I might consider competing at the Melbourne Olympic Games."

So 1954 ended with Landy in limbo but with an honour from the queen in the New Year's Honours List. Landy received an MBE (the award of Member of the British Empire), one of the few sportsmen to receive one that year (there was nothing for Bannister, though he was eventually knighted for his services to medicine in 1975). After teaching the final term of the Australian school year at the Geelong Grammar campus in Corio, Landy was to spend 1955 at the country campus at Timbertop. This was a rural campus of the school, where (then) year 10 students completed a year in which normal academic work was supplemented by a wide range of pursuits, the more physical of which, such as cross-country runs and long hikes, replaced conventional school sport.

In Landy's absence, the national titles were held in Adelaide in stinking hot conditions. The 880 yards and mile were both won by Don Macmillan, who had returned from England and, like Landy, was teaching at his old school, Geelong College. John Plummer was second and Lawrence third in the mile, which was also notable for the rare, if not unique, disqualification of a runner for two false starts. Normally, this is the exclusive preserve of highly-strung sprinters, but this time the opprobrium fell on New South Wales runner Alex Henderson. As Al Lawrence tells it: "A heat wave that had been baking Adelaide showed no signs of breaking and the temperature was measured at 120°F [48.9°C]. The mile went ahead as scheduled.

"The race began sensationally. Alex Henderson broke twice at the start and was disqualified. The disqualification was the first in the history of that particular distance in Australian athletics and forever christened Alex Henderson with the nickname of 'nerves.'"

Dave Stephens won the three miles, easily defeating Plummer and Keith Ollerenshaw. He also won the six miles — which had been scheduled for 1pm but was rescheduled after protests from the athletes — by over two minutes from Ollerenshaw and Neil Robbins.

The 1955 titles were also notable for the appearance of a prodigious young talent. Two invitation junior races were held, over a mile and 880 yards. As Al Lawrence tells it: "Twenty minutes after »

Dave Stephens

Dave Stephens was another Williamstown teammate of Les Perry, Geoff Warren and Neil Robbins. So far, so conventional — but little else was prosaic about this most mercurial of personalities.

As a student at Williamstown High School, Stephens had been a sprinter — a handy one, but not brilliant. By December 1952, he was a 22-year-old middle-distance runner, finishing third behind Landy and Perry in Landy's breakthrough 4:02.1 mile. By January 1955, Stephens was the Victorian, then Australian, champion at three and six miles and a year later, he set a world record for six miles.

Allied with his undoubted talent was an equal ability to confound. "He was a cheerful sort of bloke," says Landy, "but he was very erratic with his performances ... when he wanted to he could really burn. He was a great talent."

Joe Galli wrote that a feature of Stephens's running was his relaxation. "It has to be seen to be believed. Seemingly, there is no effort to his running. He bowls along, feet barely off the track and giving virtually no back-kick. His stride is almost a shuffle. Yet it is an extremely effective shuffle; it takes him along like a surge of flood water, winning him races against good men by astounding margins. Nothing appears to happen to Stephens in these surges; the tempo of arms and legs looks the same. Yet he is moving faster!"

Stephens had a milk round and was quickly dubbed "The Flying Milko". Geoff Warren tells how his mates used to reckon the seven-mile round had several essential elements of training built into it. "We reckoned that [with] the training every morning for some hours, and the lifting, his job gave him the work he needed. I think there was no-one more surprised than Dave when it transferred to success on the track."

Stephens attended the World Youth Congress Games in Bucharest in 1953 and struck up a friendship with Emil Zatopek. He visited the champion in Czechoslovakia and came back with some written training schedules. Zatopek mentioned the young

Australian in a 1955 interview on the emerging generation of track distance runners. "Stephens, who still writes to me, was perhaps the biggest surprise," Zatopek said. "I did not expect such a great improvement from him as he made last year. I must say it is possible that Australians are justified in regarding him as their future long-distance 'hope'." Stephens was also influenced by Cerutty, completing the Zatopek, Cerutty, Perry connection.

In turn, he influenced others. Bruce Simmons, a Melbourne runner who was a friend of Ron Clarke's, recalls training with Stephens at Caulfield Racecourse. Stephens wore light slippers held securely on his feet by elastic garters. One by one, the lesser runners copied him. After Stephens won a race, he was asked about his unusual choice of footwear. "Can't afford shoes," he replied, whereupon a Melbourne sports store supplied him with a few pairs. One by one, again without a word being exchanged, Simmons and his colleagues threw the slippers back under their beds.

» the senior title, [the] junior mile was won by a skinny, spindle-legged sixteen year old from Western Australia in 4:21.8, heralding the arrival of Herb Elliott on the Australian athletic scene."

Elliott beat Ron Clarke easily in the mile and also won the 880 yards, far ahead of Clarke and another highly-regarded young Victorian, Doug Henderson. He ran Australian junior records in both. Later that year, Cerutty visited Elliott's Perth school and "discovered" him, predicting that Elliott would run a four-minute within two years. The master coach may have been going through a lean patch, but he still knew the value of a good yarn.

Later that year, Elliott broke bones in his foot when he dropped the end of a piano while moving it. It kept him out of the pre-Olympic year and exposure to senior competition at possibly too young an age. Landy has no doubt as to Elliott's ability, however, even at that age. "He was a super-talent. Herb Elliott was a colossal runner. He would have been very competitive with the athletes today, very competitive."

Across the Pacific, Wes Santee finished his Marine Corps basic training late in 1954. In the 1955 US indoor season, he featured in a series of indoor miles against domestic rival Fred Dwyer and Danish star Gunnar Nielsen. Santee won at Boston ahead of Nielsen in a world indoor record 4:03.8, but a week later Nielsen won the famed Wanamaker mile at New York's Madison Square Garden, beating Dwyer and Santee in 4:03.6. On 2 April 1955, at the Texas Relays in Austin, Santee raced outdoors for the first time. On his own, he ran through 440 in 59.2, 880 in 2:00.0 and the three-quarter mile mark in 3:01.0. He picked up a little, but not enough, breaking the tape in 4:00.5, a new American record but short of his goal of four minutes.

Santee had now run 4:00.5, 4:00.6 and 4:00.7. Had he run something with a three in front, it is safe to say that his exact time, like Bannister's on 6 May 1954, would have been drowned out by sustained cheering, too. But Santee was not to get another chance.

Within two months, a San Francisco newspaper was reporting that Santee was under investigation for accepting excess expense money from a series of US meetings. He was banned from competition. He expected to win on appeal, but early in 1956, the Melbourne Olympic year, the life ban was upheld.

So Santee joined Bannister and Landy in retirement, only, unlike them, he *was* retired, rather than leaving the sport permanently or temporarily of his own free will.

Now, inevitably, others started to approach four minutes. Fittingly, Bannister was present to witness the next sub-four minute mile. Just as fittingly, one of the men to go under four minutes was Chris Chataway, who had played an integral role in Bannister's raced and provided an important competitive stimulus for John Landy in his world record race.

The occasion for the fourth four-minute mile race was the British Games at the White City Stadium on 28 May 1955. Chataway, the Empire Games three miles gold medallist, in case anyone had noticed, was on the line. His fastest mile remained the 4:04.4 he ran behind Landy in Turku. Joining him was Brian Hewson, a young Londoner who had so far focused mainly on the half mile. It was also his first real race of the 1955 season. Hewson had come under Franz Stampfl's guidance when his original club coach at Mitcham Athletics Club fell ill. He joined the group of Stampfl athletes — Brasher, Chataway and Bannister among them — in training sessions at the Duke of York Barracks in London's exclusive Chelsea.

"It wasn't open to the public," Hewson recalled on a visit to Melbourne for the 50th anniversary of the 1956 Olympic Games. "Just a few of the athletes, or friends of the athletes, with Franz went there. It was just like being in a village, not central London." Hewson found that Stampfl's greatest asset was his ability to instil belief into his charges. "He inspired me; he made me believe in myself. You've got to believe you can do it."

Laszlo Tabori was also on the starting line. The Hungarian athlete had run 4:05.2 in 1954, but was regarded as only the third best miler in his club. His club, however, was the Budapest Honved club, the army-backed club that had also been the basis of the famous Hungarian football (soccer) team of the 1950s. The race was intended to follow the prototype set by Bannister and the two Chrises at Oxford the year before. Replacing Brasher as the rabbit for the first half mile was Alan Gordon. He led through the first lap in a tick under 60 seconds and the second in 2:00.8.

If it started as a set-up, the British Games mile turned into a race. When Gordon started to struggle to hold the pace, Hewson was supposed to take the lead. But he hesitated, losing valuable time and momentum. Finally, he surged ahead and led at the bell in 3:02. Chataway was half a second behind and Tabori followed a step back in 3:02.7. Now, like Landy hearing and fearing Chataway behind him in Turku, or Landy striving to shake Bannister off in Vancouver, racing instinct took over. Hewson pushed the pace along the back straight, Chataway beside him and Tabori at his shoulder. Hewson still held his half-second edge at 1500 metres but, with 80 metres left, Tabori dashed past. The Hungarian went on to win by five yards, Chataway catching Hewson on the line for second. The times were: 3.59.0 for Tabori and 3:59.8 for the two British runners. They had become the third, fourth and fifth members of the sub-four minute mile club.

Others were clearly poised to follow. As ever, the emphasis in Europe was as much on the 1500 as the mile. In Helsinki at the end of July, two Hungarians and two Finns faced each other in a Finland–Hungary 1500 match (the battle of the indecipherable languages, perhaps?).

Rozsavolgyi and Iharos shared the pace, swiftly leaving Olavi Vuorisalo and Matti Huttunen behind. It was Rozsavolgyi at 400 (56.9), Iharos at 800 (1:55.7) and 1200 (2:57.2). Iharos was slowing, but he held on strongly to win in 3:40.8, taking a full second off the world record Landy had set in Turku (though Landy did not sprint to the 1500 line, of course).

Just over a month later, in Oslo, Tabori and Gunnar Nielson equalled the new world record, Tabori just getting the win as both men were given the same time.

Jim Bailey, who had made the Australian team for the Vancouver Empire Games in the 880 but been injured and run out in the heats, had somehow found himself on scholarship at the University of Oregon. Unorthodox in nature and erratic in his training, Bailey had worked consistently for the first time in his career under the supervision of Oregon coach Bill Bowerman. He won the US national collegiate mile title in 1955 in 4:05.6, a substantial improvement on his Australian best. Bailey's mercurial nature would again come to the fore throughout a tumultuous Olympic year in 1956.

Landy may have been off the scene, but he was hardly out of the news 18 months out from the Melbourne Olympics. In June 1955, he was invested as a Member of the Order of the British Empire in a ceremony at Government House. There was also the great cereal packet controversy. As Landy's film star status continued undiminished, a cereal company used his image on the packet of one of its products. Landy explained to the Victorian Amateur Athletic Association that he had not consented to the use of his picture and that the firm's manager had been asked to cease using it, but had refused. He and his family had sought legal advice.

Another, more significant, change occurred in Melbourne that year. Franz Stampfl, who had been interned in Australia during the war, accepted a full-time coaching position at the University of Melbourne. His position was a joint venture between the university's Department of Physical Education and the Victorian Amateur Athletic Association (report of the VAAA to the 65th annual meeting, 23 May 1956). Melbourne now had the world record holder in the mile (Landy), the coach who had master-minded two of the four sub-four minute mile races ever run (Stampfl), the charismatic and inspirational Cerutty, and was host of the following year's Olympic Games. It could truly claim to be the epicentre of world middle-distance running. When Stampfl arrived in Melbourne on 11 August, almost exactly a year to the day since Bannister had beaten Landy in Vancouver, he was inevitably asked about Landy's future. Stampfl said that Landy was still a young man with potential for improvement and he saw no reason why he should not make a successful comeback. "I wish I could get the chance to coach him," he told journalists as he inspected Olympic Park. "John Landy is still the world's greatest miler. I'd love to see him come back for the Games next year," Stampfl said.

Landy remained coy about his intentions. By August, rumours that he was training at Timbertop were circulating in Melbourne. *The Age*'s Bruce Welch rang to check. "I have been keeping fit," Landy told him. "I have a run now and then, but I am not doing any special training. I cannot play football here and running is about the only way to keep fit."

Olympic fever was finally starting to build in Melbourne. The Hungarians — Tabori, Iharos and Rozsavolgyi — were coming to Melbourne late in 1955 with coach Mihaly Igloi to race and inspect the Olympic city. Three Americans, sprinter Bobby Morrow, shot putter Parry O'Brien and half-miler Lon Spurrier, were coming to New Zealand and Australia in January 1956. These athletes wanted to see the faraway city that was hosting the Olympics. But what really caused Australians to focus on the 1956 Olympic Games was the very real threat to take the Games away.

Several years' bickering over venues, delays in construction and — probably — the simple wish that the Games had been awarded to a city closer to home led IOC president Avery Brundage to threaten to move the Olympics during an unannounced trip to Melbourne in 1955. Calling the successful bidders "a group of pretty smart Melbourne citizens", Brundage suggested they had hoodwinked the IOC. "I don't know how they did it," he said. "For six years we have had nothing but squabbling, changes of management and bickering. Melbourne has a deplorable record in its preparation for the Games — promises and promises."

Subsequently, Brundage would boast variously that he had thrown a "hand grenade" and an "atomic bomb" that had galvanised the organising committee into action. Even in those far-off days, there was probably no real prospect of the Games being moved elsewhere on less than 18 months' notice.

Up until the Brundage visit, no-one had got terribly excited about the Olympic Games, says John Landy. "It didn't really impinge on people. We went through 1952–53, with people almost saying 'so what'. There was no fervour, no PR to build it up. It was only when it got very close that people said 'Geez, we're putting on an Olympic Games.' When I was running well in '54 the quest for the four-minute mile was paramount; nobody seemed to be worried about the Olympic Games. When it got to '55, things really started to hot up."

Brundage's grenade may have made a loud explosion, but it probably was more a case of venting pent-up frustrations or internal IOC politics than any real concern that Melbourne would not be able to do the job. In any case, things settled down after he left.

Meanwhile, things were starting to happen at Timbertop. Perched at the foot of the Australian Alps, just under 200 kilometres northeast of Melbourne, the campus is isolated. It is also undulating to downright hilly. Even today, advice to parents of prospective students suggests the students prepare by getting in a few walks or, better still, runs over hilly terrain, because there is not too much that is flat.

Into this environment, at the end of January 1955, came John Landy. Physically and mentally, he was in need of a break. "I ran a few races … but they were pretty disappointing. I decided to give it away, with the options of it either being permanently or that I might come back for the 1956 Olympics. It was decision-making time. I'd run out of steam. I'd been running continuously since the end of November 1953 to August 1954 — non-stop, competing, overseas and so forth, and I think I just went into a flat period."

Strange things began to happen in the sub-alpine environment. Landy, who has a great love of the outdoors, began to deconstruct his passion for physical activity, as expressed mainly in his running, and then reconstruct it in harmony with the surrounding environment. "When I went to Timbertop, I didn't do any running for a while. I had to take the kids on long hikes, that sort of thing. [Then] I started to run again and said, let's just see how it develops."

At home, Landy had Central Park on his doorstep and adapted his training to suit. He now did the same thing in the bush, though the options were much more restricted. He had choices in Melbourne, he had no choice but to use what was at hand at Timbertop.

"Conditions were, by any standards, very primitive. There was no flat ground. I arranged a program that was based on the terrain. I did a bit of physical exercise too, calisthenics, simple stretching, that sort of thing. But the process was based on three things — stamina, speed and strength. I felt if I could somehow quicken my sprinting, but at the same time get a lot of long running and build myself up physically, with exercises and so forth, it didn't really matter that I didn't have a track, or even flat ground."

Up and down, around the paddocks, and along the bush tracks Landy ran. He regularly covered a rugged six-mile cross-country course. He found one spot to do repetitions of just over a quarter-mile, albeit on a steep slope, and another, alongside a creek, where he could do short sprints. He also did 150-metre uphill sprints along one track, timing his stride so as to be able to hurdle a thick tree root that dissected it. "It worked absolutely excellently," said Landy. "I was going back to the way I originally started and [the way I] ran so well in 1952–53, training intuitively. Later I went through a period of always wanting to run on tracks, and timing everything I did, [but] this was going back to the basics."

Landy knew he was getting fit. It doesn't take a rocket scientist to realise that. He knew he had a bit of speed there, but what is speed to a mile world record holder? How fit was he? How fast?

His resolve to run in Melbourne was firming. "About halfway through the year I thought, I'll see how I go," but he was still reluctant to commit "unless I was really able to demonstrate that I could stand up to a hard season, but also that I was running faster and therefore I'd be able to be in at the kill in a likely fast finish."

Landy's attitude to press inquiries was starting to soften. Publicly, he was indicating that he would test himself with a view to having a go; privately, the balance was probably the other way, he *would* have a go unless his test runs were a disaster.

He came back to Melbourne at the end of the school year in December and met the visiting Hungarians, but did not race against them.

Early in January 1956, Landy went to Olympic Park. He knew the groundsman — Dick Crossley, who was for a long time one of Victoria's top distance runners and a member of Cerutty's club in Malvern — and had sympathised with his efforts to produce a silk purse from a sow's ear of a track for so many years.

Now the Park had been re-surfaced with a world-class cinder track as part of the Olympic build-up. Landy put on a pair of spikes for the first time since 1954, and virtually the first time since he had raced Bannister. He ran a time trial over 880 yards, his first timed run of the year.

The result astounded him. "I said to Dick Crossley: 'I'll take this bloke [Lon] Spurrier on if I can run a good time.' I broke the Australian record. The first time I'd put spikes on for 13 months, I ran 880 yards in 1.51.0, in a trial, with absolute ease." (Lon Spurrier, an affable crew-cut American, had set the world record for 880 yards the previous year in California. He was the middle-distance representative who accompanied sprinter Bob Morrow and shot putter Parry O'Brien on a familiarisation visit to the southern hemisphere and, more specifically, Melbourne.)

At his 1952–54 best, Landy's credentials at the half mile were spotty. He had decent speed, a carryover from his days as a handy school sprinter, but had translated it to 880 only rarely. He had won the Australian title in 1953 and led Len McRae to a national record in 1954, but he had also finished a disappointing sixth to Jim Bailey in the 1954 national titles.

It was not the sort of background that would see him push a »

The Hungarians

From a socialist country they may have been, but that did not stop Wells, the irreverent sports cartoonist in *The Age*, portraying Sandor Iharos, Laszlo Tabori and Istvan Rozsavolgyi as "Kings of Speed" on their arrival in Melbourne.

The three Hungarians, guided by their enigmatic coach, Mihaly Igloi, swept all before them through 1955 and 1956. If a vacuum was created in world middle-distance running when Bannister retired and Landy took a year off, these three filled it to overflowing.

Iharos set world records at 1500 metres, 3000 metres, two miles, three miles and 5000 metres (twice) in 1955, and two more at six miles and 10,000 metres in 1956. Tabori equalled Iharos's record at 1500, before Rozsavolgyi sliced another fifth of a second from it to claim it on his own, albeit still for Hungary. "Rozsa", as he was invariably nick-named, also set a world mark for 2000 metres.

When Tabori and Iharos beat Dave Stephens in the first of three races on the new cinder track at Melbourne's Olympic Park in December 1955, a newspaper reported: "In their white uniforms, [the Hungarians] hung behind Australian distance champion Dave Stephens like two great birds waiting to swoop on their prey."

Swoop they did that night, but Stephens turned the tables on them in two more memorable races before the Hungarians completed their Olympic familiarisation trip.

Like Australia, Hungary punched above its weight in sporting terms. In Berlin in 1936, it was third on the Olympic medal table; fourth in London in 1948; third again in Helsinki in 1952; fourth in Melbourne; and in Rome in 1960, even after the full impact of the unsuccessful 1956 rebellion, still seventh.

Hungary's socialisation in 1949 grafted a central system on to an already successful sports tradition. In football, this created the legendary Army team, Honved FC; in athletics, it helped Igloi create his team at the same club.

Igloi's training, as much as he would discuss it, was

interval-based, though in greater quantity and over more varied distances than the traditional method. His system was as one with his person: he ruled, his runners followed. "Only my own conception of their work is valid," Igloi wrote in the program notes for meetings in Melbourne in December 1955. "I make an evaluation of my runners every day, every week. If one system works well I try it on others. I never plan more than a day ahead. Everything depends on the athlete's daily condition — and only the trainer knows that."

People in Melbourne did not care much about this in 1955. Having become accustomed to seeing John Landy challenge an unseen world in a series of solo runs over the previous two years, now they acclaimed Stephens "the Flying Milko" as he took on, and beat, the world's best in front of their eyes.

The first meeting, over 3000 metres on 10 December, went to script. Iharos made the race, but Tabori took the win on the line, 8:47.3 to 8:47.4, with both leaving Stephens (8:52.0) behind in the final sprint. Rozsavolgyi handled an 880 yards field easily, winning in 1:52.0. Landy, who had come down to Olympic Park to meet and talk to the visitors, commented: "We've seen the Hungarians and we know just how great they are." It also showed the standard he would need to reach should he come back, Landy added. "It won't just be a matter of my running 4:02 for the mile here. I'll have to be down to 3:58 or 3:59."

Yet three days later, Stephens reversed the result over 5000 metres, beating Tabori by 30 metres and Iharos by another 25 in 14:07.2. It was 27 seconds slower than Iharos' world record set at the end of the European season a couple of months earlier, but convincing nonetheless. "Stephens Now Among World's Best," trumpeted one headline, and Igloi commented: "If he can maintain the same rate of improvement next year as this, he can win the Olympic 5000 metres." Four days later, Stephens won again over three miles, this race billed "the decider". Now *The Age* ran a front-page picture of a happy Stephens with his arms around Iharos' neck after the finish of the race. "Stephens is a truly great runner," Igloi said now. "Iharos was not at his best but we have no excuses."

Dave Power finished third in a race as notable for the bizarre changes of pace as anything else. It was slow, until Stephens threw in a 60-second lap coming up to two miles. He slowed again, allowing Iharos and Power to pass. Seemingly beaten, Stephens charged back in the last lap, leaving Iharos to shake his head in wonderment.

"Rozsa" and Tabori made sure the visitors did not leave their last Australian meeting empty-handed, finishing first and second in the mile. Rozsavolgyi won in 4:03.0, with Tabori just edging yet another emerging Australian — Merv Lincoln — for second place as both clocked 4:04.6.

For Lincoln, it was an improvement of over seven seconds. More was to come as the Melbourne Olympic year got under way.

» world record holder close, but a couple of days after his trial run, he did precisely that, jumping Spurrier at the bell, leading into the straight and just failing to hold him off at the line. Both were given the same time of 1:51.8. "He beat me by that much," Landy says, pinching his fingers. "[It was a] very slow first lap of 56–57 seconds and ended up running 1.51.8 for 880. I think the point was that I was able to get to a very high level of performance by my standards, without any aids whatsoever, not even running in spikes, not even running on a track, which really made me think about physical conditioning for running.

"I'd got to a stage which I hadn't got to in previous years with a more systematic, timed approach to training. I'd just gone back to basics in the bush and, all of a sudden ... I was running very well. I had it both ways: speed and fitness. I was quick and I was fit."

10

Highs and Lows
on the Road to Melbourne

Who would have thought it? On 25 January 1956 — a day before Australia Day — a world distance record was run at Olympic Park in Melbourne. And the athlete was *not* John Landy.

Dave Stephens, the irrepressible "Flying Milko", ran 27:54.0 for six miles, four seconds under the record held by the great Emil Zatopek. Had Stephens run on for an extra 376 yards, there's no doubt he would have broken the great man's record for 10,000 metres, too. Zatopek had set the six-mile mark en route to 10,000 in Brussels eighteen months earlier. Les Perry was second to Stephens, some 90 seconds behind. Geoff Warren was third, a further twelve seconds back.

The record made front-page news. *The Age* ran a picture of Stephens breaking the tape and another of a section of the small crowd that stayed after a women's invitation meeting to watch the race, which was for the Victorian title. It was bitterly cold, the report said, with a strong wind. Across the other side of the continent, in Perth, it was 106°F (41°C).

"I'm shocked how easy it was," Stephens said, adding that he could have run even faster. "I ran a lane wide for the last three miles because the track was so badly cut up." He ran 13:59.0 for the first three miles, 13:55.0 for the second.

Training mate Fred Lester had talked him into having a crack at the record, despite the conditions, Stephens said, writing him a schedule for 28 minutes. Lester had emigrated from Germany to Australia in the 1930s and was a national-class marathoner. (He was secretary-general of the Victorian Marathon Club, the club founded by Cerutty, Perry and others to promote distance running, for almost the entire period from 1961 to 1990.)

The race was on a Wednesday night. Stephens had rested up. "I knocked off work as a milkman on Monday morning," he said at the time. "I've done nothing but sleep and train since. I think the rest helped me. I hope my old mate Emil will be pleased. You know it's a case of pupil beats master."

Zatopek would have heard about the loss of his world record pretty quickly. If Stephens — who had corresponded with him since visiting Czechoslovakia in 1953 — did not telephone to tell him, Les Perry probably would have. Had neither done so, Joe Galli would have sent the news via his Czech journalist contacts.

Bruce Welch wrote that it was the greatest performance in Australian athletics history. Understandable, but this under-valued Landy's single-handed pursuit of excellence in the mile. Once again, John Landy had been beaten to an honour. The man who had thrilled crowds of up to 20,000 with his world record mile chases at Olympic Park deserved the honour of establishing the first distance world record there. Just as Bannister had beaten him to the world record and the first sub-four minute mile, now a fellow countryman deprived him of another accolade. Such is life, Landy would have said, and been genuinely pleased for Dave Stephens.

Anyway, if there was now a 1956 Olympic bandwagon rolling in place of the one-man band of earlier years, John Landy was still in the vanguard. Like Steve Moneghetti and Cathy Freeman years later, Landy struck some sort of special chord with Melbourne spectators.

The three morning newspapers had given him poster headlines after his comeback run. "LANDY AMAZING HALF-MILE", screamed *The Sun*, the mass-ciculation tabloid. *The Argus* opted for the simpler: "THE GREAT LANDY". *The Age* landed somewhere in between with the obvious, but true: "BRILLIANT COMEBACK BY LANDY". One report referred to him as "the mighty Landy".

His performance against Spurrier — especially off such a limited preparation, convinced Landy he could do well at the Melbourne Games. "This run has shown me where I stand," Landy said. "It has given me the incentive to go on and prepare for the Games. I am really delighted."

Ten days later, an interclub record for three miles consolidated Landy's intentions. In yet another solo run at Olympic Park, he clocked 13:39.0, lapping every other runner in the race except Les Perry, who was almost 300 metres behind. "What doubts Landy might have had about his ability to get back into his world-record breaking form of 1954 after his tussle with American Lon Spurrier on 4 January were dispelled on Saturday," Bruce Welch reported in *The Age*. What the race demonstrated yet again was Landy's ambition to run fast times with or without the stimulus of competition. His time was less than two seconds slower than Stephens had run a few weeks earlier in defeating the Hungarians.

Olympic fever was building, too. The same edition of *The Age* reported that swimmer Lorraine Crapp had shattered the world records for 800 metres and 880 yards at the North Sydney Pool the day after Landy's run. She had broken the world record for 440 yards in the same pool a week earlier. And, in a front-page story, the paper reported that contractors building the new Olympic grandstand at the Melbourne Cricket Ground had agreed to a July completion deadline following an agreement on payment of overtime to workers who, in turn, had agreed to work a six-day week. Total additional cost of the overtime agreement was put as £19,100, a pittance by today's standards. With the agreement of a deadline, however, clearly even the much-maligned contractors and building unions were catching Olympic fever!

Around the same time, 22 November 1956, the Games' opening ceremony day, was declared a public holiday. It was also suggested that the Melbourne Cup, Melbourne's stop-the-city horse race held on the first Tuesday of November each year, could in 1956 be held on a Saturday to minimise any clash with the Games. Ultimately, the Cup stayed put.

Landy was to run the mile at the Victorian championships three days later. It was to be his first mile race since he lost to Bannister in Vancouver, but he made it known it would be a different type of race. He would not lead. "I will not race against the clock … I will not do a fast time unless someone else sets a fast pace for the first half-mile."

Perhaps Landy feared that Lincoln, who was coached by Stampfl, would apply similar tactics against him as Bannister had in Vancouver — simply follow the pace and hope to capitalise. Lincoln had improved almost seven seconds in his race against the Hungarians. Who knew how much more he had in him?

Certainly Landy was preparing for the sort of race he expected in Melbourne at the end of the year. "It is suicide to take the lead before the half-mile in international racing."

On Saturday 28 January 1956, the day of the race, the evening paper, *The Herald*, ran a front-page story by "a staff reporter". The story was intended to provide a "presence" on the big race for the early editions; it ran alongside the race report in later ones. The "staff reporter" reported he rang Landy at home that morning. "He was in bed when I phoned him at 9:45am, but he showed no sign of pre-race temperament."

Think about this for a minute. A reporter rings on the morning of a significant race, not the athletics reporter, whom Landy would have known, but a reporter from the news desk. And Landy gets out of bed to answer the phone. Imagine this happening with Craig Mottram? You can't. Indeed, it is difficult to conceive of it happening with contemporaries like Bannister or Santee, either. But that was John Landy. Like Zatopek, like Perry, always open and available to any and all questioners and questions.

That afternoon, Landy would give Australia the first sub-four minute mile on its soil. After six near-misses, he ran 3:58.6, faster than Bannister's Oxford breakthrough, faster than Bannister's winning time in Vancouver (which, in any case, was obviated by Landy), faster than Tabori, Chataway and Hewson in London — the only faster time his own world record run in Turku.

Yet it was not a "Landy run". From the gun, Landy dropped to the back of the field rather than employ his customary dash to the front. After a lap, he was tucked on the inside of Geoff Warren in seventh place, with Lincoln just behind. Ahead of them were Tony Guinan, a young runner from the Sandringham club; Robbie Morgan-Morris, another Cerutty protégé; John Stavely; and Ron Clarke. (The other runners in the race were Don Macmillan, Les Trigg from South Australia, Melbourne University duo Tom Roberts and John Howes, and Tom Worrell.) Guinan ran the first lap in 58 seconds, with Landy at least a full second behind. At the half-mile, Guinan (2:01) still showed the way, but was about to surrender the lead to Landy. Then, and still with a lap to go at 3:01, Lincoln was within a few yards and holding on.

Landy struck with a surge down the back-straight and sprinted right away in the final 100 metres to win. He covered the last lap in 57.6 seconds, easily the fastest final lap he had ever produced in a mile race. At 1500 — in an Australian record (which had to be set *in* Australia) 3:43.2 — he was actually 1.4 seconds slower than in his world record race. At the finish, the margin was only half that.

Ten thousand spectators packed onto the Olympic Park terraces to witness the first sub-four minute mile in their country. They saw one world record, too: Clarke was third in 4:07.6, a world junior record. He also broke the 1500 record en route.

Landy told them he could have gone faster. "I'm certain I can do better. I would have been happier if the time had been 3:57.0. The way I started, I thought I had no chance of winning … but I finished well and that pleased me most." Lincoln, who took himself to the verge of four minutes with 4:00.6 in second place, put it simply: "I tried to have a go at John with about half a lap to go, but I had no possible chance of catching him. He's too good." Stampfl acclaimed Landy "the nearest thing to a certainty for the Olympic 1500 metres".

Landy outlined his fresh approach to *Age* athletics writer Bruce Welch. "I did all my thinking about running when I was up in the country last year," he said. "Now I have a plan, more a set of principles and when you adopt something like that you have to adhere to it strictly." Welch reported Landy was "more relaxed, he sleeps better, he has coordinated his body better to respond to his iron, superbly-disciplined will". This last observation must have been Welch's. It is hard to imagine it coming from Landy. Though he *was* quoted as follows: "I have achieved a peace of mind, and training is even reasonably enjoyable now. There's no strain."

At a stroke, too, he had reversed the public image of the Melbourne Olympic Games. Publicity had been dominated by union disputes, construction delays and petty squabbling, culminating in Avery Brundage's fulminations about taking the Games elsewhere. Now, Landy had put the focus back on sport. Wilfred Kent Hughes, the organising committee chairman, enthused: "[He] is worth £100,000 to us in publicity."

Landy, in any case, had not yet completed his burst of New Year activity. He ended the first month of the 1956 Melbourne Olympic year in the same manner as he had started it — with a personal best over 880 yards. "On the basis of my 3:58.6, I should come up like a rocket," he told *The Argus*. He did, too. Running in the final of the Victorian championship, Landy ran 1:50.4, almost a full second and a half faster than against Spurrier, to beat a resurgent Don Macmillan and Doug Henderson. At 800 metres, just over five yards short of 880 yards, he was timed at 1:49.8. Both times were the fastest ever run in Australia.

Landy still found a nit to pick. "I still cannot get started properly in the first lap," he told *The Age*, suggesting that he might have to do some running against the clock to pick up his speed.

Even 50 years later, there is still a tinge of ambivalence when he talks about the 800. "I could have run much better over 800, but I struggled with my first lap," he said in October 2006. "I used to run 56 for the first lap. If you want to run a fast time in the 800 you've got to run two seconds faster for the first lap than the second. I was running 56, and even slower, and coming home in 54."

Macmillan's form was also encouraging, the report predicting he would be a "formidable opponent by the Australian titles in March". Dave Stephens, still feeling the effects of his world record five days earlier, ran the three miles without pushing himself. His 13:47.8 saw him three seconds ahead of Les Perry and well clear of Geoff Warren.

While the return of Landy and Stephens's world record naturally dominated the news reports, the rest of the country was not standing still. In Sydney, Al Lawrence was continuing his march to the Olympics; John Plummer had made a comeback to push for one last chance at an Olympic team; Dave Power had moved up in distance, with success. Alex Henderson remained a competitive threat in the 880 yards and the mile and newcomers Albie Thomas and Pat Clohessy were starting to make themselves noticed.

Power had won the first of what would be four national cross-country titles in Perth in 1954. The significance was that he beat Plummer, his mentor. The winning New South Wales team was made up largely of clubmates. "Dave Power and I ran against each other so many times," Plummer said in late 2006. "The first time he ever beat me was in Perth. He cleaned up there. [Of] the team of six who went to Perth to represent New South Wales, five were from Western Suburbs." Power won his second national cross-country title in Hobart in 1955.

As the pre-Olympic domestic season got under way a couple of months later, a surprising number of young men nurtured hopes of winning an Australian singlet in events from 800 metres to the marathon. It was certainly higher than the number many had foreseen a few years earlier. Al Lawrence reasoned at this stage that his best hopes lay in the 1500. Landy was "retired" and not yet making serious noises about coming back. The mercurial Jim Bailey was at the University of Oregon and had won the US national collegiate title, Merv Lincoln had yet to emerge and he figured he had an edge on Plummer and Henderson. It seemed the most open event.

Or it did then. But a series of races in the early part of the 1955–56 season forced Lawrence to reconsider. Pat Clohessy, christened (probably by Lawrence) the "Tamworth Flash", came down to Sydney and beat Power in an interclub three miles in a New South Wales record 13:47.8. At that stage, Dave Stephens was the only Australian to have run faster. A week later, Clohessy caught the train to Sydney for interclub again. This time he shook Lawrence's confidence, out-sprinting him in the mile in 4:12.2. A fortnight later, Lawrence got his own back — but only just. He needed a 56-second final lap to narrowly defeat Clohessy, 4:10.2 to 4:10.3.

Both Lawrence and Clohessy were invited to run against the visiting Hungarians, Lawrence in the 1500 and mile, Clohessy in the 5000. It would be a watershed for both. For Al Lawrence it was simple; he was outclassed by Rozsalvolgyi and Lincoln in the 1500.

On the Sunday following the third and last meeting involving the Hungarians, John Landy and his parents invited the athletes to a social gathering at Central Park Road. Late in the afternoon, the athletes decided (as serious runners inevitably do) to go for a light run across the road in Central Park. Lawrence stopped after a mile, feeling exhausted. On returning to their accommodation, Dave Power advised Lawrence to take a look at himself in the mirror. "My face and neck were covered in ugly red–blue spots," recalls Lawrence. So was the rest of his body. Lawrence had Rubella (also known as German measles).

But Lawrence had already come to the even more painful realisation that he was training for the wrong distance. "I did not have the basic speed to be a world-class miler and I did not possess the necessary ingredients to make the Australian team in the 1500 metres."

Clohessy, too, suffered some disillusionment against the Hungarians. Running barefoot on the grass — something he did only infrequently — in Tamworth a few days before the 5000 meeting, he trod on a thorn. The wound became infected and Clohessy's attempt to run in Melbourne caused the poison to spread through his system. It would be a year before he returned to full health and fitness.

Pat Clohessy was born in Melbourne in 1933. His father worked in the Postmaster General's Department and moved around as the postmaster at several NSW rural towns as Pat grew up. He began running at Muswellbrook, where he had a coach, then the family moved to Tamworth.

It was suggested to "Clo" (probably by Al Lawrence when he came to Sydney for some early races) that he contact Landy for training advice; thus began a relationship between Clohessy and Landy, mainly by correspondence, which would continue throughout Clohessy's career. Given that Clohessy went on to coach, his most famous pupil being world marathon champion and world record-holder Robert de Castella, it also was the start of a Landy legacy that would extend to the present day.

Landy's basic advice to Clohessy was to work on his fitness gradually, to adapt to his environment, to consider his rural isolation an asset rather than a handicap, and to think for himself rather than blindly follow the schedules he detailed in his letters. He outlined precisely what he did at Timbertop — like Zatopek, no secrets — and counselled him how best to combine the training for the mile and three miles with their conflicting demands on stamina and speed.

In Melbourne that December, however, the best thing Landy could do for Clohessy was get him to a good doctor to heal his foot. This Landy did, taking him to Dr John Bartram, an Olympic sprinter in 1948. (Bartram must have been his own best patient; he continued in general practice in Melbourne's eastern suburbs until 2006!)

Albie Thomas was making spectacular progress, too. With the Australian titles coming up in March (the final Olympic Trials would be later in the year), the chief selector for the New South Wales team risked provoking some ire in Melbourne when he said: "Victorians seem to think the three miles will be a match race between Landy and Stephens. But Sydney's little Albert [sic] Thomas will give them the shock of their lives. Thomas has run the fastest three miles in Australia this season.

"Stephens holds the Australian record, 13:31.8, but hasn't got near that this season. Landy just now is an unknown quantity as a three-miler, but I think he is capable of running 13:20. Thomas is capable of much better time than his 13:36 and he will hang on with Landy and Stephens. In doing so, his time must come down."

The NSW selector also pooh-poohed the notion that 21-year-old Thomas was being pushed too far, too quickly. "They kept runners in cotton-wool 30 years ago, but this is 1956 and athletes are proving every day that the harder they work the better their performances."

Thomas was working hard. Just turned 21, he had never even placed in a national title before. But he had a good competitive attitude. "The tactic I used," he said in 2006, "was to hang on as long as I could before I got dropped out the back door. I hung on, and hung on, and hung on a bit more until one day with 200 to go I was behind Power, or someone, and I had a go. And that was a state two mile record.

"You'd get improvement by trying to run with the good athletes, and they'd pull you out. The older one draws you out and you get some experience and learning from them. And that's what I got from Perry and those."

Thomas had not done much at state level, either, but he started to in 1956. In late January 1956 Al Lawrence recovered from his measles to win a classic state six miles title from Thomas and Dave Power. The three of them were side by side through the last lap before Lawrence and Thomas edged away from Power. Lawrence won in 28:39, with Thomas 0.8 behind and Power a further six seconds back. After that, Lawrence won the three miles from Power and John Plummer.

But Landy fired a shot across the three-milers' bows. He had already run his "easy" 13:39. Now he lined up in an interclub race. Paced for six laps by a young Ron Clarke, Landy reeled off consecutive — and remarkably consistent — miles of 4:29, 4:29.5 and 4:28.9, beating his nearest rival, Ron Blackney, by almost a minute. His 13:27.4 took over four seconds off Dave Stephens's record.

The "milko" was on hand to congratulate Landy. "I don't mind how fast John runs. If he can make me run faster I will be happy for it will give me opposition," he said. Landy praised Clarke's contribution. "There's the boy who's going to be better than me," he told the press. "He's really got great possibilities. Clarke got me going. When he dropped out I felt terrible — just like a man on a desert island. And at times I wanted to quit."

Once again, though, Landy was running the second half of a race out on his own and he wondered what he might do with competition. "I still can't get the best out of myself during a race," he said, "and when I am out by myself I tend to say, 'What the heck.' I might go better with someone to beat." (Note that Landy was still full of his new-found confidence — he said someone to *beat*, not *race*.) In 2006, Landy said: "I found the three miles hard to do. But I was confident that if I could hold the pace for three miles, or 5000 metres, I'd be quite damaging …"

Damaging indeed. Dave Stephens was already thinking he would have to break the world record to beat Landy if the latter ran the national three-mile title. Sandor Iharos held the three mile world record at 13:14.2, but Stephens told *The Sun*'s Jack Dunn that even beating that time might not be enough to win a race against Landy. "Even if John makes me run 29 seconds faster than ever before for the distance, and I am beaten, it does not matter," Stephens said. "If I can run 20 seconds faster that will do me. It will not matter if I finish first or last if I can improve that much against Landy."

What Landy's run, or more exactly, the ease of it, did ignite was the debate over which event was best for him. Landy admits it was the possibility of winning the longer race that interested him. "I would probably be the fastest man in the Olympic 5000 and I must say I was quite interested in running it. I didn't like the event, frankly, but it seemed to me I could do both the 1500 and 5000."

In fact, the double would have been very difficult, given the Olympic timetable. A common rule of thumb athletes apply in deciding whether to attempt a double is that their stronger event should be the first of the two. Further, an athlete running two events because he or she reckons they can win both, or win the first and have a good chance in the second, is a world away from deciding to run two events so that they might enhance their chances of winning one. The latter way of thinking leads classically to falling between stools!

For Landy, if his stronger event was held to be the 1500, he faced a 5000 heat and final first, with the final on the day before the 1500 heats. All of this was long before the time of helpful adjustments to the schedule to accommodate star athletes, of course. Landy admits now the dilemma cost him, and describes trying to prepare for both as "the seeds of my problems. In trying to do both I probably over-trained. I ran into Achilles tendon trouble and I think it was that ambition to run the two events that was probably the mistake I made. I should have concentrated on the 1500."

For the moment, however, Landy was on a roll. He would clash with Lincoln and Clarke in the mile at the Australian championships on 10 March 1956. "I'll do my best to make it a sizzler for you," he promised in one preview article. Another predicted the race would be "one of the greatest sporting events to occur in this country".

Indeed, it was, but not in the sense in which *Sun* journalist Jack Dunn was suggesting when he wrote those words. Like everyone else, Dunn expected that given reasonable weather (which he got) and a reasonable pace (which he didn't get) John Landy would better his own world record.

The 1956 Australian mile title, as Landy says to this day, was "a much ballyhooed event". Indeed, it was voted "The Sporting Moment of the 20th Century" in a turn-of-the-millennium national poll. The finishing time — a mediocre 4:04.2 and the only post-Turku mile John Landy ran in which he did *not* break four minutes — were secondary to his extraordinary action within the race.

The most vivid post-race picture is not one of world record celebration — much as the 20,000 crowd would have loved it — but of Landy squatting on the infield inquiring anxiously of Ron Clarke's wellbeing, flanked by a St John's Ambulance officer and Dr John Bartram on one side and the Governor of Victoria, Sir Dallas Brookes, on the other.

Landy did not lead from the gun. That task fell to Robbie Morgan-Morris, a young runner who had trained with Landy and was a protégé of Cerutty. Adrenalin took him through a first lap of 59 seconds, prudence saw him slow to 63 for the next lap for a half-mile time of 2:02. So far, so good and not that dissimilar to the earlier 3:58.6 in which Tony Guinan had led in 58 and then 2:01. But this was the national championship and others were lurking, too, including Plummer and Alex Henderson.

Coming into the straight on the third lap, Clarke led Landy, who had Lincoln to his outside. Henderson was next on the inside and Plummer looking to improve on the outside. Still the pace was not on.

Forty yards later, Clarke was down, Plummer leaping away from him into the lead, Henderson and Landy attempting to pass either side of the spreadeagled Clarke and Lincoln now at the back of the group of five and the most severely checked.

No-one knows who caused the fall. Reports were, and remain, conflicting. It is not important anyway, because what followed was truly remarkable. In leaping Clarke, Landy caught him with his spikes, gashing his right arm. Now, having regained his balance, he trotted back to check on him. It was, Landy says, "one of those instinctive things you do in a hundredth of a second. You might say 'embedded instinct' — what you'd do in a car crash or something."

In his own account, Landy attributes a lot of the responsibility to himself. He says he doesn't get that excited about the incident, or its implications. "In fact, I get quite embarrassed because it shouldn't have ever happened. I didn't contribute to it directly in the sense that I didn't trip Ron Clarke up, but I *should* have been leading the race. This was one of the situations where I thought, 'I can't keep doing this thing, leading from early in the race.'

"I probably could have broken the world record if I had gone all out, but the point was I felt that would have been getting nowhere in preparation for the Olympic Games. I thought, 'I'm not going to run the 1500 metres like this in the Games. I've got to get some feel in practice races for coming home very fast.'

"Clarke fell out in front of me. It all happened pretty quickly and I had to get into long jumping mode. My spikes tore down his shoulder and arm. He had a tetanus shot after the race. People thought I went back because he fell, but I spiked him pretty seriously in the arm. He yelled out. Instinctively I stopped."

As he bent down to Clarke, Clarke yelled at Landy to keep running. In regaining his running, Landy took a couple of steps on the grass infield. Now, conscious of Neil Robbins's fate in the six miles at the 1953 national championships in Perth, he was fearful he would be disqualified.

"Clarke yelled out 'get going'," Landy says. "The field was well ahead (some say 70 metres, but it was probably 30 or 40). I panicked. I was also ashamed that it had happened, because I felt in a roundabout way that I had probably contributed to it by not actually doing what people expected me to do, to go for the world record. So I had a whole lot of mixed emotions. I thought 'I'll try to redress it, because there were 25,000 people there, I'll have to redress it, I'll do the best I can but I expect to be disqualified anyway.'"

However, history would tell another story. Amazingly, Landy was back in contact with the leaders within less than 200 metres. He then coasted (his word), before unleashing his final sprint past Henderson. "The last lap wasn't particularly fast. It might have been about 55 seconds, but there was a period when I actually coasted. I probably had to run about 26 seconds for 200 metres to get near the field, then I coasted. But I came home very fast. I ran the last 109 metres [the difference between 1500 and the mile], in 14.5 seconds which is very fast, even today.

"So it wasn't that I ran flat out for the remaining distance, because once I had the field in my sights, I had a 'rest'. Surprisingly Merv, who should have won it, didn't have a good day. Henderson was out in front; he must have thought that he was going to win it."

If the others were surprised Landy did not set the pace, they should not have been. He had told Bruce Welch (reported in that morning's *Age*): "I will not set the pace. Why should I? Why should I make myself a sitting shot?"

The incident had a huge impact, epitomised by the reaction of Harry Gordon. Now the official Australian Olympic historian after a long career as a newspaper executive, Harry Gordon was then a sportswriter for the Melbourne *Sun* and he wrote an open letter praising Landy's sportsmanship. "The fellows in the press box don't have many heroes," it began. "Often they help to make them — but usually they know too much about them to believe in them. Yours was the classic sporting gesture. It was a senseless piece of chivalry — but it will be remembered as one of the finest actions in the history of sport."

In his column in *The Argus*, Franz Stampfl declared it "the most gallant thing I've seen in a lifetime of international athletics". A prominent Melbourne clergyman echoed that view. The Reverend Alan Moyes, who was there on the day, said later that it was "the most incredibly stupid, beautiful, foolish, gentlemanly act I have ever seen".

Landy says now: "People see more in it than it deserves. Harry Gordon, who is a great writer, saw more in it, but other scribes hardly commented on it. I thought that was the way it would be treated." You get the distinct impression that what Landy regrets is not the incident itself or his reaction, but the fuss that it caused and continues to cause over 50 years later.

Two days after the race, despite a sore foot and ankle as a result of treading on the track plinth during the fall's aftermath, Landy ran against Stephens in the three miles. For all the talk of a world record pace when they met, Stephens had struggled since his six miles world record. He had only done six hard training sessions in the six weeks since. Making things even, Landy was not the runner he had been two days previously. He took over in the second half of the race and won by almost 15 yards from Lawrence and Power, but he was uncharacteristically exhausted by the effort to run some 15 seconds slower than his recent national record.

Standing on the victory dais, Landy looked like a boxer who has just taken a solid body punch. "I was very tired, just putting one foot after another," he said later. Despite that, Landy said he intended to attempt both the 5000 and the 1500 at the Games later in the year.

No doubt Landy took his own counsel, but Franz Stampfl advanced the same view. Writing in *The Argus*, the coach commented that, despite the demanding competition schedule the double would demand at the Games, all Landy needed was "one more solid winter build-up and he will astonish the world". As it turned out, a solid winter build-up was one thing Landy would not have.

At the end of March, Landy was talking of running some cross-country races. Stories appeared in the press and he told Pat Clohessy in a letter: "I am contemplating running some cross-country races myself. I feel that with the long winter it may provide an added incentive. I am not sure about this … and I may slip off for a short holiday in May." Ironically, this was in the process of advising Clohessy not to race cross-country too frequently. In a further irony, the "short holiday" was an ill-fated racing trip Landy would undertake to the US.

Before all this, Landy ran 3:58.6 once again in a mile at Olympic Park on 7 April. The trend of VIPs of escalating importance watching Landy continued. This time it was The First Sea Lord, Earl Mountbatten who watched the race. Again, there was a dash across town, this time from the race meeting at Caulfield Racecourse. A hastily arranged "red carpet" of hessian bags was laid down for the earl, who surely had seen rougher conditions at sea.

"I never thought I'd see the day when an athlete could make a below-four minute mile look quite ordinary," Stampfl wrote in his newspaper column. "But John Landy did at Olympic Park on Saturday." Landy described himself as "a sort of rejuvenated plodder" and suggested his main target in the Games would be the 5000.

Four days after this race, the destination of John Landy's "short holiday" was revealed. Maurice Nathan, then a Melbourne City Councillor and chairman of the Victorian Promotions Committee

— top priority the 1956 Olympic Games — announced the star miler would run twice in California in May.

The trip was a ploy to counter the adverse publicity for the Games generated by IOC president Brundage the previous year. Landy was a huge name in the USA, where the mile was at least as big as it was in England, but no-one had yet run one in under four minutes. American fans had been frustrated by Santee's failure to win the race for the first sub-four, and outraged by his subsequent suspension. They had watched the Landy–Bannister race on television, enthralled.

What better way to redress Melbourne's image with influential American fans than to have the man who could make sub-four minute miles look "ordinary" come over and run the first such mile on American soil?

Nathan had floated the possibility of a visit late the previous year. He had the support of the premier of Victoria, Henry Bolte. The pair pressured Landy. "I was more than encouraged," says Landy. "Henry Bolte and the government were worried about negative publicity after Avery Brundage came out and said the Games should be taken away [from Melbourne] if things didn't improve. Things weren't going well and Maurice Nathan was terribly keen to get me to go. Bolte was aware of it, and supportive."

Pete Rozelle, later to become famous as the chief executive of the American National Football League, came to Australia to help persuade Landy. And Landy needed persuading. He had resumed his teaching position at Geelong Grammar. He was ready to begin his winter build-up to the Olympics. "Pete was a hell of a nice bloke. He came from California and when Bob Hope owned the Rams, the football team representing Los Angeles, he was the manager. Then he went to work in public relations with Ken Macker in San Francisco. They had the Qantas account. They obviously saw the value in getting me over there, because I had a name in America.

"They came out to Australia and really put the pressure on me. This was within two or three weeks of my last race of the Australian season. I thought, 'this isn't going to help at all'. I said, 'What's required?' and they said a four-minute mile would be great!"

Ultimately, Landy was persuaded. It is not hard to infer it was against his better judgement, even though he rationalised his way through it. The premier and Councillor Nathan farewelled him at a pre-departure dinner, also attended by the Lord Mayor of Melbourne and the US Consul-General. A low-key visit this was not!

The publicity round continued as soon as Landy set foot on US soil. He was feted, fawned over and all but overwhelmed. His every move was reported on two continents. Privately, the concerns were building. Landy was racing less than a week after his arrival — "I had three days to adjust". In Finland, he had had three weeks. The tracks were hard and he developed blisters on his feet. And Ron Delany, an Irishman attending Villanova University on the east coast, was added to the field. Delany was the form mile runner of the US season.

And the hustle and bustle of promotional appearances meant he had to draw up a rigid schedule to allow him to train. Regardless, every Melbourne paper featured the race on its posters. "Blistered Landy: I'll Beat Four Minutes," was one.

Strangely enough, this did reflect Landy's inner thoughts. "I was at the stage where I could routinely run sub four-minutes at will and I was confident I would do it." Jet lag, crowded schedule, blisters and all.

Landy's first American race, in the Los Angeles Coliseum, had been planned and promoted well. The race was slotted into the schedule for the dual meet between the two Californian sport powerhouse colleges, USC and UCLA or, as they were more formally known, University of Southern California and University of California at Los Angeles. "They got 41,000 people in the Coliseum, which they claimed was the biggest crowd ever, at that stage, to attend an athletics meeting in the US," says John Landy. Forty million more watched on television — the race being timed to follow the nationwide telecast of the famous Kentucky Derby.

All 40,041,000 of them got their great race, got America's first sub-four minute mile, saw John Landy break four minutes, saw an Australian win but Landy lose, and left or switched off their television sets disappointed that there was still no American sub-four minute miler.

In an amazing boilover, Jim Bailey, the talented but erratic Sydney runner who had stayed on in the US after the Vancouver Empire Games, hung on to Landy, challenged him, and beat him. Bailey ran 3:58.6 — his best had been 4:05.6 in winning the previous year's NCAA title — and Landy ran 3:58.7. Twice now John Landy had run under four minutes on the north American continent; twice he had lost.

The Bannister-Landy race had been seen as a summit meeting between the two best milers in the world. Not this one, however; few gave Bailey any chance. Landy usually beat him easily.

John Landy describes a race that was "a bit of a disaster". It took on a strange quality from the gun. Delany, who never led a race before the finish line if he could help it, hared off from the start. "That's not Ron Delany's way of running," John Landy said. "Within 600 metres he'd blown up."

Landy took the lead before halfway and, as in his recent Australian races, picked up the pace in the third lap. He ran a tick over 59 seconds, reaching the bell in 3:01.5.

Cornelius Warmerdam, the famed US pole vaulter universally known as "Dutch", was positioned along the back-straight to let Landy know how he was going in what had been expected to be a solo quest for a sub-four minute mile. "Warmerdam said 20, or something like that, which was how far in front I was," says Landy. "Then 15 the next lap, then two [on the final lap] — but I didn't take much notice, being convinced I was well in front."

Bailey had chased Landy down, however, and the message from "Dutch" Warmerdam that Landy did not grasp was that the gap was down to two yards, not much more than a stride. Oblivious to the danger, Landy raced on, until he felt a tremendous "whack" on the backside.

His initial thought was that a stray discus had bounced off the infield and struck him. "I turned around to see what happened and Bailey [went] "away" up the straight. I'd beaten him a few times in Australia, always been able to beat him except once in a national 880 title, so I thought I could handle the challenge. But he held me out in a fair finish by about one metre. It was a bit of a shock."

No more so than to Jim Bailey. "'No ... it can't be true,' gasped shocked Jim Bailey," ran the headline in *The Argus*. "I didn't think I'd beat John Landy or get down to anything like 3:58.6."

The Argus covered its own shock a little better. Previewing the race, the paper had run a colour photo of Landy in his Geelong Guild singlet headlined "The Kangaroo Kid". In reporting the result, it simply went for the plural, describing Bailey and Landy as "The Kangaroo Kids". The paper also carried the most discerning comment on the race, its columnist Franz Stampfl observing that the race was a great tragedy for Landy because "the prestige and confidence he has built up since Roger Bannister defeated him in Vancouver in 1954 has been shattered".

Bailey certainly believed he could repeat the triumph. "Jim: I Can Beat John Again" was the poster headline in *The Herald*. A picture of Landy with his head buried in his hands added to the gloom.

Perhaps it should not have come as such a shock, particularly when Bailey got into contention in the third lap. Sydney contemporaries all describe him as a better runner than people gave him credit for, with John Plummer observing: "You wouldn't want him with you with 400 to go." Bailey says his main goals in the race were to provide Landy with as much opposition as he could — and »

Jim Bailey

For most of Jim Bailey's running career it seemed he would just as soon have a fight as run. The legend "DQ" (signifying disqualified) appeared opposite his name in results almost as often as did a time.

Variously described as knockabout and "a lair", Bailey epitomised what some Victorian athletes saw as a more robust style of racing in New South Wales. Sharp elbows and sharp tactics were the order of the day. He was not without a sense of humour, once introducing himself as "the most disqualified man in Australia".

"That was normal for me," he said in 2006 of one racing incident. "I didn't mind a little contact and if I wanted to go by someone I didn't always give them as much room as I needed. I was a bit of a showman."

Perhaps Bailey's attitude was formed as much on the football field as the athletics track. "I played a lot of rugby. I thought I was pretty tough. I'd gone to a very strict, old-fashioned Catholic boarding school out in the sticks of New South Wales. We had one athletics meeting a year. I was the mile champion of the school, but you could be the mile champion and not run under five minutes in those days.

"I came home and started playing junior league at the Catholic Youth Organisation rugby league. We used to train really hard, these crazy sprints up and down the length of the oval. Originally the idea of joining the St George track club was to keep fit for football."

Bailey showed some talent early. At the age of 19, he dead-heated in the Australian 880 yards title with West Australian David White (who went on to finish fourth at the 1950 Empire Games). Officials ordered a re-run to decide the title, but Bailey did not take part so was relegated to second place. Two years later, the 21-year-old Bailey won the 880 title in Hobart. Two years later again he was disqualified in both the 880 and mile in Perth, the latter after clashing with Les Perry in what was described as "a king hit", then he beat Landy to win the half-mile the following year in Sydney and was second to him in the mile.

It was enough to earn him selection in the team for Vancouver. He left Australia with the intention of returning. "I think we had to sign a letter saying we'd stay with the team, not leave the team and come back with the team." But fate intervened in a typical Bailey manner — injury. "I broke a couple of metatarsal bones in my foot between the heat and the finals of the 880. I seemed to be cursed with these damned things that happened on big occasions.

"I was excused from the team because there was this local doctor in Vancouver looking after me. A couple of Canadians who were students at the University of Oregon felt sorry for me I guess and invited me to come down to Oregon. There I met [coach Bill] Bowerman. He broached the idea [of] coming to Oregon on a foreign student scholarship. I said 'I'm probably sick of running, I've had a lot of disappointments and I'm 25. I can't tell you that I have much desire of continuing to run.'

"Well, that's up to you," Bowerman said, telling Bailey it was not a condition of the scholarship offer.

"Within a few weeks I was healed and got on the track," Bailey continued. "It was the first time in my life that I ever had facilities available and was free for a couple of hours an afternoon to get on the track."

Bowerman was the first coach Bailey had ever had; Oregon was the first place where his running took on an organised nature. Up to a point, anyway. "[Bowerman] used to put training schedules up on our space in the locker-room. Sometimes I stuck to them, sometimes I didn't. I was older than most of the kids. I was kind of a prima donna. I didn't like working out; the only thing I liked was if I won on Saturday."

On 5 May 1956, Jim Bailey had the best Saturday win of his life. Ultimately, it was a win that would cost him, but that was for the future. At the time, he had rocketed from obscurity to Olympic medal contention.

» to audition for an invitation home. "I knew if I performed well they'd have to invite me to the Australian Olympic trials."

So why give Landy "a belt on the backside"? Bailey says it stemmed from his view that it was Landy's day and his momentum was about to carry him into the lead. "I knew that if I didn't do anything I would carry past him, maybe surprise him. So when I got alongside him I belted him on the backside and said 'go John.'"

Landy vowed to do better at his remaining race the following week at the Fresno Relays, and wondered aloud whether he might be a runner of fast times, but not a racer. "I don't have the temperament of a race winner, I just like to run fast times."

Bailey did not race in Fresno, but Delany lined up again. "His [Delany's] coach sent him back to California as if to say 'You've got to keep trying,'" says Landy. "I liked him [Delany] very much, still do, we're good friends. I had a bit of a talk to him about running."

Where the Coliseum meeting, with the competition between the two big colleges, was an event, Fresno was more of "a connoisseurs' meet", says Landy. People went to the Coliseum to see a big race; they went to Fresno to play their own part in it, however small. "Someone said, 'There'll be a thousand stopwatches on you,'" Landy recalls. "They were probably right."

The publicity was just as remorseless. The Melbourne *Herald* featured a report from the "Herald Special Service" suggesting that Fresno was "in fever as great run nears". Alongside a radiophoto of Landy and Delany jogging together on the track, the article acclaimed the world mile record holder as "the biggest thing since the seedless grape to hit this beautiful, solidly prosperous city of 115,000 in the middle of California's grape district". Backing up the reputation of Fresno as a haven for athletics enthusiasts, the report continued that "nearly any passer-by in the self-styled 'raisin capital of the world' can rattle off two sets of statistics with equal ease — on raisins, and racing on the latest white clay track where Landy will run tomorrow."

Landy ran his sixth sub-four minute mile — 3:59.1 — in beating Delany by just over ten seconds. "I had no spark," he said, but he had now broken four minutes in six out of eight races over a mile, the exceptions being the Australian mile title when he went back to help Clarke, and his heat of the Empire Games.

Besides newspaper reports, four Melbourne radio stations were in Fresno to broadcast the race live (as they had in Los Angeles the previous week). That catered for the Australian perspective, but what of the American one?

Sports Illustrated, perhaps the most famous sports magazine in the world, then as now, assigned a senior writer to cover the races and write a profile on Landy in consecutive issues. Paul O'Neil confirmed the popular view on Fresno. "Kids in Fresno," he wrote in the 21 May edition of *SI*, "can recite the latest clockings in the 100- and 220-yard dash the way kids in Brooklyn recite baseball averages." O'Neil described Landy as "running like some tanned Inca courier" as he left his opponents trailing in his wake. The race, he continued, "ended one of the most astonishing and admirable adventures in the history of athletics in the US".

He detailed Landy's odyssey: "In a single fortnight he had flown 9000 miles from Australia to the US, had not only accepted a burden of press conferences, newsreel performances, radio shows and television spots which would have staggered a candidate for the US Senate, but had won his auditors to a man with his poise, his patience and an articulate honesty. In accepting, without reserve, the responsibility of serving as an 'ambassador' for Australia and a sort of salesman for the Melbourne Olympics, he had virtually promised to run two four-minute miles in eight days. And, for all the nervous strain of his incessant extracurricular activities, he had done so — a feat without precedent in the annals of track. If he had been beaten by a jump in the surprising race with Jim Bailey he had also made the pace and thus opened the door of fame to his fellow countryman."

Later, O'Neil reports that Landy was "appalled" by the stone-hard nature of the Coliseum track and that he was very apprehensive about running on it. But he doubted whether either the surface, or the demanding schedule had affected his running. He also refused to attach any significance to the fact that his feet were cut and blistered by his heavy training. In a comment evocative of his view about the cut foot in Vancouver, O'Neil quotes Landy as saying: "There is no gray — just black and white — in this injury business. If you're hurt badly enough to limp, you can't run at all. If you aren't, it makes no difference."

Landy also hinted at the loss of confidence engendered by his loss to Bailey and the conclusion he drew from it. "I'm mortally afraid, now, that nobody, including myself, has the margin of superiority to be able to make the pace and win."

On the same day as the Fresno race, Jim Bailey ran 4:06.4 elsewhere. (He also announced his engagement to Janet Somers of Falls Creek, Oregon.) Landy had a short break in Florida, where he stayed with a relative, before returning to Melbourne and, almost immediately, teaching at Geelong Grammar's Corio campus. "I'm tired … stale … I want to rest," he said.

A few days after Landy's return to Geelong, Ron Delany and Gunnar Nielsen of Denmark became the seventh and eighth sub-four minute milers in history when the Irishman just edged past the Dane at the Compton Invitational, 3:59.0 to 3:59.1. Landy's world record was surviving all assaults — including his own — but more and more men were becoming capable of breaking it.

Landy returned home with more worries than the growing number of actual and potential sub-four minute milers around the world. Incipient problems in both Achilles tendons — under control before he left Australia — had been exacerbated by racing and training on the hard American tracks.

The problem would dog Landy all the way through to the Melbourne Olympics and be largely responsible for the lack of confidence with which he would approach the Games. There is a »

Search for a Cure

Like every other element of John Landy's career, his battle with tendonitis was painfully documented. Actually, it was more a case of his pain being fully documented.

Harry Gordon, in his column "This is the Score", noted that everyone seemed to have a cure for the ailment — except John Landy. He then proceeded to offer two himself, one from English runner Gordon Pirie, the other from Australian sprinter Winsome Cripps. Pirie's proposed remedy was described merely as "very painful"; the Cripps cure consisted of a six-week course of shortwave radiation followed by a cortisone injection, outlined in detail, along with quotes from the sprinter.

One charming element of all this pressure was the number of offers of assistance that poured in from all parts of Australia and, in some cases, overseas. "The cures were wonderful," John Landy said in 2006. "Mum used to keep a list of all the cures. One suggestion we took seriously was a large dose of aspirin, but that affected my digestion so much that we gave it away. Some blokes sent things like Tiger Balm. It was funny."

To this day, John Landy has a file of about 50 of the cures. They came from everywhere. Within Australia there were letters from the far north, the deep south and the extreme west of the country. Famed ultra-distance runner Arthur Newton, whose ideas on training informed Arthur Lydiard, among others, wrote from England. Other offers of assistance came from New Zealand and the US. Medical and paramedical professionals offered their services (mostly for free), quacks offered their theories, housewives proffered traditional remedies. The Scientology Efficiency Training Centre even wrote from its Sydney headquarters.

In his letter, Newton suggested Landy "cut out the frills and look straight at the thing. What causes it? Undoubtedly 'stretching' the tendon. Why should it stretch? Because you wear ordinary footwear with considerable heels and running shoes without them," he wrote. As a short-term expedient, Newton advised adding rubber heels to Landy's running shoes.

He concluded (this was by now October): "All the very best of good luck, and remember me to [Gordon] Pirie if you see him."

Several other correspondents suggested build-ups of various sorts. Others thought massage would do the trick, or compresses (mostly "borax', sometimes combined with doses of crude molasses), or hot sea-water baths. The suggestion of large doses of aspirin came from a New Zealand stationmaster. As always, working on the railway provided plenty of idle time for theorising. Another letter, from the manager of the railway refreshment rooms in Townsville, endorsed arnica, a natural anti-inflammatory agent.

One rambling letter, giving an address of "Mental Hospital Sunbury", outlined a whole philosophy of treatment (not to mention government). The writer closed with: "My name must not be made public." Scrawling a symbolic smile, he added: "I must be like the Cheshire Cat — vanish!"

A woman wrote from South Australia offering not a specific remedy, but relaxation of the body and soul as advocated by American preacher and positive thinking advocate Norman Vincent Peale. "I am far from a young girl, just wishing to hear from you or anything like that, far from it," the writer reassured Landy.

Ken Macdonald, a Victorian runner who had made the 1950 Empire Games team, wrote of his own experience that year. He had tried various remedies, including regular infra-red rays, but in the end had found relief when he visited George Saunders, the Olympic team physiotherapist and masseur. Another woman wrote from Brisbane, recommending the services of her husband who had been an osteopath in England but had not practised in Australia. "My husband does not know of this," she concluded conspiratorially. "He would call it soliciting, and a breach of medical ethics, but I would call it a human act."

What strikes you immediately on reading the letters is the obvious and utter sincerity of the writers. Naïve many of them may have been, but well-meaning, too and, for the most part, standing to gain nothing.

» tradition of great Australian sporting champions — the racehorse Phar Lap, the boxer Les Darcy, both of whom died in the US — being done in by trips to America. Was Landy a third victim? He thinks not, but it is at worst an open question. "The Achilles problem affected my whole Olympic program. I wouldn't say it was caused by the US trip," John Landy says, "but it didn't help. The tracks I was running on were almost as hard as running on that road [points outside] and my shoes weren't cushioned. The US visit certainly didn't help but I think it's simplistic to say that was the reason for my Achilles problems."

If racing on the rock-hard US tracks was not the origin of John Landy's Achilles tendonitis, it certainly exacerbated it. Moreover, the US visit took a valuable month out of his build-up to the Melbourne Olympics. He did not choose to go to America; rather, he was pressured into it. Paul O'Neil quantified the extent of Landy's US commitments in *Sports Illustrated*. Chris Brasher did so again after the Melbourne Games. John Landy would never use the impact of the American trip as an excuse, but equally there is no doubt it was a negative factor in his final preparation and ultimate Olympic performance.

Time and confidence were ebbing away from Landy by the day. If an athlete is attempting a record, he or she can always postpone a competition. But the Olympics come round once every four years. Ready or not, you must compete on a fixed day.

"It was the most difficult period of my athletic career, because so much was expected of me," says Landy. "I lost confidence because I couldn't train regularly and how I got up [to run] was a bit of a miracle. Once I got through the pain barrier it was OK. I could run in a race, there was no problem with that. But I couldn't train consistently; I'd have to have days off and time off. So the chances of running the 5000 started to evaporate quickly. I pulled out of that with about three weeks to go. There was no way I was going to be able to do justice to that event; I just couldn't do the training."

11

The Games

In September 1956, Al Lawrence bought his first car, a Morris Minor. "The fact that I couldn't drive wasn't that important."

Fellow Botany Harrier John Russell, who worked at the same paper mill as Lawrence, volunteered to teach him to drive and transport him to and from their various training venues. "It was convenient for John as well," says Lawrence. "He had been selected to run the marathon in Melbourne — so it was a very good situation for us both."

Lawrence and Russell decided driving from Sydney to Melbourne would be a good idea. "I always travelled poorly by air," Lawrence says. "We ambled leisurely down the Hume Highway (the highway, now mostly motorway, connecting Australia's two largest population centres). John did most of the driving — he told me he wanted to arrive safely in Melbourne." The pair had a couple of overnight stops to break up the almost 900 kilometres trip. Popular spots were at Gundagai about halfway between the two cities, where the weary traveller would nod off to sleep to the sound of road transports rattling across the long wooden bridge over the Murrumbidgee River, or closer to Melbourne, at Albury, on the border between New South Wales and Victoria.

"I can't remember the name of the town," says Lawrence of one stop, "but we found a private boys' boarding school on the outskirts and asked the headmaster if we could loosen up and run a little on their grass oval. The whole school was allowed out of class to watch the Olympians 'strut their stuff', cheering wildly each time we jogged by or stopped to perform some ridiculously easy exercises. 'Run a few short sprints for them, John,' I told him. 'Give them something to remember the Aussie Olympians.'

"'Bugger you, Allan, I'm a plodder! I run marathons. You run a couple of fast quarters for them,' Russell shot back.

"'I have to race at Puckapunyal tomorrow. I don't want to be buggered for the race.'

"'Ah, come on. Nobody's going to be there. It's a military base.'"

Lawrence ran several brisk quarters, and the kids seemed to like the show. "Then we went back to our hotel, had a meal, and went to bed," Lawrence continues. "We slept in and checked out late in the morning."

Lawrence and Russel stopped in Puckapunyal later that day. Known as "Pucka" to generations of schoolboy army cadets over the years, the town is a sprawling army base just outside Seymour, some 160 kilometres north of Melbourne. It was one of several unlikely venues for pre-Games meetings.

"When we arrived in the middle of the afternoon," Lawrence recalls, "we found a surprise waiting for us: Dave Stephens was also entered in the three-mile race. 'The Milko' looked lean and fit. He immediately went to the front and had me hanging on. After a mile a loud voice began assailing me each time we went down the back-straight: 'Take a lap, Lawrence. Share the load.' I must admit that after a couple of laps, I began to feel intimidated enough to go by Dave and, against my usual tactics, lead for the next mile. Apparently, it pleased the fan: 'That's better, Lawrence. Run as a team.'

"The fan might have been satisfied, but the new tactics left me uncertain how to run the last lap. I was fortunate to barely edge Dave in 13:47.2. 'The Milko' ran the same time."

Since the Olympic Trials in late October, Stephens appeared to be regaining top form. Commenting on Stephens's race, Percy Cerutty said: "Stephens will be in the first three in the Olympic 10,000 metres — or the last three!"

"Although I knew Percy had no power of clairvoyance, I respected his opinion, and I marked Dave Stephens down as a definite threat in the Olympic 10,000 metres," Lawrence recalls thinking at the time.

Lawrence and Russell completed the journey to Melbourne and into the Olympic Village. They were not the only two Australian athletes to arrive at their Olympic competition unconventionally. I recall talking to a 1956 Melbourne Olympian who lived in North Carlton, an inner Melbourne suburb, and was competing at the Royal Exhibition Building, the magnificent domed building constructed for Melbourne's first International Exhibition almost 70 years earlier. Basketball, weight-lifting and wrestling were conducted there. This athlete stayed at home, caught the tram down Nicholson Street to the venue, competed and caught the tram home again to sleep in his own bed — some Olympic experience that was.

In the weeks before the Games, athletics meetings were held at Melbourne suburban venues such as Oakleigh, Olympic Park and Melbourne University, but the meetings that gained most attention were those held in country Victoria, on cinder tracks at Puckapunyal and the Flinders naval base, and on grass tracks in Bendigo and Geelong. The Geelong meeting, held under lights at Kardinia Park, attracted 15,000 spectators. Julius "Judy" Patching, chief starter during the Games, says the meetings outside Melbourne were popular with athletes and officials, who enjoyed seeing the country, as well as spectators, who relished international competition. "It was all part of getting everyone in the groove."

In the Olympic Village, in the northern suburb of Heidelberg, Lawrence and Russell were allocated a room "somewhat isolated from the main team accommodation". The reason soon became clear. "John Landy had the room opposite us and we spent many pleasant hours relaxing and discussing our opposition," Lawrence writes.

"John was a great boost to my confidence." Unfortunately, Landy's morale also needed boosting and there was no-one to do that.

Landy's confidence was waning by the day as he struggled to throw off his Achilles tendon injuries. Athletes with chronic injuries know the syndrome all too well. Some days are fine; others are not. Something helps one day but is useless the next. Some treatments and remedies produce short-term gains, only for the improvement to prove illusory. It is all two steps forward, one back and all the time the clock is ticking.

In early October, Landy raced for the first time since the US trip. "I ran two slow two-mile races. I ran in bare feet. I was pretty hobbly, I couldn't stretch out much. Both races were on grass which made it possible to run barefoot." The second race was faster than the first. Landy told reporters his tendons appeared to be healing. "For the first time in three months I feel like I can walk like a normal man. I certainly didn't feel sharp, although I tried to hurry up a bit when my mile time of 4:34 was announced." He did, running six seconds quicker for the concluding mile.

Some decent time trials over 1200 metres also indicated Landy was slowly building back to form. Then, a week before the Games, a disastrous two-mile race at Geelong knocked his confidence back to rock-bottom. Landy, who had said a few days before the 15 November meeting that he would not race again before the Games 1500 heats, changed his mind. Perhaps he had been encouraged by his improved training form, but he was discouraged by the outcome. He finished 11th out of the 13 starters in a race won by Chris Brasher, the initial pacemaker in Bannister's sub-four minute mile, who would go on to win the Olympic 3000 metres steeplechase.

Brasher ran 8:45.6. "My previous best was 8:58," he told the media. "I have been here three weeks and it seems to have done me good. I should be able to run the fastest steeplechase in my life at the Olympic Games."

Hoping to run faster than his two earlier races, Landy instead ran considerably slower, but it was how he felt that mattered more. Franz Stampfl reported Landy as telling him "this could be the end", and Stampfl wrote off Landy's chances of winning a medal in the Games 1500 "UNLESS YOU BELIEVE IN MIRACLES". (This last phrase was capitalised in the report in *The Argus*.)

Other reports were less dramatic, but scarcely so. "I'm just not fit," Landy told Bruce Welch of *The Age*. "I just can't relax. I am obviously not running well. I'm just not fit." In the mass-selling *Sun*, Jack Dunn wrote a piece directed "to the men who organised John Landy's tour of America to boost Melbourne's Olympic Games". "It certainly was a great publicity stunt," Dunn wrote, "Oh! BUT THE CONSEQUENCES." Again, the capitals emphasised how dire things were, at least in media-land.

Landy was clearly distressed. He still describes the run as "devastating to me. It was the first time I'd run against international competition since my visit to the US. It was absolutely devastating. Brasher and the others were so far in front, I was way back. Whether I could even run the 1500 was doubtful. It did nothing for my confidence at all."

Despite the emergence of Jim Bailey and Merv Lincoln in Landy's event, and the performances of Stephens, Lawrence and others, it was still to Landy that Australians looked for a track gold medal in Melbourne, just as they looked to Cathy Freeman in Sydney 2000. "The public still thought, because I had the carryover from '54 and earlier in the year, they still thought that somehow or other I would do it," says Landy.

Landy, literally, could not win. The Australian public overwhelmingly wanted him, willed him, to win, no less a pressure for being well-meaning. At a personal level, driven by the same principles that had motivated him to make the Empire Games race against Bannister, there was his own feeling that he must ensure a memorable race. Depressingly, in his state at the time he knew he could neither guarantee a win, nor deliver a great race.

The realisation weighed heavily on him. "I was full of doubt and worry and yet everyone kept saying, 'good luck, you can do it'. I just thought 'this is dreadful and it's going to be so hard to deliver', because I just had not done the necessary training."

As Landy was on a downward trajectory, Merv Lincoln was on the up. Consciously or otherwise, the wily Stampfl had something to gain by writing off John Landy's medal chances in the Olympic 1500 metres. He coached Lincoln, and his athlete stood to gain should the favourite falter.

Lincoln had come from nowhere to run 4:00.6 behind Landy in the first sub-four minute mile in Australia earlier in the year. A month or two earlier, as the 1955–56 domestic season started, he had virtually not been heard of.

In 1954, while doing his (army) National Service training, Lincoln had entered, and won, his battalion mile because some of his friends were going to run. He wore sandshoes and won in 4:40 on a grass track. "That race fired my interest in athletics," Lincoln told Canberra author Brian Lenton (in an interview for *Through The Tape*, Brian Lenton Publications, 1983). "Then I came to Melbourne and ran very well in the university championships, and inter-varsity, which convinced me I'd like to put more effort into running."

When Stampfl came to Australia in 1955, Lincoln was teaching at Stawell High School. (Stawell was the hometown of the Easter Gift, the famous professional foot-race run off handicaps over 130 yards.) Lincoln started running Melbourne interclub in the summer of 1955–56. "Some of my friends told Franz I was very keen on athletics … He wrote me a letter … we very quickly teed up a meeting."

Guided by Stampfl, Lincoln rapidly improved. In the opening round of interclub, he defeated Don Macmillan in a mile, running 4:10. "I led all the way on the five laps to the mile oval … I knew I was on the right track with my training." Lincoln also won the mile at the Puckapunyal pre-Olympic meeting against an international field that included Chris Chataway, Murray Halberg, Jim Bailey and Ron Clarke. "It was blowing a gale, and I led for the last three laps to record four minutes four seconds."

Yet misfortune was poised to strike Merv Lincoln, too. Ten days before the Games opened, he tore the tendons underneath his right foot during a track session at Melbourne University.

Jim Bailey also had his worries. In keeping with this tempestuous character, they were as much of his own making as anything else. A few weeks after the Coliseum race that had propelled him to international attention, Bailey again faced Ron Delany. It was in the NCAA (National Collegiate Athletic Association) mile. Bailey was defending champion, but this time he was the one in for a shock at the finish. "I was leading with maybe 100–150 yards to go," he says. "Delany went by me so fast, so suddenly, that even if I'd had the ability I wouldn't have been able to go with him. He would have been only 19 or 20 at the time. I was close to my 27th birthday and had been banged up playing football since I was twelve years of age."

If the loss dented Bailey's confidence, he never showed it — outwardly, at least. He came back to Australia a month or so before the Olympic Trials in October. His hopes were high, and he wasted no time expressing them publicly, a fact he regrets now. "I came back with some expectations, that's for sure. I shot my mouth off as soon as I got off the plane." Bailey's refrain was the familiar one that had followed his upset win over Landy. "I would have no trouble beating John Landy again," he said on arrival in Sydney. While this might have made good theatre in the US, it offended many in Australia.

"That was the way I was," Bailey explains. "People took it as arrogance, but I wasn't arrogant. I felt that I didn't have either great speed or great stamina and I'd always had these injured knees from football. But I was cocky enough, and my honest feeling was that I was in better shape when I arrived back in Australia than I was in that race with John. I said, 'I'm in better shape. If I race him again I'll beat him by a bigger margin.' The Melbourne newspapers really went for me. I had the experience at the trials — I can't remember at the Games, it's still just a blur to me — of 15,000 people booing me."

Bailey won the 800 and 1500 at the selection trials, and was selected to run both in the Games. The trials were conducted over two weekends. The 800 was run on the first weekend and Bailey featured in an incident with Don Macmillan before winning in 1:51.2. Bailey had looked across at Macmillan as he drew level and clearly said something to him. "Bailey simply laughed and waved me goodbye," Macmillan said in a newspaper report.

Bailey's version of the incident was similar: "I turned around and laughed at 'Old Mac'. The expression he gets — the worried look, you know — makes him look like an old horse."

Whatever the facts, Bailey's action attracted widespread hooting from the crowd, as did his perceived arrogance in taking a victory lap (he insisted it was a warm-down). He was warned and rebuked by the track referee, but escaped disqualification. "Oh well, that was normal for me," says Bailey. "I didn't mind a little contact. I was a bit of a showman. The crowd was really turned against me by some of the newspaper reporters. I had a really low opinion of some of the writers." He could not have been referring to Bruce Welch, who wrote in *The Age* that Bailey "did nothing to warrant the isolated hooting that broke out even before he hit the tape".

Bailey defeated Lincoln to win the 1500 metres the following weekend without further incident. Bailey ran 3:44.4, doing nothing to belie the impression that he was a real medal prospect.

But, in the end, the Olympic Games were a disaster for him. He was run out in the semi-finals of the 800 metres and then failed to front for the first heat of the 1500. He had decided to withdraw, but no-one in the crowd knew of his decision until he did not appear on the track with the other starters. Team management did not know, either.

Bailey had respiratory problems. In typical Bailey style, he dropped in at the Olympic Village press centre the following day to explain. "I can hardly breathe and have hardly had any sleep for a week now," he told the journalists, who were a little taken aback to see him. Adding that he had tried to run twice the day before the heats but been unable to complete a 440 in less than 66 seconds, Bailey said: "You can call my trouble either hay fever or sinus … but whatever it is I just can't run because of the damn thing."

Melbourne scarred Bailey. He says now that personal problems at the time exacerbated what was basically an underlying psychological one. "My fiancée, my bride-to-be, was having last-minute doubts — that put me in rather a bad mood just before the Games. Then I got into a car accident in Sydney; I turned a car over rather spectacularly. It didn't do any damage physically but it shook me up a bit. Psychologically, I went to pieces when I got there with the reaction of the crowd. It was terrible. I just wanted to get off the face of the earth."

Al Lawrence, Dave Power and Dave Stephens opened the batting, so to speak, for Australia on the Melbourne Cricket Ground, competing in the final of the 10,000 metres on the opening day of Olympic competition. There were no heats for this gruelling event.

Lawrence's confidence had been boosted by his runs at Puckapunyal and Geelong (where he came third), his nerves soothed by Landy's invaluable analysis of his opponents, and his race plan was clear in his mind.

To no-one's surprise, world record holder Vladimir Kuts, the Ukrainian representing the USSR, set the pace; to the surprise of few, Britain's Gordon Pirie followed in his tracks, a step behind. Lawrence and Power led the chasing pack, which at times closed up on the leaders, at other times dropped back as Kuts applied another of his trademark surges. »

Bailey's Shoes Win Gold Medal

There was one happy sequel to Jim Bailey's otherwise sad Melbourne experience. As Bailey was packing up at the Olympic Village, he tossed an almost-new pair of training shoes into the rubbish bin. His roommate, distance runner Dave Power, was amazed at this profligate waste and asked: "Don't you want those shoes, Jim?"

"No, I'm finished with running for good," a disconsolate Bailey replied. "You can have them if you want them."

So Dave Power acquired a new pair of shoes. In the manner of the day — indeed, a manner that would last until the big shoe companies got into mass production with the 1970s running boom — Power got several years' wear out of the shoes, repairing them from time to time with Shoe Goo and such products. "I trained in those shoes and after many re-soles won the Empire Games marathon in them at Cardiff two years later."

Power's win in the marathon completed a gold medal double as he had earlier won the six miles.

So Jim Bailey never won a gold medal for Australia, but his shoes did.

» Kuts eventually broke Pirie, physically and mentally, coming into the last mile and went on to win. A shattered Pirie dropped back to eighth place. Lawrence fought the silver medal out with Jozsef Kovacs of Hungary. They entered the last lap together, Lawrence trying to balance the demands of the competition against the persistent "knife-like pains" in his right calf. Lawrence led Kovacs in the final straight, but the Hungarian got past him to take the silver medal by a second. Lawrence's bronze medal was Australia's first medal of its home Olympics.

Power finished a creditable seventh, the last man to sprint past a staggering Pirie. Dave Stephens ran a bizarre race, at times holding his side as if cramping, at times waving to the crowd as if to say everything was fine with him. Things had not gone well for him, with injuries and illness, and he was not the runner who had beaten the Hungarians a year ago and broken the world record for six miles at the start of the Olympic year.

Albie Thomas did not emulate his more-experienced New South Wales colleague Al Lawrence's mode of transport to Melbourne. He flew. In fact, he had been "flying" for a couple of years. Thomas had improved rapidly — from 15:24.8 for three miles in 1954, to 14:07.4 in 1955, then to 13:36.0 in 1956; but the 21-year-old had not even run a place in an Australian title before he gained selection for the 5000 metres in Melbourne. With a spot already reserved for Landy, Thomas clung to Lawrence throughout the race to secure the remaining place. A week later, Thomas finished fourth behind Lawrence, Power and Dave Stephens, just missing a spot in the 10,000 metres.

Cerutty, who coached Thomas by correspondence, had assured him he would make the team, but Thomas had not been game to risk being left both without a blazer and without tickets. He gave them to Nola, his girlfriend then, and now wife of 50 years. "Nola used my Games tickets. I had purchased them never thinking I would be in the team." Nola got good value from the tickets. Thomas won his heat of the 5000 metres comfortably and, while no-one was going to beat Vladimir Kuts in the final, he finished fifth, displacing Les Perry (sixth in Helsinki) as Australia's best Olympic finisher in the event.

The run of Australian success continued in the 3000 metres steeplechase. That race was notable for the victory by Chris Brasher — a victory that was not confirmed until the appeal jury overturned his disqualification by the track referee for interference as he took the lead. Brasher was "the third man" in Bannister's sub-four minute mile, taking the pace for the first two-and-a-half laps before Chris

Chataway took over. Brasher was very much the third man among the British steeplechasers, too. His colleagues John Disley (with whom Brasher later founded the London Marathon) and Eric Shirley were more fancied.

Neil Robbins was a club-mate of Perry, Warren and Stephens at the powerful Williamstown club, and he trained with Franz Stampfl. Ron Blackney was injured, Graham Thomas was bumped off the track in his heat and never recovered his balance, and it was left to Robbins to take seventh place in the final, breaking the national record as he had done earlier in his heat.

During the Olympics, Landy's celebrity status, continued unabated. He sought quiet places to train and was able to concentrate on his preparation. He was short of races, but would just have to make do. But he was not in the physical shape he had been in when he came down from Timbertop to stun Lon Spurrier at the start of the Olympic year; nor did he have the confidence he had built with his startling series of runs in Australia.

The day before the 1500 metres heat, Kuts completed his distance double in the 5000 metres watched by Landy, Roger Bannister and the Duke of Edinburgh. The Duke maintained the informal atmosphere of the royal tour by eschewing the Royal Box, but neither Bannister nor Prince Philip had a race to run the next day.

The third heat of the Melbourne Olympic 1500 metres on 29 November was essentially John Landy's first serious race since Fresno in May. All he had done, or been able to do, in Melbourne in the lead-up to the Games was test his state of fitness. The inescapable fact was he failed more of those tests than he passed.

The qualifying conditions were simple: three heats, and the first four in each would go through to the final two days later. Jim Bailey stunned the crowd by failing to report in for the first heat; Merv Lincoln thrilled them by winning the second in what would turn out to be the fastest of the preliminary round.

Middle-distance heats are often physical affairs and Landy copped his share of buffeting in the final heat. But he came through strongly enough to take third place behind Neville Scott of New Zealand and Brian Hewson of Great Britain. Gunnar Nielsen of Denmark took fourth, the vital last spot in the final, with Dan Waern of Sweden in fifth, just missing out. Hewson described it as "the roughest race I've been in".

Landy ran wide most of the way, avoiding the worst of the interference inevitable in a slow-run race. Briefly in the final straight, it looked as if he was struggling to go through, but he qualified easily enough. His performance sparked a debate as to whether he had been saving himself. Lincoln thought so; as did Ron Clarke, who was watching from the stands. Others — mainly those paid to write in newspapers — weren't so certain. Landy said nothing after his heat, asking the Australian team manager to tell "the press boys" he would have something for them after the final. What he said then — "I was so flattened … I had doubts if I could face up for the final" — indicated he had been all-out.

The media had a new Australian favorite. Lincoln won his heat by 20 yards in the fastest time. "It's better to be sure than sorry," he said. "I was more or less waiting for footsteps behind me all the time." Delany qualified comfortably, well behind Lincoln. His training form had not looked impressive, but those in the know were convinced that he was a threat in the final. His old school coach in Ireland noted sagely: "If Ronnie's there with 300 yards to go in Melbourne, he has a wonderful chance."

Flattened or not, Landy had survived the heat tolerably well. Not so Lincoln, whose foot became inflamed. Typically, it was Landy who accompanied Lincoln as he sought treatment. He had a pain-killing injection and another was organised for 30 minutes before the final.

Over 100,000 people crammed into the MCG for the final of the 1500 metres on Saturday, 1 December. Almost to a man or woman, they wished Landy well. "One hundred thousand people had honored champions of its [sic] own and other countries," *The Age* reported the following Monday (television had been introduced to Melbourne for the Games, but not Sunday papers!). "[The crowd] reserved its heart for Landy as he walked out to take his place in the field for the 1500 metres final."

Landy's confidence had always grown from his physical fitness, not outside support, however well-meaning. A month before the 2006 Commonwealth Games, he appeared on the MCG for a photo with Craig Mottram and commented on the crowd support that the first Australian athletics team to compete there since 1956 could expect. Landy said he had found the unconditional support of the crowds "almost overwhelming. People were just wishing you well, [but] it works two ways. If you're very confident I think it would give you something; if you've got some doubts, it emphasises that and you wonder: how am I going to do it?" No prize for guessing which category John Landy fell into.

Still, he was there and others were not. Bailey, who had beaten him, had not fronted for the heats. Istvan Rozsalvolgyi, the world record holder, had not progressed through the heats. He had been injured and was demoralised at the turn of events in Hungary. Josy Barthel, the defending champion, was run out in the heats.

Merv Lincoln's chances dwindled when the doctor who was to give him the pain-killer was held up. The injection was finally administered minutes before the race. "I went out in a totally confused frame of mind," Lincoln told Brian Lenton 25 years later. "Obviously, [the injection] didn't have time to work. [Melbourne] was a lost opportunity. I think I had a pretty good chance. I was feeling quite unbeatable and it's something you rarely experience."

It all fell to Landy again. The biggest crowd ever to watch an Olympic 1500 metres final was hushed as the field went to the line.

The arrival of one member of the 104,400 crowd had attracted more attention than anybody other than Landy. The Duke of Edinburgh made front-page news in that day's evening edition of *The Herald*, albeit tucked just below the report on the 1500. "The Duke of Edinburgh drove up to the Olympic Main Stadium this afternoon in his Lagonda drop-head sports coupe," the paper reported. "The hood was down and the Duke was at the wheel ..."

Landy had talked with Lincoln the previous night. "Merv and I discussed the possible form the race might take. I said it was quite likely that no-one would set the pace, which is quite common in an Olympic 1500, and you'd have a first lap of 61 or 62 or 63. I said in that case, as he looked much more likely to do well than I did, I'd get out and lead. But in fact I was hanging on. The first lap was 58.6."

Murray Halberg of New Zealand led. Halfway around the second lap, the pace slowed and Lincoln moved gradually to the lead as 800 was reached in just on two minutes. Good pace, but they had slowed to get there.

Thus far, the race had followed the same pattern as Landy's races early in the year. He had developed a new tactic of striking during the third lap, that point in the race where the competitors have absorbed the shock of the first two laps and are mentally settling back in preparation for the final sprint. He had employed it in his two 3:58.6 miles in Melbourne and his two races in the US (unsuccessfully against Bailey).

It didn't work this time. Landy was caught wide and back as Lincoln retained the lead through the third lap. The "second Australian" still led at the bell with 400 to go in 2:46.8, but he was starting to feel the strain. As the field turned into the back straight, Lincoln surrendered the lead to an unwilling Hewson.

Hewson had not wanted to be in front at this stage, but he knew that to surrender the lead now would be fatal. So he went for home, leading almost into the final straight. Landy was starting to move from the back of the pack, where Delany had been "tracking" him, but he was forced five wide and baulked at running that far out on the bends.

Delany, on the other hand, was coming through on the inside and he burst through the ruck to take the lead in the final straight. He was running so fast — 53.4 seconds for the final lap — that with the preferred run, no-one could catch him. Landy, out wide and clear at last, finished faster than anyone else. His 54-second final lap brought him from near last to third, just failing to catch silver medalist Klaus Richtzenhain of Germany.

After the race, Landy was effusive in his praise of the winner. "I couldn't understand why they weren't talking about Delany after the heats," he commented. "I thought [he] was a certainty in the final. Delany was unquestionably too good. He's a magnificent runner. I just didn't have it. I thought I had no chance at all before the race and only in the last straight did I begin to hope."

Landy says now a medal was as much as he could have hoped for. The lead-up to Melbourne was "the most difficult period of my athletic career, because so much was expected of me. I lost confidence because I couldn't train regularly and how I got up to win the bronze medal was a bit of a miracle."

Delany outlined his feelings in his book *Staying the Distance* (2006, O'Brien Press): "It was the happiest day of my life. I had set out to win the Olympic 1500 metres crown, and ... I had achieved my goal. The rest of my athletic career would always be a sort of anticlimax. I was plagued by injuries later on and I never again had the same driving ambition. But on that day in Melbourne I was grateful to so many people — my parents, my early coaches in Ireland, Jumbo [James 'Jumbo' Elliott, his coach at Villanova University] and John Landy — who had inspired me with confidence and example."

Fifty years earlier, Delany had expressed similar sentiments on the MCG. He talked about how meeting and talking with Landy during the latter's American tour had helped. "Before I met John I was just another mile runner. He told me I could run faster and showed me my capabilities. He taught me how to relax and cut five or six seconds off my time for the mile."

The questions in 1954 were, firstly, could Landy have won with different tactics; and secondly, would he have won but for the cut foot. This time it was whether the trip to America had ruined his chances. There seems little doubt that it severely compromised them. Landy says he was developing tendonitis before he went to the US, but on his return he referred to the tracks on which he competed as "very hard. The one at Fresno is pure clay, as far as I can see. I don't say they're not good, but I didn't like them."

Landy has always refused to blame the US trip for the woes that followed, but in 2006, he said: "It didn't help. The tracks I was running on were literally the same as running on that road," he pointed outside, "and my shoes weren't cushioned." Interestingly, New Zealand's Jack Lovelock, the 1936 Olympic 1500 metres champion, had not run as well as expected at the 1932 Los Angeles Games four years earlier. One of the factors affecting his performance was bursitis, which he attributed to training on the hard US tracks (*Jack Lovelock: Athlete and Doctor*; Dr Graeme Woodfield, Trio Books, 2007). From Landy's own experience, he warned Herb Elliott to beware of the hard tracks before the rising young miler went to the US in 1958.

Landy was pressured into the trip to promote the Melbourne Games. Premier Bolte and Councillor Nathan applied that pressure. In light of Landy's subsequent injury problems, had it been horse racing they may well have been charged with not allowing Landy to run on his merits in Melbourne!

That said, it is entirely possible Delany would have won the Olympic 1500 metres anyway. He ran just six tenths of a second »

Ron Delany

A talented tennis player, Ron Delany turned to athletics in his mid-teens and quickly discovered his gift for running.

Delany's talent was obvious. As a 19-year-old he ran 1:50.2 for 800 metres to make the final at the European Championships (in which he finished a distant last). He then followed a trail that has become familiar to Irish middle-distance athletes since: leaving Dublin to study at Villanova University in Pennsylvania, USA. There Delany trained under legendary track coach James "Jumbo" Elliott. He moved up to the mile in 1955 and was undefeated at the distance in indoor competition in the 1956 winter.

As noted already, Delany ran in John Landy's two US races and was soundly beaten in both. He uncharacteristically led in the first race, in Los Angeles, and blew up. "If I hadn't run too smartly, I at least spent my time off the track wisely listening to Landy's advice on how to run the mile," Delany wrote in *Staying the Distance*. "John pointed out flaws in my action, which I worked on subsequently, and he assured me it was only a matter of time before I, too, would join the four-minute club."

Delany bounced back to dethrone Jim Bailey as national collegiate champion, demonstrating the potent sprint he would use in Melbourne. "[He] went by me so fast, so suddenly, that even if I'd had the ability I wouldn't have been able to go with him," said Bailey, no mean finisher himself.

In June, running in Compton, Los Angeles, Delany fulfilled Landy's prediction, running 3:59.0 for the mile, crossing the line less than a metre in front of Denmark's Gunnar Neilsen. He ran in a new pair of spikes. "I got a pair on credit about 15 minutes before [the start] from a shoe salesman. He made me pay up afterward, too, my last $10 in fact ..." (*Staying the Distance*.) Landy sent a telegram. "Heartiest congratulations. Don't take up 5000 metres. Leave me a chance. Kindest regards, John Landy."

Then things went awry. Delany was badly spiked in a race in Paris in July and although he returned with a respectable

4:06, he then slumped to 4:20 in a race in front of his home crowd in Dublin.

As usual in Ireland, there was no shortage of advice, some of it that Delany should not go to Melbourne. Fund-raising was another problem to be overcome, but eventually Delany arrived in Melbourne as part of a small team of twelve that would take home no fewer than five medals.

Insiders knew Delany posed a threat in the Melbourne 1500 because of his devastating finish. He described the race in *Staying the Distance*: "In a crowded field of twelve one had to avoid trouble and I did this by running at the back of the pack. At the bell the entire field was fantastically gathered within a mere six yards. I was back in tenth place but I was very much in touch with the leaders … I knew I could not afford to allow anyone to break into a lead at this vital stage so I moved out wide to allow myself a clear run about 350 yards from the finish.

"As we went down the backstretch for the last time, Hewson was forging away in the lead. Suddenly Landy sprinted and I reacted immediately, slipping into his wake and following him as we passed the struggling figures of the other competitors. I knew if I were to win I would have to make one and only one decisive move … and about 150 yards from the finish I opened up with everything I had. Within ten yards I was in the lead and going away from the field. I knew nobody was going to pass me, for my legs were pumping like pistons … My heart swelled with joy as I approached the tape ten feet clear of the rest of the field, and as I burst through I threw my arms wide in exultation. I could hardly believe I had won. My eyes swelled with tears, and I dropped to my knees in a prayer of thanksgiving. John Landy, who finished third, came over to me, helped me to my feet and warmly congratulated me …"

Delany was third in the 1500 metres at the 1958 European championships, behind Brian Hewson and Dan Waern. Achilles problems hampered his preparations for the defence of his title at the 1960 Rome Olympics and he was forced to withdraw from the 1500 after failing to make the final of the 800. He hung up his spikes in 1962, aged 26.

» slower than Istvan Rozsavolgyi's world record set just three months earlier. And he did it with a last lap of under 54 seconds.

Olympic champions can be thought of as covering a spectrum: at one end, there are those whose gold medal crowns several years' dominance in their sport; at the other end are those who have their day of days with perfect timing. Delany probably falls closer to the latter end (albeit injuries are a mitigating factor). But if 1 December 1956 was Delany's day of days, it was one of such brilliance it may have beaten any other runner in the race at his best anyway.

While the drama of the 1500 metres was being played out on the MCG, the marathoners were making their way from the stadium to the turnaround point in suburban Oakleigh and back. With poignant timing, as John Landy ran his last major race, his friend and the man who had inspired many of the 1956 team, Les Perry, was running the marathon. Never one to die wondering, Perry stuck close to the leaders for almost 20 miles before, feeling sick and leg-weary, he could run no further. Time, and the distance, had conquered him.

"Too hot, too hard and too old," he said after he pulled out at 20 miles at which point he was still in the top ten runners in the race. "It was the toughest race I have run in," Perry told reporters.

The marathon was won by Alain Mimoun of France, second so many times to Emil Zatopek on the track. Mimoun fulfilled his destiny in 1956 in more ways than one. During his stay, he visited Mt Alexander near Bendigo, because it was near the Victorian goldfields. It proved a good omen, so much so that he named his son Alexander a few years later. Mimoun retained such a love for Melbourne, and Australia, that almost 50 years later, when Australia played France in the final of the rugby world cup, he supported Australia while his wife supported France!

Despite the organisational hassles and squabbles in the lead-up, and international conflict in Hungary and the Middle East, the Melbourne Games proved an outstanding success. The Olympic

Games was a watershed event for Melbourne and Australia, proving Australians could organise a world event.

Similarly, for John Landy and his fellow middle and long-distance athletes, the Games confirmed they could compete on a world stage. Soon enough, they and others would go on to even greater success.

12

The Legacy

In 1983, a global athletics meeting was held in Helsinki for the first time since Les Perry, Don Macmillan, Bob Prentice, John Landy and Percy Cerutty had ventured there for the 1952 Olympic Games. In a poignant touch, Emil Zatopek was present, too. Not surprisingly, given his feats of 1952, he had been invited by the Finns. The surprise, and it was a pleasant one, was that Zatopek was allowed to attend at all; it was the great runner's first trip out of then Czechoslovakia since he had been sent to internal exile by the Czech government for having been a supporter of the short-lived reformist socialist government led by Alexander Dubcek. The tanks rolled in, snuffing out the so-called "Prague spring" of 1968, and Zatopek was sent off to work in a remote rural forest area.

Fittingly, an Australian did great things in Helsinki that 1983 summer. Surging up a long hill fewer than five kilometres from the finish on Helsinki's main boulevard, Mannerheimintie, Robert de Castella broke clear from his Ethiopian shadow, Kebede Balcha, to win the marathon.

"Deek" had been fancied to win in Helsinki, made favourite by the uncritical embrace of his fellow Australians, just as John Landy had been in 1954 and 1956. He had set a world record at Japan's Fukuoka marathon in 1981, won at the 1982 Brisbane Commonwealth Games and defeated the American, Alberto Salazar, in Rotterdam earlier in 1983 in what was widely regarded as a match-race between the two best marathoners in the world. (In fact, Carlos Lopes of Portugal, who would become 1984 Olympic champion, had upstaged the well-beaten Salazar by running de Castella to two seconds.)

There was a closer link between de Castella and John Landy, however, than the mere coincidental one of carrying the burden of favouritism. The connection ran through de Castella's coach, Pat Clohessy.

Clohessy was not only de Castella's coach, but the biggest influence on Australian distance running through the era from roughly 1976 to 1996 that produced Olympic finalists like Bill Scott, Chris Wardlaw and Dave Fitzsimons, and middle-distance stars in Pat Scammell and Simon Doyle. He became a great coach at least partly because he never fulfilled his potential as an athlete. Born in Melbourne, Clohessy grew up mostly in rural New South Wales where he received some coaching from Cliff Johnson in Muswellbrook. From then on, however, inasmuch as he had a coach, it was John Landy. At the suggestion of fellow New South Wales runner Al Lawrence, Clohessy had written to Landy in 1955.

Landy's reply initiated an arrangement accurately described as coaching by correspondence. He wrote out detailed schedules that the enthusiastic and over-motivated Clohessy followed to the letter and beyond (in similar fashion to Geoff Warren emulating Zatopek's supposed running in heavy army boots). At a personal level, Clohessy was amazed at and grateful for this interest from one of the world's best runners. "Here was I, a kid from the country, and John Landy was taking time to write to me," he says. Fortunately, the correspondence continued over several years, so Clohessy ultimately had the benefit of Landy's conversion back to the natural running that Landy was forced to undertake in the mountains at Timbertop in 1955.

Clohessy ran for Australia at the 1962 British Empire Games in Perth, finishing seventh in the three miles, but his greater success came in the US for the University of Houston. From 1961 to 1963, he won two national collegiate three mile titles and the AAU national three mile title. Together with Clohessy's exposure to New Zealand coach Arthur Lydiard and his athletes — principally 1960 Olympic champions Peter Snell and Murray Halberg, and marathoner Barry Magee — on a 1961 European tour, the Landy letters formed the basis of Clohessy's complex training system that combined elements of Lydiard, the Swedish system of fartlek, and intervals. So, in a very real sense, Robert de Castella is part of John Landy's legacy in Australian athletics.

In fact, a line can be drawn from the Olympians of 1952, through Herb Elliott and Ron Clarke to de Castella and his era and then, through Chris Wardlaw's own coaching and influence, to Steve Moneghetti, and now Craig Mottram and his coach (through to the Beijing Olympic Games), Nic Bideau. Another offshoot starts with Merv Lincoln and Franz Stampfl and runs to Ralph Doubell, Australia's gold medallist in the 1968 Olympic 800 metres, as well as the only man to have made a close approach to the Australian record Doubell set in winning that race, 1982 Commonwealth Games 800 gold medallist Peter Bourke. The Landy legacy continues to this very day. If you would trek the difficult path from Australia to the top in world athletics, what better role model could you have than John Landy?

Cerutty and Perry may well have fired his ambition and shown him the way, but twice — once when he came back from Helsinki and again in 1955 — he demonstrated that the isolation of Australia was not an insurmountable handicap to reaching the top of the world. The first time, Landy crossed the street from his family's home in Central Park and utilised what he found there; the second, he adapted the far less obviously suitable environment of the Australian sub-alpine bushlands to his needs to return to the track with a personal best at half-mile. Both times, he showed by personal example that world-class performances could be achieved by Australians, in Australia, training in Australian conditions.

Clohessy is in no doubt as to Landy's influence — and never has been. In *Deek: The Making of Australia's World Marathon Champion* (Robert de Castella with Mike Jenkison; Collins, 1984), Clohessy says: "Before Landy's time our runners were very aware of Australia's isolation and they felt somewhat inferior to the Europeans who produced most of the records, won most of the medals and came up with all the new training ideas. Landy's excellence broke this feeling of inferiority. His world mile record in Finland in 1954 was very important for Australia. On a personal level he helped countless runners with his advice and counselling and I get a lot of satisfaction from the feeling that I am carrying on his work."

The Landy legacy can be examined in several areas: what his contemporaries thought of him; his wider role in the Australian running community and his position as a role model; and his contribution after he retired.

First, however, let us get Landy retired. Before the Melbourne Games had even finished, there were two athletics meetings starring Australian and international Olympic athletes in Sydney. The first, at Sydney Sports Ground on Sunday 2 December 1956, saw Isabel Daniels, a member of the bronze medal US women's 4×100 metres relay team, run within a tenth of a second of Marjorie Jackson's world record for 100 yards. She ran in heavy rain without removing her sweat jacket.

The second, also at the Sports Ground and held three days later, was the traditional British Empire versus the USA match in which John Landy was involved in his second, and last, world record, albeit an unofficial one. "We'd been up all night," says Landy. "I ran 4:02; I don't know how I did it. We beat the Americans." Indeed, the British Empire team of Murray Halberg and Neville Scott of New Zealand, Britain's Ian Boyd and Landy ran 16:26.4 to beat the Americans by almost 200 yards. Again, Landy took a "world record" off Roger Bannister, who with British teammates Chris Chataway,

Bill Nankeville and Donald Seaman had set the previous mark three years earlier. This one did not count officially, however, as all members of a world record relay must be from the same country.

In an article written on Landy's retirement, Chris Brasher talked of the socialising among the athletes in Sydney and reflected on the pressures — in Brasher's view — nudging John Landy towards retirement. "I last saw him late one night in Sydney, his room full of friends and good talk and song. John, prising open the beer bottles, making sure that everyone's glass was full, occasionally joining in with a comment or a new verse, relaxed and temporarily happy. Dissatisfied with his own performance in the Olympic Games, he knew that he couldn't run again as he had done in earlier years. Always there would be pressure from outside that every time he ran he must win. He had known defeat by the greatest runners in the world, yet he also knew that he could under different circumstances defeat them. He had to make up his mind whether or not to go on to convince himself of this, knowing that he could never again enjoy his running because of this weight of outside pressure." (Chris Brasher, *The Observer*, 3 March 1957.)

Landy and his teammates came back to Melbourne to participate in a closing ceremony that, with its innovative mingling of teams as suggested by young Chinese–Australian boy John Ian Wing, set a happy precedent for all subsequent closing ceremonies. "I came back and walked in the closing ceremony, which was fantastic. [It was] very emotional, a very, very fine finish. It was one enduring contribution of Melbourne to the Olympic movement, because it's been duplicated not only in every Olympics since but in every major Games — the Commonwealth Games, the Pan American Games, the European championships, they all have this final day inter-mingling and it started in Melbourne. Melbourne had a terrific atmosphere in terms of friendliness and crowd encouragement. It was great."

Landy had told press and friends that he would continue to

run, at least until the end of the 1956–57 season. Now that he had regained it, he said, it would be a shame to waste his fitness. But the tendonitis got no better. "The leg trouble just got to a stage where I couldn't go on. I just thought I'd give it a rest for a couple of months, which I did, and then I tried to come back. I had a couple of 880 runs and I ran 1.54. I had done no training." In what proved to be his final race, Landy lost over 880 yards to Geoff Fleming, a good runner who was many times a finalist in Victorian titles but not in Landy's league. "I quit, my time was up," says Landy. It was belated recognition, he adds. "I should have quit straight after the Games."

John Landy's world record in the mile lasted almost three years in all, until Great Britain's Derek Ibbotson ran 3:57.2 in July 1957. Landy's one involvement in competitive sport after he gave up athletics was a half-hearted attempt to come back to Australian Rules football with Old Geelong Grammarians in the Victorian amateur competition. "I played a few games with them in 1959–60," he recalls. That, too, ended with a realisation of his limits. "We played Kew one day. I was at full-back and I got Ian Mort. It was a real baptism of fire. He kicked a few goals and gave me the run-around." (Not that this was any disgrace: Ian Mort was a gifted player who went on to play for Hawthorn in the top Australian Rules competition and was a member of their 1961 premiership side.)

Others were coming to the end of the road as well. Les Perry did keep running after the 1956 Games, mainly in Victorian road and cross-country races. His contribution continued in other areas, too. He moved to Heathmont, in Melbourne's outer eastern suburbs. Though remaining a member of Williamstown, he was also one of the founders of the Ringwood Athletic Club, which has produced home-grown Olympians including David Culbert, Werner Reiterer and Kyle Vander-Kuyp, as well as being the club of other champions including sprinters Cathy Freeman and Lauren Hewitt and Commonwealth Games discus champion Scott Martin. Perry made an attempt to return for the Rome Olympics. He won the 1959 Victorian marathon, held over the Olympic course from the MCG to Oakleigh and back, in 2:45:17. As he had also won the Victorian title over the Olympic course in 1956, this gave him more wins on it than Alain Mimoun but not, alas, the gold medal.

Perry also continued to contribute through the Victorian Marathon Club, but his most significant contribution to Australian athletics may have been to take his new neighbour out for a run around the hilly suburban streets of Heathmont one night.

Ron Clarke once described how Perry and another fit veteran runner, Bob Horman, who was the mayor of Ringwood, had to wait for him at the top of every hill. "You've got some work to do if you want to get fit again," Perry told the former junior world record holder in the mile. Unwittingly, this galling experience crystallised Clarke's ambition to get back into athletics and set him on the path to becoming the greatest distance runner in Australian and, arguably, world history, re-defining the limits of performance in the 5000 and 10,000 metres.

Dave Stephens continued to be dogged by the injuries that had hindered his Games preparation and limited by his own erratic personality. He made a promising comeback a few years after Melbourne and, in 1960, won the Victorian six miles title and was placed second and third in the three and six miles, respectively, at the national titles in Perth. But the comeback petered out again.

Al Lawrence, Dave Power and Albie Thomas continued to dominate Australian distance running, eclipsing the Victorians between the Melbourne Games and the return of Clarke in the early 1960s. Lawrence went to the University of Houston in the USA, one of several Australians to find success there (others included Pat Clohessy and Barrie Almond). Lawrence made the 1960 Olympic team, but did not duplicate his Melbourne success. Power won the six miles and marathon at the 1958 Empire Games in Cardiff, won a bronze medal in the 10,000 at the 1960 Rome Olympics and silver medals in both the six miles and marathon at the 1962 Perth Empire and Commonwealth Games. Thomas went on to set world records for two and three miles and also record the fastest mile by an Australian in Australia, a record that was to last many years. He ran in two more Olympics, though without the same success as 1956.

Besides Landy, the other athlete to go virtually straight into retirement from Melbourne was Jim Bailey, the man whose defeat of the champion, combined with the rock-hard US tracks, did so much to derail Landy's Olympic campaign. Bailey departed from Melbourne a dejected figure. His marriage soon after the Games doubtless restored his spirits somewhat but, athletically, he was at a low ebb. He hardly ran again, and when he did, did not compete well.

Fifty years later, Bailey told me in a phone interview that his performance in Melbourne was "a tragedy". How does he feel about it? "It's a lingering disappointment; [I feel] embarrassment, humiliation, regret."

Bailey lived in Sydney for some time in the 1970s. Even in America, he was occasionally tracked down for various Olympic anniversary commemorations. "I enjoyed anonymity for a long time," he said. But he had not thought of coming back for any until the 50th anniversary. He was looking for "some sort of closure", he said. Bailey repaired his relationship with John Landy before coming out, at least from his own side. "I did get one thing off my chest. I wrote to Landy and congratulated him on the terrific race he ran in the [Olympic] 1500. He came from behind and got up into third. People used to say that he had no finish, but he did. He ran a good race."

Bailey also had a "Landy legacy" of his own. Despite his Olympic performance, he was voted Oregon "champion of champions" by Oregon sportswriters for 1956, ahead of other college and professional sports stars. The honour was bestowed almost entirely on the basis of his win, and sub-four minute mile, at the Los Angeles

Coliseum. "I really must thank Landy for this," Bailey said by way of acceptance. "Without that one race, who would even know me?"

John Landy's position among his contemporaries evolved through his career. When he took his first serious steps towards Olympic selection in 1951, he was very much the understudy to Don Macmillan, both within Cerutty's group and on the track. "Macmillan's tail-light" he was dubbed by Ben Kerville of *The Sporting Globe*. Doubtless this was not intended as the disparagement it implicitly was. Nevertheless, Landy rapidly progressed to a position of independence and leadership. He was as much in thrall to Emil Zatopek in 1952 Helsinki as Cerutty or Les Perry, but he went about learning from the champion in his own way, through observation, and he put those observations into practice. His improvement from 1952 Olympic also-ran to the world's leading miler was achieved entirely as a result of his own efforts.

Landy did not seek a leadership role, but his performances and character catapulted him into one. The notion of athletics as the pursuit of excellence is like all ideals in that it is generally aspired to, but seldom attained. Landy went close to it, as US journalist Paul O'Neil noted in 1956. "Landy is a complex human — an intellectual with a compulsion for the arena, and a stoic disregard for pain and exhaustion; a reserved and sensitive man whose mind is repelled, but whose spirits are kindled, by the roar of applause and the incandescent glare of publicity. The mile is much more than a race to Landy: it is, one gathers, almost a problem in aesthetics. 'I'd rather lose a 3:58 mile,' he says, 'than win one in 4:10.' He has never betrayed by the slightest word or gesture anything but the utmost admiration for those who have beaten him. But he burns to win." (Paul O'Neil, *Sports Illustrated*, 21 May 1956.)

Pat Clohessy's view that Landy's world-record mile in Finland liberated Australian athletes from their inferiority complex is quoted earlier. Clohessy characterises Landy's legacy into various categories

— pathfinder, innovator, inspiration, generosity, national influence and global influence. "Landy not only climbed the mountain himself," Clohessy said early in 2007, "but he encouraged, inspired, even assisted others who sought his advice." These others included Ron Clarke, Herb Elliott and Clohessy himself. Clohessy lauds Landy as "a pioneer [who] set a high standard on the running track and even higher standards in innovation and inspiring others. John was inspiring in his positive approach, facing new challenges and seeing advantages in training on your own if your career situation determined that."

Clohessy also categorises Landy's "propensity to help others" as "legendary, even unsurpassed. His influence pervaded the Landy era and far beyond, indeed set in motion the Landy, Clarke, Power, Thomas, Lincoln and Elliott world era." And further, "John Landy's pioneering spirit, his innovation, his high standards, his no-excuses approach, his use of the available environment, his inclusion of long running and Timbertop hill sprints, all linked by his generosity in passing on advice to others has left a legacy that has inspired and pervaded the rest of the twentieth century and indeed beyond."

Clohessy emulated Landy's use of the "available environment" in devising sessions for Simon Doyle in Canberra's Stromlo Forest, utilising the hills and dirt trails, away from the sterility of the 400-metre track. Doyle ranked number two in the world at 1500 metres in 1990, still holds the national record for 1500 metres and was Australia's first sub-3:50 miler (Craig Mottram has since broken Doyle's mile record). Yet in his letters to the young Clohessy in Tamworth, Landy emphasised that he should not simply duplicate any of the training schedules he sent him, but find his own way. "I would advise you," Landy wrote, "never to take a great deal of notice of anyone with regards to your own training; rather, go out and find what suits you by a period of trial and error." Landy also wrote that: "Training on your own is the greatest asset you can have; it teaches you to be self-reliant." »

Barrie Almond

Barrie Almond was another New South Wales runner to benefit from John Landy's generosity towards his fellow athletes. A schoolboy champion sprinter — he won the New South Wales Combined Intermediate under-15 220 yards in 1949 and the Combined High Schools open 440 in 1951 — Almond gradually made his way towards the middle-distances, eventually excelling at the half-mile. If he was not exactly dragged kicking and screaming into the longer event, he was certainly given several nudges, the last, decisive one by John Landy.

Like all Australian 18-year-olds of the time, Almond did his national service training, in his case six months in the air force. "Nasho" was one of the elements Ron Clarke blames for wrecking his 1956 Olympic campaign. In most cases, including that of Almond, the compulsory training put a halt to careers.

When Almond went back to Botany Harriers, clubmates Al Lawrence, Bryce Mackay and John Russell encouraged him to try the 880 yards. He got as far as the 440, but no further. In the second half of 1955, John Landy paid a visit to Sydney to fulfil a speaking commitment. Landy had befriended Bryce Mackay during the 1954 Empire Games, the two meeting up in Europe and, as he usually did, he rang his "mate" to let him know he was coming to town. Mackay, as he usually did, told Landy he would meet him at the airport.

The catch in the arrangement was that Mackay did not drive. No problem; the irrepressible "Macca" who, among other things, was a stringer for the Sydney newspapers, invariably knew someone else who did. This time, he put the word on Barrie Almond, who was delighted to comply. Mackay had organised a drink and something to eat at a Sydney hotel. Almond remembers it well. "At age 20, I was awestruck listening to John and 'Macca' reminiscing on Vancouver and their subsequent trip to Europe."

When the conversation turned to what event Almond ran, Mackay jumped in before Almond could reply, saying that Almond was a sprinter wanting to move up to the half-mile, and asked what training should he do. Over the meal and a beer, Landy outlined a training program for Almond. Advice which had fallen on stony ground when it came from his clubmates suddenly took hold when it came from one of the world's most famous athletes.

Barrie Almond was one more athlete to benefit from John Landy's willingness to help any athlete, any time. When Landy met Ron Delany two years later, it would have been more out of character had he *not* offered him help and advice. "He talked about what the Finns did," Almond said in 2007. "He suggested a program that included a series of 330s [330-yard repetitions] a couple of times a week and some 165s [165 yards, half that distance], fartlek a couple of times a week and, once a week, go for a long run with these guys. Since these were god-like words, I trained very diligently for about ten weeks with the program. After a while I could sense the running strength coming."

Simple enough, yet for a sprinter of some talent but uncertain dedication it was all the motivation Almond needed. He adopted the 880 and improved steadily. In one of his first runs, Mackay nominated him to run in a half-mile race at half-time in an Australia versus England rugby match. The Sydney Cricket Ground was a quagmire that day, but Almond surprised himself by winning in just over two minutes. In 1956, Almond reached the final of the 880 at the Australian championships — the titles of the famous Landy–Clarke mile — and trained hard through the winter for the Olympic selection trials. The 880 was scheduled for the first of the two weekends over which the trials were held. As Almond remembers it, the final was a farcical jog with a fierce sprint home. There was just one problem: it was such a farce the selectors ordered a second race the following weekend. Almond did not qualify for the team in either race, but at the Australian championships in March 1957, he ran Herb Elliott to less than half a second in the 880 yards, losing narrowly, 1:49.3 to 1:49.7. Two days earlier he ran fourth in the mile, though this time a more substantial twelve seconds behind Elliott's 4:00.4.

The long running did not go to waste, either. Almond joined

Lawrence and Pat Clohessy at the University of Houston. At the 1959 Amateur Athletic Union national cross-country championships, Lawrence won and Almond finished sixth. Not a bad effort for a bloke who messed around with the sprints.

And all down to giving John Landy a lift from the airport to the pub!

» In another letter, Landy — as he did for Al Lawrence in the 1956 Olympics — offered his thoughts on how best to run against Clohessy's domestic opponents. One paragraph sums ups his attitude to helping all who ask. "Most of these fellows I have mentioned (Power, Lawrence, Stephens, Perry, Macmillan and Bailey) are my friends and naturally I have no desire to see them beaten … I like to take an impersonal attitude — try to do your own best and if you don't make it enjoy the other fellow's success." In other words, it is easier for one athlete to improve if all athletes are improving at the same time.

An October 1956 letter gives some insight into Landy's injury struggle. "You must excuse me for taking so long to reply to your letters," he begins. "I have been very worried these last few weeks with bad tendons and have not written a single letter in a month!" Landy also writes ruefully of the role of luck in reaching peak fitness on a particular day such as at the Olympic Games. "Allowing for all this, I think one should aim to achieve something in athletics over a period of two or three years rather than stake everything on one or two very big meetings."

Landy's no-excuses approach also struck Dave Power in Vancouver. Regardless of whether you felt the cut foot was a big factor or agree with Landy's view that it was irrelevant, Landy's refusal to put it forward as an excuse impressed his fellow runners. "Running with that cut in Vancouver and not saying anything about it, who wouldn't be inspired by that," asks Dave Power. High praise indeed from one described by his friend Jim Bailey as "a tough little bastard". Power also talks of how Landy's break-through runs inspired his contemporaries to lift their sights. "When John ran 4:02, we just wouldn't have thought it possible. If we ran 4:12 then, we thought we were going great guns. He lifted us to another level. When he broke the world record it was greater than sliced bread."

Albie Thomas makes the point that Landy was a lot tougher than the 'gentleman John' image inspired by his good sportsmanship and acts such as picking up Ron Clarke. "People looked up to him in a different way to being a nice bloke, and a gentleman," says Thomas. "You'd have to say he was inspirational, but he wouldn't be out there beating a drum about himself. He liked his personal life, he wasn't pushy. You had to respect what he'd done. When you read of '54, he cuts his foot and still lines up and races, doesn't say anything. That's got to get you respect."

John Landy's ability to mix well with people at all levels is a major factor in the role he played in Australian athletics both during and after his own running career. Landy is, and always has been, reluctant to venture down biographical or autobiographical paths, but his genuine interest in others, combined with an uncanny knack for retaining key facts about them, are readily observable.

When *The Age* set up a picture story with Craig Mottram and John Landy, who at that stage was nearing the end of six years as Governor of Victoria, at the Melbourne Cricket Ground in the months before the 2006 Commonwealth Games, Governor Landy arrived in his official car. Mottram strolled across the MCG parklands from his Richmond home with Garry Henry, the assistant coach who regularly accompanies him to training camps and competition sites around the world. Craig introduced Garry to John Landy. "Oh, yes," said the governor by way of recognition, "the 2:10 marathoner." Landy had correctly remembered that Henry ran 2:10:09 at the 1980 Fukuoka marathon.

From personal observation, too, Landy is far more down-to-earth and *Australian* (there is no better word for it) than his image as some sort of paragon of sportsmanship and virtue would suggest. Australians directly exposed to this in the 1950s would have recognised his qualities. For all the praise, considered and unconsidered, that Landy's gesture in checking on Ron Clarke engendered, Australians valued as much, or more, Landy's tenacity in his lonely pursuit of the four-minute mile, the total honesty of his racing and his refusal to make excuses once he had put his toe on the line. "That's got to get you respect." Albie Thomas was talking about the cut foot in Vancouver when he made that observation, but it is equally apt of Landy's entire attitude.

It is often said that Australians love winners only — an observation that is to some extent true. But ahead of that they recognise and value whole-hearted commitment in their sportsmen and women. This is something John Landy the athlete had by the buckets full. It also explains the popularity of other largely non-winning athletes such as Ron Clarke, Raelene Boyle and Steve Moneghetti.

In one of the many newspaper profiles written on Landy after he broke the mile world record, his mother observed that "Among his family and close friends, John has a wonderful sense of humour." Paul O'Neil noted similar traits in his *Sports Illustrated* profile done during Landy's 1956 US visit. "[Landy] proved himself a humorous and extremely sociable fellow, albeit one with a sardonic eye.

"When [Pete] Rozelle announced, amid a long-distance call to Melbourne, that Australian newspapers were reporting the tour on page one daily, Landy muttered: 'Sickening.' As Rozelle recounted his ambassadorial triumphs, Landy marched up and down the room, grinning accusingly and lifting an imaginary pitchfork."

To an Australian pressman in Fresno on that trip who reported that he'd just seen a real cowboy, Landy asked: "What's he look like?"

"Tight blue jeans, cowboy boots, black shirt and a big hat," came back the description.

"Oh, I know him — Wes Santee," Landy shot back.

As Brasher noted, Landy was a convivial host to some Empire and US athletes in Sydney in 1956. Another contemporary recalls Landy as a superb story-teller and a mimic. In any event, his ability to socialise was not an issue.

In assessing what followed John Landy, it is easy to forget that he was the athlete who put Australia on the map, athletically. By the time the Olympic flame was doused at the Melbourne Cricket Ground, the Games had superseded what went before. But it was only in the last 18 months before the Melbourne Olympics that the event had come to the forefront of the public's attention. There was not the long promotional and marketing build-up then that is such an integral part of recent editions of the Games. Indeed, as John Landy says himself, Australians, and more particularly the people of Melbourne, only became acutely aware of the Games when IOC president Avery Brundage threatened to move them elsewhere. Before that, Landy was the face — the whole body, in fact — of Australian athletics. His fame grew out of the chase for the four-minute mile, and it made him a household name around the world like no other Australian athlete and few international athletes had ever been. Landy, Bannister and Santee were as widely known around the world in 1953 and 1954 as Zatopek, Blankers-Koen and Owens ever were at the peak of their powers.

Were this just reported locally, it would be easy to dismiss it as a peculiarly Australian preoccupation with a small country's place in the world, but the publicity generated by John Landy's visit to the US in May 1956 shows this not to be the case. Landy was feted right up there alongside major US sporting events like the Kentucky Derby. He was photographed as often with film stars like Douglas Fairbanks and Bob Hope as he was with Ron Delany and other athletic opponents. He was as big in mass appeal publications like the *Saturday Evening Post* as he was in specialist sports magazines like *Sports Illustrated*.

When Merv Lincoln and Herb Elliott went to the US in 1957 and 1958, their passage was so much easier because of the pathways smoothed by Landy. Nor were emerging Australian athletes viewed with scepticism because Landy had been through that and dispelled it. The salt passed to Arthur Daley had served to season his substantial slice of humble pie. Like Kenyan and Ethiopian athletes years later, it was assumed relatively unknown Australians were worth backing because Australians must be good.

The major development of the 1956–57 domestic season was the emergence of Elliott. He had been inspired watching the Games, principally by Vladimir Kuts' double in the 5000 and 10,000 metres. After the Games, Elliott convinced his parents he should stay on and train with Cerutty at Portsea. He was still feeling some pain in the foot he had broken the previous year, but he was assured that there was no danger of the fracture opening up again. He continued to train hard as he moved towards racing.

After a half-mile race at a Portsea carnival, Elliott opened up with a world junior record mile of 4:06.0. Landy, who saw the race, praised Elliott as "the most fantastic junior I have ever seen". Cerutty could not help himself, commenting pointedly: "Elliott will rewrite the record book in a few years if he sticks at it. You will forget Landy ever existed." This was half right, of course. Herb Elliott did rewrite the record books. But he was totally wrong on the other. Fifty years later, people were still recalling the chase for the four-minute mile and Landy's leading role in it. Cerutty's gracelessness knew few bounds.

In a very real sense, Cerutty needed Elliott to come along. By 1956, he had alienated himself from not only the athletic establishment but also from most of the athletes he had influenced. He was having most success with athletes like Thomas and Power whom he saw only a limited number of times a year and then only for limited periods. However, even with Elliott in his camp, Cerutty would continue to feud with virtually everyone else. People who disagreed with him were dismissed contemptuously. To a certain extent, he needed enemies to rail against; part of this was show, but he did it too often, to too many people, over too long a period of time. Once Elliott was off the scene, Cerutty went into decline, too.

That was for the future. For the present, things were very much on the up. Elliott and Lincoln did not clash often in the 1956–57 season. This was understandable given Lincoln had ended his Olympic campaign injured, while Elliott, who did not turn 19 until 25 February 1957, was coming back off his severe foot injury. Elliott won the 880 yards and mile at the Victorian championships, beating Jack Douglas in the former and the tough New Zealander Bill Baillie, who was living in Melbourne and running for the Box Hill club at the time, Ron Clarke and John Murray in the latter. Elliott and Lincoln met just once, in the mile at the Australian championships at Olympic Park on Saturday 9 March 1957. Elliott led and the pair were still close together at 1500, when Elliott unleashed a fierce sprint to win, 4:00.4 to 4:02.6. Two days later, he beat Barrie Almond in the half mile to record a national middle-distance double in his first senior titles.

That was pretty well Elliott's season. The precocious 19-year-old started his first serious build-up, running miles around Melbourne's Tan Track (the four-kilometre gravel path around the Botanical Gardens), and on the weekends ran the circuits, sand dunes and golf courses at Portsea. One salutary experience was Elliott's first, and only, ten-mile cross-country race in 1957. The race was run at Collingwood, on the very fringe of Melbourne's centre, and ran into and around the national park adjoining the Yarra River. It was one of the areas where Cerutty used to meet his athletes a few years earlier. If the event and the Collingwood Harriers track might have had some emotional attachments, the sentiment ran out as soon as the starting gun went off. A team of New Zealanders, headed by Murray Halberg and most of them trained by Arthur Lydiard, was competing. Two weeks earlier, the Kiwis had dominated the Australian cross-country title, Halberg winning the race outright.

The New Zealanders smashed the Victorians all over again. Halberg won in 52:18, over half a minute faster than the course record held by Les Perry. Teammates Kerry Williams and Pat Sidon took the minor placings ahead of the first local, Don Brain of Chelsea. Then followed three more Kiwis — Melbourne 1500 finalist Neville Scott, Jeff Julian and Mervyn Hillier — before Elliott struggled home in eighth place, over two minutes behind Halberg.

The fact that Halberg and Scott, both at that stage potential 1500 rivals at the 1960 Rome Olympics, were that far ahead could have had a demoralising affect on Elliott. "I'm still not fit," he told journalist Alan Trengrove in a report in *The Sun*. "This is a much tougher business than middle-distance running," he added, but already he was fired up. "I think I'll run in more of these kind of events. They'll be good for me." Cerutty agreed, telling Trengrove: "It will teach him that he has to harden up a lot yet." Elliott kept on training through the 1957 winter and spring, but a recurrence of his foot injury delayed his start to the 1957–58 Australian domestic season.

For Merv Lincoln, who had run the Melbourne Olympic Games, the end of the post-Olympic domestic season was really the start of his year. A fortnight after his defeat by Elliott in the national title, he was ready to make his own tilt at a four-minute mile. A new cinder track had been constructed at Melbourne University, reputedly using some of the cinders from the Olympic track at the MCG. A mile with a Stampfl connection naturally had pacemakers, in this case Ron Clarke and Frank Henagan, a Stampfl protégé who worked at the university. They towed Lincoln through the first three laps in 59, 61 and 60 seconds respectively. He took over halfway up the main straight with 500 yards to run, and worked hard to come home in 3:58.9.

Lincoln said he had got the most out of himself on the day. "I exerted myself to the limit," he told *The Age*, but just as Elliott might say one thing and Cerutty would say another, Stampfl was not content to let his athlete speak for himself, either. He said they had "battled really hard for this, and this is a great reward for Merv". Lincoln, he added, could run 3:55.0 within the next 18 months (give or take a fraction of a second, he was right).

In May, Lincoln headed off to the west coast of the US for a series of five races. The Franz Stampfl connection would not have hurt, nor would Lincoln's status as an Olympic finalist, but he was following the trail Landy had cut the year before. On 24 May 1957, Lincoln won the mile at the Coliseum Relays in 4:01.0, leaving Brian Hewson, Laszlo Tabori (now, along with coach Igloi, living in the USA) and Derek Ibbotson behind. Ibbotson, the emerging British star, got into trouble on the final bend in the race, so the following night at Modesto he stalked Lincoln and won a tactical race in 4:06.4, producing a 55.2 final lap after a dawdling pace. Lincoln then finished off his whirlwind tour with wins at Compton in 4:05.0 (Tabori third), Bakersfield in 4:04.4 and then the AAU national title in Dayton, Ohio in 4:06.1. In the latter, he ran a 56.2 final lap to beat leading Americans Bob Seaman and Don Bowden, who earlier in the year had run 3:58.7 in becoming the first American to break four minutes.

(A little aside on Ibbotson, who was a Yorkshireman who had come late to the mile. His debut came in the 1956 Emsley Carr Mile, one of Britain's traditional middle-distance races, in which he broke four minutes in beating an unfit Ron Delany. His 3:59.4 equalled Roger Bannister's British record — which, like the Australian record of the time, had to be set in Britain. After winning a bronze medal in the 5000 metres in Melbourne, Ibbotson returned to Britain and put in a solid winter of training. Although the results — at least in terms of times — did not show it in his short US visit, they soon did.

On 19 July, 30,000 crammed into London's White City Stadium to see a mile race featuring 1500 metres world record holder Stanislav Jungwirth of Czechoslovakia, Ibbotson and Ken Wood of England, and Olympic 1500 champion Delany. Before the race, Ibbotson asked half-miler Mike Blagrove to set a pace of about 1:56–1:57 for the first half mile. Blagrove delivered enthusiastically, if a little unevenly, scooting through in 55.7 and 1:56.1. Ibbotson, feeling tired, was having second thoughts but a slower third lap gave him a second wind. He went through three laps in 3:00.3, a full stride behind Jungwirth. Ibbotson got the decisive break in the back-straight. He won in 3:57.2, 0.8 faster than Landy's official world record, with Delany second in 3:58.8, then Jungwirth (3:59.1) and Wood (3:59.3).

Controversially, Ibbotson's record was disallowed, not because someone had acted as a pacemaker, but because Ibbotson had asked him to. The International Amateur Athletic Federation had tightened its rules on pacemaking, without providing any greater clarity, unfortunately. In any case, it was no use closing the stable door; the horse had well and truly bolted. "If Jungwirth or Delany had won, would there have been the same fuss?" Ibbotson asked at the time. "I doubt it because neither spoke to Blagrove." Eventually the IAAF relented and allowed the record which, by that time, had been bettered in any case.)

At the end of 1957, hoping to build on the momentum of the Melbourne Olympic Games and the success of the Landy "twilight meetings", the Victorian Amateur Athletic Association brought Stanislav Jungwirth to Melbourne to race Merv Lincoln. Elliott was recovering from another foot injury and unable to run. Six days before Christmas, Lincoln and Jungwirth raced over 1500 metres in Melbourne. Lincoln comprehensively outkicked his main opponent to win, 3:46.5 to 3:48.1. Jungwirth had been ill and he explained to reporters that he was on the improve. "Lincoln was just too good but I think I am finding form after my illness and should do better tomorrow [when they were to race over a mile]."

The Melbourne public did not want explanations, however, plausible or not. At roughly the same point of each of the previous five years they had seen unknown John Landy run 4:02.1 and ignite the chase for the four-minute mile (1952); Landy just fail to break four minutes (1953); Landy ill and apparently broken by 18 months of unremitting racing (1954); Dave Stephens beat the Hungarians and Landy on the verge of a comeback (1955); and had basked in the afterglow of a successful Olympics (1956). They feared they were being sold a pup.

Only 400 were in the crowd to see the 1500. The VAAA faced a loss of £1500 on Jungwirth's visit. Worse, it appeared they may have been looking for a style of running Merv Lincoln could not deliver. They wanted Landy, or someone who ran like him. Bruce Welch articulated the feeling in *The Age*. "It appears the public do not like Lincoln's style of running to win and wants fast times as in the Landy era," he wrote.

Salvation was at hand. A week later, Steve Hayward reported on Elliott's progress and plans for the season in *The Herald*. Elliott, he wrote, may adopt "Landy-style front-running technique" in his coming clashes with Lincoln. "I plan to go fast early and hang on to as high a rating as possible," Elliott was quoted as saying in the article. "If I'm left in front it won't worry me … after all there is more chance of running without distraction — and thus gaining full concentration — when in front." Elliott was speaking a day after he had run a 1:52.4 880 yards at Portsea on Boxing Day, his first race after missing two months with a foot injury. It was a handicap race and he had rounded up the out-markers with a 52.8 first lap before sweeping past them in the second. Three weeks later he ran a touch quicker at an interclub meeting at Olympic Park.

A month before his 20th birthday, Elliott was ready to turn his attention to the mile. At Olympic Park, he followed Coburg clubmate Geoff Fleming through 880 yards in laps of 59.0 and then 62.0, for 2:01.0. On his own, he reached the bell in 3:02 and pushed all the way to the line in 3:59.9. Elliott became the world's youngest sub-four minute miler by a month or two (Don Bowden had just turned 20 when he did it), and the fourth Australian to achieve the goal after Landy, Bailey and Lincoln.

Cerutty caused something of a fuss by insisting on being on the oval after the race. One official objected to his presence, but he was eventually allowed to stay after pointing out that Franz Stampfl had access to the infield. According to newspaper reports, he threatened to pull Elliott out of the races with Lincoln if he (Cerutty) was not allowed to stay.

The enmity between the two coaches added a further element to the natural rivalry between their athletes. It had been smouldering ever since Stampfl arrived in Australia and now it burst into flames. The root cause was the disparity between the professional coach, Stampfl, and Cerutty, who had to scratch to make ends meet and who, moreover, had played a part in the career of pretty well every good distance athlete Australia had produced in the post-war period. When Elliott had beaten Lincoln in the previous year's national title, Elliott had inscribed a picture of the finish with the words: "A victory of Cerutty–Elliott against Stampfl–Lincoln. We've proved to the public what we've always known."

When John Landy was at his peak, Australia had one-third of the chase for a sub-four minute mile; the other two — Bannister and Santee — were elsewhere. All three operated independently of each other, though they were aware of and motivated by what the others were doing and even might be doing. Bannister ran in the contrived race at Motspur Park in 1953 because Santee *might* — the mere possibility was enough — break four minutes later that same day in the US. What was building up in Australia now between

Herb Elliott and Merv Lincoln was a rivalry that, like that of Hägg and Andersson, would play out between two athletes from the same country. Throughout 1958 and into the early part of 1959, Elliott and Lincoln would race each other frequently, would run fast times on almost every occasion and would be, simply, the best two milers in the world.

After Elliott broke four minutes, running wide most of the way because the inside lane of the track was breaking up, Cerutty described the performance as "only a pipe-opener". Both he and Elliott predicted further improvement — and soon. Already the meeting between the two milers, set down for 30 January at Olympic Park, was being seen as a clash of the coaches and their vastly different approaches. Welch's report on the 3:59.9 race repeated a quote from Stampfl that Lincoln was ready to beat "anyone in the world", to which Cerutty's riposte was: "Put your money on Elliott." Indeed, more than a little side money was being wagered on the outcome. The prospective clash had some of the elements of Landy–Bannister, with Elliott more in the front-running Landy mould, Lincoln in the Bannister sit-and-kick role. Elliott would certainly be the aggressor, though not necessarily straight from the gun.

Lincoln understood Cerutty's resentment of Stampfl. In a 1983 interview with Brian Lenton (*Through the Tape*, 1983), he commented: "It was a pity that Percy should have been upset about Franz coming to Australia and getting an appointment at Melbourne University as a full-time track and field coach with a nice salary going into the bargain. Poor old Percy had tried very hard in Australia to make ends meet. He had to get his income from other sources and coach part-time. Cerutty saw Elliott's victories over me as vindicating his superiority as a coach over Stampfl." Lincoln also told Lenton that the relationship between himself and Elliott eventually settled, but added, "However, if Percy or Franz came on the scene a few days before races then things changed again."

To the non-technical, the differences between the coaches were not that important, but the "battle of the coaches" line was manna to journalists and played well in the media. Writing on the eve of the Elliott-Lincoln race on 30 January, 1958, Bruce Welch commented: "No race since the war has created so much intense argument on coaching method … It is no secret that Stampfl and Cerutty do not see eye to eye on a lot of things. The extent to which their training methods differ is not clear to anyone except Lincoln and Elliott … because Cerutty prepares many of his runners at Portsea and away from tracks, the nature of his routines is hidden."

Whether it was the talk of Elliott adopting "Landy-style tactics" or the extra layer of rivalry embodied by the coaches, the race drew the biggest crowd since the pre-Olympic twilight meetings. Anywhere between 15,000 and 20,000 crammed into Olympic Park. Nor did they leave disappointed. Elliott defeated Lincoln narrowly, 3:58.7 to 3:59.0. The race also received "Landy-style" coverage. "Two crash the mile barrier", *The Sun* reported the next day in a front-page picture of the two protagonists turning out of the straight in front of a packed main grandstand with a lap to go. Elliott wasn't excited about his win, the paper reported. "In fact, he was disappointed — because he hadn't cracked Landy's record."

Lincoln had got onto Elliott's shoulder coming into the last bend: "I thought that I had him approaching the home bend," Lincoln said, "but he accelerated." Despite being the leader most of the way, Elliott said he had not been worried about Lincoln's finishing capabilities: "Lincoln's burst did not worry me. I have run 220s and 440s faster than he has."

Inside the paper, sportswriter Jack Dunn reported that Elliott had not only run close to John Landy's national record. "He also emulated Landy," wrote Dunn, "when he:

- brought amateur athletics back to the enthusiasm of the John Landy era;

- recouped the VAAA for most of the money it lost over the unsuccessful visit of Stanislav Jungwirth;
- showed that Australians can bring thousands to see top-class competition without the expense of overseas stars."

The following day's *Sun* carried a perceptive analysis on Percy Cerutty by sports columnist Alan Trengrove, then and now one of the world's foremost writers on tennis. He knew a thing or two about coaches; Australia's tennis coach at that time was Harry Hopman, a strict disciplinarian whose approach brought outstanding results but who was by no mean everyone's cup of tea. Trengrove wrote that Cerutty was a man who looked like an artist but was "an athletics coach — and surely the most extraordinary one in the world". Comparing Cerutty to one of Australia's irascible tennis stars, Trengrove noted: "It's a fact that over the years he has gone through more athletes than Mervyn Rose has tennis racquets." Yet to have sparked the imagination of Landy, Macmillan, Perry, Stephens, Warren and now, Elliott, Cerutty "must have something". Noting that all those athletes except Elliott had broken with the coach, Trengrove suggested that "Cerutty's weakness lies in his very strength — his dominating personality. It is not surprising that he clashes with officials, pressmen and the very athletes he helps to produce. He just doesn't compromise. Eccentric or not," Trengrove concluded, "he knows how to create athletes."

Lincoln and Elliott met again at Leederville Oval in Perth two weeks after their first clash. This one was even closer, Elliott just getting the upper hand in a desperate sprint to the line after his rival had headed him in the straight. Both men were given the same time, 3:59.6 — then the first sub-four minute mile run on a grass track. It would be the closest Lincoln ever came to beating Elliott. "I have a press cutting which shows he was given it by eight inches [20 centimetres]," Lincoln told Lenton. "I didn't think I'd won but at the same time I didn't think Herb won either. You get a feeling as you go over the line together and I thought this must be a damned dead heat."

Timing is sometimes held to be everything in politics. Timing, or the lack of it, was certainly everything in Merv Lincoln's career. He had the misfortune to strike the tail-end of Landy's career, which made a virtual segue into the start of Elliott's. At state, national and international level he always found either Landy or Elliott waiting for him. He ranked second in the world behind Elliott in 1958, yet won only one national and one state mile title throughout his career. His highly successful US tour of 1957, with four wins in five races, was the one period of dominance in Lincoln's career.

After the Perth race, Cerutty expressed concerns that the two-man duels were taking too much out of Elliott, who was doing all the leading. The pair met for the final time in the domestic season at the national titles and dawdled around for two laps before Elliott ran the third lap in 60 seconds and the last in 52.8 to win. He had won from the front in Melbourne; he had won coming back from being passed in the straight in Perth. And now he had won off a slow pace. Lincoln was getting desperate for a win over Elliott. He kept trying. The two were both invited to the US and the head-to-heads continued, despite the presence of Bowden, Tabori and Delany.

Now Elliott encountered his own pacing controversy. He won the first race of the tour — the Coliseum Relays — in 3:57.8, better than Landy's official world record but not as fast as Ibbotson's yet unratified 3:57.2. But a young American half-miler named Drew Dunlap had led for two laps before dropping out. Elliott then led every step after that to beat Lincoln by over 20 metres. Dunlap's coach said he had entered him in the mile at the last minute because he wanted a warm-up run for the half-mile later in the program and another of his runners, who had been entered, could not run. World record or not, Elliott made an impression. Leading the chorus of praise was a familiar name — Arthur Daley of *The New York Times*.

Quoting a top American coach, Daley hailed Elliott as a combination of Delany the racer and Landy the runner. "He's both a racer and a runner. You make the rules and he'll run that way. I used to think Delany was the best miler I ever saw. But now I'll take Elliott. He moves with such lack of effort that he has everyone gasping. This kid is wonderful."

After a modest 4:02.7 win in Modesto, Elliott returned to Los Angeles to run the Compton Invitational meeting. Delany was in the field; so was Tabori. Leading at the bell in 3:01.4, Elliott burst clear to come home over two seconds clear of Tabori in 3:58.1. After a couple of weeks' training, Elliott and Lincoln both ran the AAU titles in Bakersfield, on the edge of the Californian desert. They spent most of the time avoiding each other, and Elliott won the race 3:57.9 to 3:58.5. Lincoln was the only runner in the world getting anywhere near Elliott, but he could not get past him. It was the same at the Empire Games in Cardiff, but at least the first, second, third finish in the mile by Elliott, Lincoln and Thomas was reported not as another second for Lincoln but as an Australian medal sweep. For Elliott, the mile completed a golden double as he had defeated the more-fancied Brian Hewson to win the 880 four days earlier.

It had already been a long year, and Elliott was feeling the strain. "It's a grind," he told journalist Harry Gordon. "Right now I don't feel like doing much racing. I've had a tough program in the US and here and I have miles lined up in Dublin, White City and Edinburgh for the next few weeks." That would change in a few days. Billy Morton was one of the more interesting characters in the sporting world of 1958. He was an Irish athletics promoter, but those words hardly conveyed adequately all that he did.

Morton had single-mindedly and almost single-handedly built Irish athletics from the ground up. He had begun promoting meetings at Lansdowne Road, Dublin's rugby venue, but his aim had always been to create a dedicated athletics venue. Morton's techniques for wooing athletes were legendary. With rationing still in place in post-war London, Morton would turn up at White City "laden like a Lipton's agent: eggs, butter, cans of fruit, all the unpurchaseables of post-war England", according to a 1958 profile in *The Observer*. Such blandishments were lost on American athletes, so Morton invented Irish ancestry for them as a means of luring them across the Irish Sea.

When Ron Delany — Ronnie to all of Ireland — emerged in 1954, Morton had found a drawcard for his meetings. A week before the June 1956 meeting, Delany broke four minutes in the US, then 35,000 turned up to see him run in Dublin. After he became Olympic champion in Melbourne, similar numbers came to two "Delany meetings" in 1957. Through the power of Delany's legs, Billy Morton got his cinder track at Santry stadium. And at one of its first meetings, just before the Empire Games, he got a world record from an Australian. Paced by Lincoln, Albie Thomas ran 13:10.8, to take just over three seconds off the world record formerly held by Sandor Iharos. (Thomas also got barrows full of blarney from Morton, which he passed on to Elliott and the other Australians when he joined them in Cardiff for the Games. Among the many stories extolling Santry's advantages was this absolute zinger: according to Morton, the trees ringing the track absorbed oxygen through the day then released it as dusk closed in, so the athletes ran in an oxygen-rich environment.)

Morton had put together a great field for the mile on 6 August 1958, a few days after the Empire Games closed. Delany was the star turn, but he also had Empire Games medallists Elliott, Lincoln and Thomas and three-mile champion Murray Halberg of New Zealand. Harry Gordon travelled to the race as well, and his previews ran in *The Herald*. Delany, badly beaten by Elliott in the US, had threatened revenge and told Gordon he was now ready to exact it. "I don't ever intend to start watching the back of this Elliott boy every time. That's all over for me ... He depends on a big finishing kick and so do I. Sometime he's going to meet someone who's strong and fit enough to pace it with him over the last lap. And don't you know I've never been so strong and fit in all my life ..."

Elliott, for his part, wanted "to beat Delany badly". Cerutty and Elliott liked to dislike opponents, at least before the start. Trouble was, Delany was a pretty likeable fellow. Needing something to dislike about him, Elliott went for his style. "Personally he's a great fellow but I don't admire his style of running. I don't like this business of sitting back waiting for others to do the work, then pouncing on the last curve."

Thomas had agreed to set the pace for the race. He tore through the first lap in 56 seconds, slowed to 62 in the second for 1:58 at halfway, just as asked. Elliott took over, but now Lincoln pulled his surprise, taking the lead off the bend as they came into the main straight. Elliott was back in front at the bell, and gradually took control. He flashed through the last lap in 55.5 seconds for a final time of 3:54.5, a fabulous 2.7 seconds under Ibbotson's mark and 3.4 under the official world record. Lincoln held his form for second place in 3:55.9; Delany just edged Halberg for third, both clocking 3:57.5. Thomas, who had been instructed by Morton that he must finish, did so gleefully in 3:58.6. Santry had just witnessed the greatest mile ever, won by — almost certainly — the greatest miler ever.

Amidst all the post-race turmoil, Elliott wondered that he had not felt as "mean" beforehand as normally. "I was downright sociable," he told Gordon. "I chatted for a long time in the dressing-room, to officials as well as athletes. I didn't feel a bit mean. The race felt easy ..." Delany was spent. Asked how he might beat Elliott he replied: "There's just one way to beat the man — by tying his legs." After the Santry mile, an Australian, Elliott, held the mile world record and another, Lincoln, was the second-fastest miler ever. Three more — Landy, Bailey and Thomas — were, respectively, sixth and equal eighth fastest ever.

Thomas held the world record for three miles and the very next night, again at Santry, he added the world record for two miles. Before the end of his fabulous 1958 year, Herb Elliott smashed the 1500 metres world record almost as comprehensively as he had the mile. Running in Gothenburg, he ran 3:36.0, taking 2.1 seconds off Jungwirth's world record.

Truly, Australians had come from nowhere to the top of the world. In the crowded and boisterous Santry dressing room, Merv Lincoln made reference to the man who had led the way. "Wouldn't John Landy have liked to be here," he said. "He can take a lot of credit for what we did here. He was the pioneer … if he hadn't inspired Herb and myself, we wouldn't even be here." (*Young Men In A Hurry*, Harry Gordon, Landsdowne Press, 1961.) Typically, John Landy does not entertain such thoughts. Asked if he took any pride in the fact that his achievements contributed to the success of the Melbourne Olympics and the years immediately after, he replied: "If I felt I had contributed to it, I was just one of the people who, early in '56 and prior to that, the public thought might be a star turn at the Olympics."

In a February 1953 interview (*Sporting Life*), Landy said: "I'm more interested in giving athletics a boost than in breaking records." In that aim, he certainly succeeded.

Perhaps he would agree that, paraphrasing an expression he himself used more than once, John Landy showed other Australians that they "had possibilities".

Epilogue

Herb Elliott's fabulous mile world record at Santry may have been the highlight of Australian athletic achievement in the immediate post-Melbourne Olympic period, but it was by no means the end of it. The very next day, Elliott led for the first half of Albie Thomas's successful attempt to set a new world two-mile record. Then, Elliott took a much-needed break in a virtually non-stop racing season from his domestic clashes with Merv Lincoln, through his US tour, the Empire Games and then the epic mile against Delany. With a group of fellow Australians — and Kiwi Murray Halberg — Elliott headed to Europe in Gordon Pirie's Volkswagen campervan.

The group eventually made their way to Stockholm, where Elliott resumed more structured training at Boson, the sports institute on an island in the archipelago. Cerutty was already there. The day after the European championships ended — with Brian Hewson winning the 1500 metres from Dan Waern and Delany — Elliott ran his first ever 1500 at a meeting just outside Stockholm. He won in 3:41.7, well clear of Halberg. From there, Elliott crossed the country to Gothenburg for a 1500 against world record holder Stanislav Jungwirth, Halberg, Rozsavolgyi, Waern and Ibbotson, among others. Not only did he win, but Elliott smashed Jungwirth by three seconds and his world record by 2.1, running 3:36.0. The next night, despite protesting that he was not a machine, he gave a pretty good imitation of one, beating Waern in a mile in Malmo. Again, it was under four minutes. Five days later again, at White City stadium in London, Elliott ran a mile in 3:55.4. Only his own world record was faster. Finally, surely near breaking point, he went back to Oslo and ran the second-fastest 1500 ever.

After that, Elliott had a low-profile year in 1959 compared to his amazing achievements in 1958. He focused on his studies to put himself in a position to train without too much distraction for the 1960 Rome Olympic Games. Still, he managed to crush Merv Lincoln's spirit — for good, as it turned out.

Elliott and Lincoln were on the same flight to the Australian championships in Brisbane. Elliott looked pretty relaxed, downing a beer and even smoking a couple of cigarettes on the way up. "I've got the blighter this time," Lincoln thought as he led in the final lap off a solid pace, but Elliott burst past to win easily, 3:58.9 to 4:04.8. Lincoln was devastated. He thought at that stage he was fitter and definitely better prepared, but still he was beaten, and decisively. "I think I lost a bit of fight after that one," he told Brian Lenton years later.

Elliott had that effect on others, too. In Rome the following year, after a preparation that he agonised over but which included a solid domestic season and wins in the USA in May, Elliott destroyed the Olympic field in similar fashion, winning by over 20 metres and running a world record 3:35.6.

Then he, too, was gone. Elliott went to Cambridge University early in 1961 and after a few desultory racing attempts decided that his desire was no longer there and he retired. Power won a bronze medal in the 10,000 metres in Rome, but Thomas, Lincoln and 800 metres runner Tony Blue all failed to make finals and Albie Thomas was a distant eleventh in the 5000 metres and did not reach the final of the 1500.

Clarke won a bronze medal in the 10,000 in the Tokyo Olympics four years later and then ran better than anyone had a right to expect in the high altitude of Mexico City four years after that. There, the highlight was the gold medal by Ralph Doubell in the 800 metres. The Stampfl-trained athlete overcame a troubled preparation to run a superbly-judged — and fast — final, defeating Wilson Kiprugut of Kenya in equal world record time.

But the successes of the 1960s were more sporadic and Australia never again enjoyed anything like the broad success of Melbourne 1956 or Cardiff 1958. Only then could we ever have claimed to be at the top of the world; only at the end of an era sparked by Percy Cerutty and driven first by John Landy and then Herb Elliott. On that one day, 6 August 1958, when Elliott, Lincoln, Landy, Thomas and Bailey all were amongst the ten fastest milers ever, Australia truly was on top of the world. It hadn't been before and hasn't been since.

Bibliography

Bannister, Roger, *The Four-Minute Mile*, The Lyons Press, 1955; republished 1981 by The Globe Pequot Press.

Bascomb, Neal, *The Perfect Mile*, Collins Willow, 2004.

Butcher, Pat, *The Perfect Distance – Ovett & Coe: The Record-Breaking Rivalry*, Weidenfeld & Nicolson, 2004.

Cain, John, *On with the Show*, Prowling Tiger Press, 1998.

Clarke, Ron, *The Measure of Success: A Personal Perspective*, Lothian Books, 2004.

Donald, Keith and Selth, Don, *Olympic Saga: The Track and Field Story, Melbourne 1956*, Futurian Press, 1957.

Gordon, Harry, *Young Men in a Hurry*, Lansdowne Press, 1961.

Jenes, Paul, *Fields of Green, Lanes of Gold: The Story of Athletics in Australia*, Playright Publishing, 2001.

Lawrence, Al, *Chew With My Mouth Shut*, unpublished manuscript, 1992.

Lenton, Brian, *Off The Record*, Brian Lenton Publications, 1981.

Lenton, Brian, *Through The Tape*, Brian Lenton Publications, 1983.

Nelson, Cordner and Quercetani, Roberto, *The Milers*, Tafnews, 1985.

Phillips, Bob, *Za-to-pek! Za-to-pek! Za-to-pek! The Life and Times of the World's Greatest Distance Runner*, The Parrs Wood Press, 2002.

Phillips, Murray, *From Sidelines to Centrefield: A History of Sports Coaching in Australia*, UNSW Press, 2000.

Sims, Graem, *Why Die? The Extraordinary Percy Cerutty 'Maker of Champions'*, Lothian Books, 2003.

Solomon, Robert, *Great Australian Athletes: Selected Olympians 1928–1956*, self-published title, 2000.

Woodfield, Dr Graeme, *Jack Lovelock: Athlete & Doctor*, Trio Books, 2007.

The Associated Public Schools Combined Sports, 1948, at Melbourne's Scotch College. Start of either the 880 yards or mile, with the college chapel in the background.

John Landy just edges Peter Quin of Xavier to win the mile. "The winner, John Landy (G.G.S.), ran an excellent mile," a report commented. Quin was disqualified for interference.

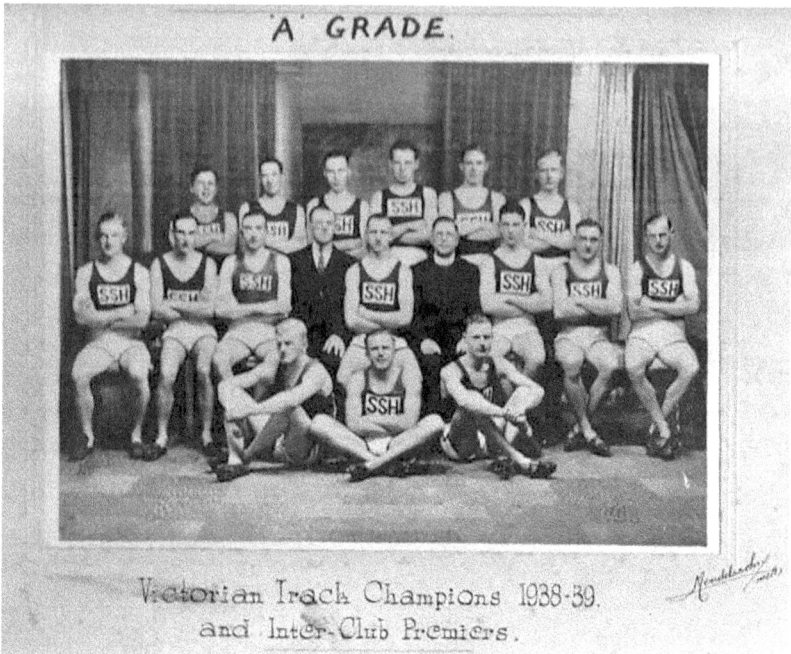

'A' GRADE.

Victorian Track Champions 1938-39.
and Inter-Club Premiers.

St Stephen's Harriers was probably Australia's strongest club in the pre-WWII years. The 1938–39 premiership team with 1936 Olympic 800 metres finalist Gerald Backhouse front row left.

Percy Cerutty demonstrates points for an admiring audience during a lecture in Perth, on the 1955 trip during which he first met Herb Elliott.

A Victorian 5000 metres championship at Bendigo, probably in 1950. Jack Davey (4th, 1950 Empire Games six miles) leads here from Les Perry, John Landy, (probably) Ken McDonald (obscured behind Landy), Gordon Hall, an unidentified runner and Geoff Warren.

Australian prime minister Robert Menzies shakes hands with John Landy after watching him run 4:02.0 at Olympic Park in December 1953. Wilfred Kent Hughes, chairman of the Melbourne Olympic Organising Committee, looks on.

Landy's performances drew increasingly larger crowds to Olympic Park. The ground is virtually empty as he runs 4:02.1 in December 1952.

The media pack is definitely in evidence as he finishes his 4:02.0 almost a year later to the day.

There is scarcely a vantage point left on the packed terraces as he runs the first sub-four minute mile in Australia, 3:58.6 on 28 January 1956.

Hurdler Ray Weinberg (second from left) is the odd one out as Roger Bannister (centre) joins Australian middle-distance runners Don Macmillan (far left), Landy and Les Perry in a training session at Motspur Park, London, before the 1952 Helsinki Olympic Games.

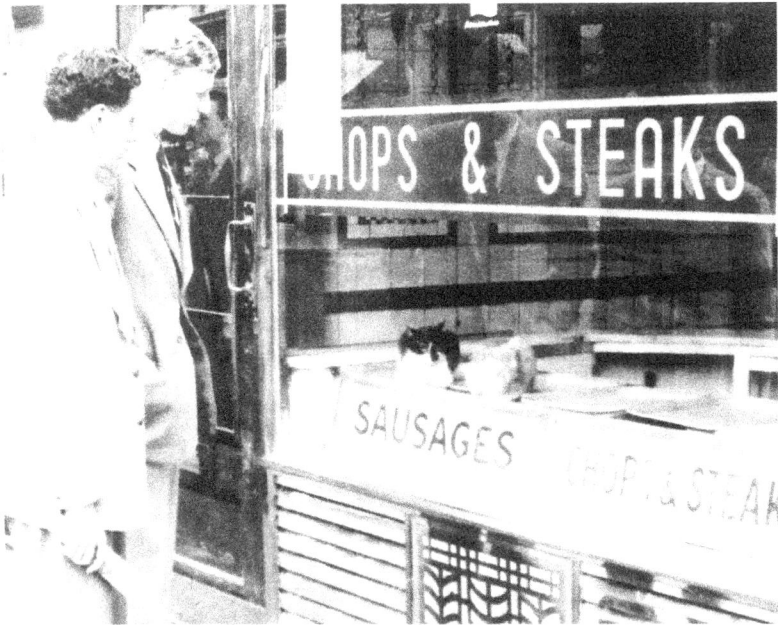

Landy and Macmillan stare into an empty butcher's shop window in London's Petticoat Lane, 1952.

The crowds flocked to Perth's Leederville Oval to watch John Landy at the 1953 Australian championships. Here, he signs autographs for a couple of young fans.

Landy breaks the tape to win the mile. The force of Landy's finish snatched the tape out of one official's hand, but Landy caught it as he burst over the line.

Landy's first trip to Finland brought Olympic failure. In this picture, he is with teammates (left to right) Bob Prentice (marathon), Ray Weinberg (hurdles), Ron Faulds (springboard diving) and Ken Doubleday (hurdles) at a team function.

Landy leads Chris Chataway en route to world records at the 1500 metres (3:41.8) and mile (3:57.9) at Turku on 21 June 1954.

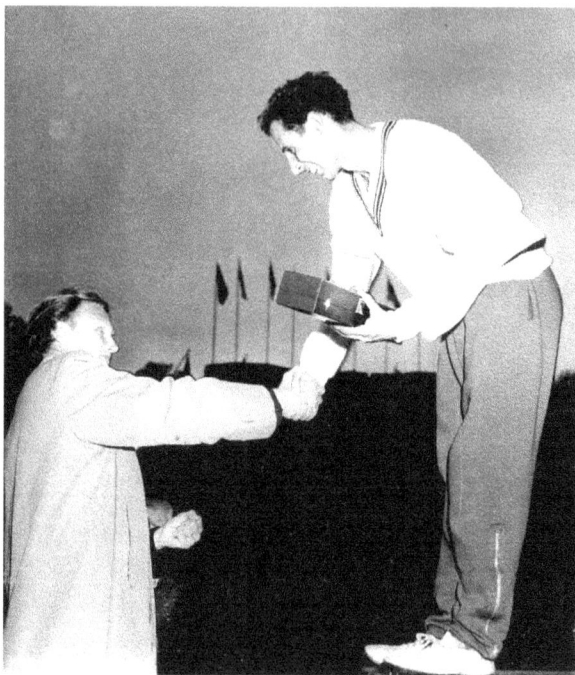

Landy receiving the trophy from former mile world-record holder Arne Andersson after winning the 1500 metres at a meeting in Gothenburg.

With his father, Gordon Landy, in Vancouver at a training session in preparation for the Empire Games mile against Roger Bannister.

Running in his Geelong Guild club singlet, Landy nears the finish of his 3:58.6 mile on 28 January 1956. Merv Lincoln slashed his previous best but was two seconds behind at the finish and Ron Clarke, just visible entering the straight, set a world junior record.

John Plummer leads the Australian three miles championship early in the race. John Landy (no. 112 in the Victorian singlet) sits mid-field, just behind Al Lawrence (to Landy's inside) and Dave Stephens (to his outside).

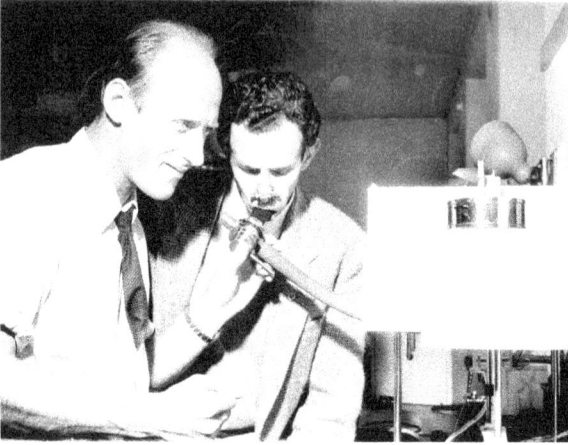

While in Stockholm in 1954, Landy visited the laboratory of pioneering exercise physiologist Per-Olof Åstrand. Here he has his lung capacity measured before running on a treadmill.

John Landy returns to racing at the start of 1956 and almost defeats world record holder Lon Spurrier of the USA over 880 yards at Olympic Park. John Murray is third.

Al Lawrence stops off for a race at Puckapunyal Army Base on his drive from Sydney to Melbourne for the Olympic Games. He is surprised to find Dave Stephens, "the flying Milko", also there for the race and even more surprised to beat him over three miles.

The famous fall in the Australian mile championships in 1956. Ron Clarke is down, John Plummer leaps to avoid being caught by his heels, John Landy and Alex Henderson prepare to go either side of the fallen Clarke, and Merv Lincoln braces himself for evasive action. Albie Thomas, a spectator of the race, captures the only shot of the fall and sells the copyright to a Melbourne news organisation for at princely £50.

Just a lap later, Landy, having gone back to check that Clarke was alright and then chased the field, is poised to sweep past Henderson into the lead. Note the crowd.

Landy tests his sore tendons in a two-mile race a month before the Games. At this stage, he found it put less stress on them if he ran in bare feet.

After a couple of test races, Landy has a more serious hit-out in a two-miler at Kardinia Park, Geelong, home ground of the Geelong Football Club. The Games opening is only eight days away. "This could be the end", he tells Franz Stampfl of his Olympic chances.

Victorian state premier Henry Bolte (left) and Victorian Promotions Committee chairman Maurice Nathan (right) farewell Landy at a civic reception on the eve of his trip to the USA. Racing on the rock-hard US tracks severely compromised Landy's Olympic preparation.

Despite his troubled lead-up, Landy qualified comfortably enough in his heat of the Olympic 1500 metres. Here he runs well back early in the race before coming through to finish third.

The legacy: it was Merv Lincoln's fate to come along at the tail-end of the Landy era and the start of Herb Elliott's dominance. He never beat Elliot (nor did anyone else), but he came closest in this race in Perth. Both men ran 3:59.6, with the official margin in Elliott's favour being described as "inches".

Ron Clarke swept all before him in 1965, setting eleven world records. Here, wearing the blue boomerang of his Glenhuntly club, he races in London.

John Landy with eight of Australia's ten fastest milers in 1994 at a function to mark the 40th anniversary of his first sub-four minute mile in Turku. Back row (left to right): Mike Hillardt, Albie Thomas, Landy, Merv Lincoln, Peter Fuller, Steve Foley. Front row (left to right): Pat Scammell, Graham Crouch, Ken Hall. (Absent: Herb Elliott, Simon Doyle.)

Ron Clarke invited the 1956 Olympic 1500 finalists to the opening of his Couran Cove resort in 1999. Right to left: Clarke, Ron Delany (Ireland, gold medalist), John Landy (bronze medalist), Laszlo Tabori (Hungary, fourth), Brian Hewson (GB, fifth), Neville Scott (NZ, seventh), Murray Halberg (NZ, eleventh), Merv Lincoln (twelfth).

Once the two fastest milers in the world, Roger Bannister and John Landy enjoy a leisurely stroll and chat on Melbourne's famous Tan track around the Botanical Gardens.